THE LIFE,
HISTORY AND MAGIC OF
THE DOG

THE LIFE,
HISTORY AND MAGIC OF
THE DOG

BY FERNAND MERY

Madison Square Press

Publishers   **GROSSET & DUNLAP**   New York
A NATIONAL GENERAL COMPANY

ARCH. R. LAFFONT

A MADISON SQUARE PRESS BOOK

Copyright © 1968 Robert Laffont, Paris

English translation published 1970 in the United States
by Grosset & Dunlap, Inc.
51 Madison Avenue, New York 10010

Published in 1970 in England
by Cassell & Company Ltd.
35 Red Lion Square, London, WC1

Published simultaneously in Canada

Library of Congress Catalog Card No.: 78-117172

First published in France
by Editions Robert Laffont
under the title *Le Chien*

Printed and bound in Italy by Mondadori, Verona

INTRODUCTION

There are some dogs which we cherish like nothing else on earth. But there comes a time when we ask ourselves: "Why are we so fond of them? Why this curious feeling of tenderness?" Then, depending on the length and strength of our friendship, it becomes either a simple, fleeting interest which we see blossom and then wither like a flower, or otherwise grow into an unexpected obsession. At the same time we feel an irrepressible urge to seek the truth, to try faithfully and impartially to see what it is that distinguishes us from this creature.

To some extent this is what I have felt since turning from my interests in medicine and biology and losing all contact with animals, after grieving over the loss of a wonderful cross-bred dog. This irritating problem has since haunted me: WHAT IS A DOG? *So familiar, being always at one's side, so dear and yet remaining a mystery to everyone.*

What do we know of its obscure origins? Of the secret of its evolution? Of its various forms? What do we know of its intelligence in the way we understand logical behavior? Is it capable of affection or is it capable only of dependence? Finally, what responsibility do we bear toward this turncoat animal, the only animal in the world which cannot really live without us?

At times the veil can be torn apart. Recently some deceptive behavior patterns have seriously defied analysis; and others equally bewildering still confound us, and put in question all that we thought we had unravelled. The reasons for our uncertainty are perfectly clear: The dog has been exposed to human behavior for too long not to be affected by it. It reacts to pleasure and suffering, pain and joy, just as humans react; but with the difference that it is happy or discontent without knowing it.

Is this not a clue which might lead us into a field of inquiry in which science, rightly, still hesitates to become involved? Can we discover something which, paradoxically, might prove that the dog has not followed man's destiny in vain? Something which would allow us to set dogs a little apart from other animals and which, indeed, in the face of scientific truth, would provide the excuse which so many of us seek for loving them?

—F. M.

TABLE OF CONTENTS

BULLOZ

THE DOG AND ITS PAST

THE DOG IN THE MIND OF MAN

THE DOG AND SCIENCE

THE DOG IN THE SERVICE OF MAN

THE DOG IN THE FACE OF SUFFERING AND DEATH

THE DOG
AND ITS PAST

1 PREHISTORY

*"In the beginning,
God created man,
but seeing him so feeble,
He gave him the dog."
(Toussenel)*

What are the origins of the dog, the domesticated dog? The dog, our friend, seems to have been waiting, in the depths of time, for the arrival upon the earth of *Homo sapiens,* waiting for the moment when it could sever forever its links with all other creatures and give itself up to man.

What is the dog? Physically we have so profoundly transformed this animal, and psychically we have so greatly influenced it, that any attempt to distinguish between its natural characteristics and those it has acquired through living with us is almost bound to fail.

It is very difficult to find a reply to these two questions. The difficulty lies partly in the extraordinary diversity of canine breeds. Indeed it seems absurd to call both the diminutive Chihuahua and the powerful, hairy bob-tailed sheepdog by the same name of "dog," but also there is the fact that though all dogs do not resemble each other, some of them have many wolf-like or fox-like characteristics.

Yet no child ever mistakes one for the other. He can always recognize a dog because he sees with the eyes of the heart. Of all the animals, surely the dog is the only one that really shares our life, helps in our work, and has a place in our recreation. It is the only one that becomes so fond of us that sometimes it cannot go on living after its master dies and so merits the name "faithful dog"—*canis familiaris*—that Linnaeus gave it.

THE DOG FAMILY CANIDAE

Taxonomists, who are specialists in zoological classification, divide the dog family into two distinct lines whose evolution seems to have run parallel: on the one hand, dogs and wolves, on the other, foxes and jackals.

Dogs, wolves, foxes, and jackals are all carnivorous, with some identical characteristics. Their dentition consists of the same number of teeth: incisors, canines, and

*Cave Rock painting.
Hill station at Sefar.
(Tessili-n-Ajjer, Algeria)*

molars, for biting, chewing, and gnawing. They have five toes on their front paws and four on the back, and each of these toes has a strong but not very sharp nail, very different from the sharp retractile claws of the cat family. They all display a certain natural propensity to live in packs. The females have the same mean gestation period, 63 days, and their young, born in large litters, come into the world with closed eyes.

These are a good many morphological similarities. But even more important for the scientific classification of the species is the distinguishing feature of interbreeding, which unites the four great Canidae in one group.

A dog bitch can be mated with a male wolf, as can a male dog with a she-wolf. The offspring of these unions will be fertile. Dogs and jackals can also be crossed, with identical results. It is possible, though admittedly difficult, to mate dogs and foxes successfully. There has even been a successful attempt, by means of scientifically supervised mating, to obtain a cross-breed in which the blood of the wolf, dog, and jackal was mixed in equal proportions.

But the true dog, however closely related to the other Canidae he may be, is nonetheless very different. There can be no doubt that it has an identity of its own. Wherever and whenever the four members of the canine family have lived together, man has never confused them and has always had different words to denote each of them.

But there is also the delicate problem of the intermediate breeds. These are all wild Canidae. Some of them are very closely related to the dog (like the Australian dingo), but they cannot be included in the genus *canis.* They will be discussed later in this chapter.

THE ANCESTRY OF THE DOG

Let us leave to the paleontologists the task of determining the distant ancestry of the present-day dog, whether it was the *myocis*

15

Moufflon hunt, with dogs.
Late Paleolithic Age.

Rock engraving.
(Collection of Yei Lubu Yoga. Niger. Tenéré)

MAXIMILIEN BRUGGMANN

of the Tertiary or the *daphocnodon* or *cynodictis* of the Upper Eocene. Let us confine our attention to the domesticated dog and try to discover when it was that this predestined canine became man's companion.

The Tertiary Era saw the emergence and development of the mammals. But we will go no further back than the Quaternary, where the presence of *Homo sapiens* is substantiated. Indeed it seems that one really can talk of a domesticated dog in the Mesolithic Age, just at the end of the glacial period of Wurm (circa 10,000 B.C.), when the earliest peoples appeared. Joléaud and Alimen have identified huntsmen and dogs in the Magdalenian frescos of Spain, and ascribe them to this era.

But let us turn to the Neolithic Age (6,000 or 5,000 years B.C.). Our knowledge of this primitive civilization is more complete and less hypothetical.

In Europe, fishing and hunting tribes came to live along the coasts of the North Sea. Gradually they became sedentary, the bands multiplied, settled areas became more numerous, and soon there were many villages. Up until then, man's detritus had been allowed to collect outside his caves. But now, from England to the Baltic, enormous quantities of left-over food, garbage of all kinds, mollusc and crustacean shells, the broken bones of game, deer, wild oxen, and boar— all this accumulated around man's dwellings.

This testimony to the stable presence of man and his way of life was to become so important that it was given the name "kjolkkenmoeddings," from the Danish word used to designate these piles of bones and debris.

The bones have marks on them. Some have been gnawed by a carnivorous animal whose jaws were not as strong as those of the Cave Hyena (now extinct). They bear the marks which a dog will leave on bones when it is left in peace to worry them.

"This carnivore," wrote Steenstrup, "was always present, in every place, sharing man's food." This then was certainly not a wild

*Dog portrayed on a rock painting
in the Algerian Sahara.
(Tin-Abteka hill station. Tassili-n-Ajjer)*

*Portuguese dog,
living descendant
of the Peat dog.*

animal, but a domesticated and friendly carnivore.

It was to this first dog, a commensal of long standing, that Rutimeyer (who first discovered its remains) gave, in 1852, the name *canis familiaris palustris*—the Peat dog. Little by little this dog had spread all over Europe. What did it look like? It was medium-sized, halfway between the jackal and the fox; it had a tapering, but not long, muzzle, a wide, deep chest, and a slight skeleton and limbs. The easiest way to imagine it is to compare it with the modern Samoyed or the Spitz.

There was another dog that resembled this dog of the pile dwellers. This was a wild dog whose many well-characterized remains have been exhumed by Anoutchine near Lake Ladoga, which at that time was part of the Gulf of Finland.

Was the Peat dog its ancestor?

This is not the opinion of Zeittler and Nauman, who see it as "nothing other than a descendant of the jackal" (*canis aureus*) which is to be found in North Africa, India, and, more rarely, in southern Russia.

Whether this opinion is well founded or not, the Peat dog was not the only one of its type. The bones of yet another dog which was alive at this time have been discovered in the pile-dwellings of Switzerland and other mountainous regions. This was a much larger, stronger dog, with a more elongated head and powerful jaws, though its muzzle was pointed. According to Trouessart, this very different creature was related to the Pale-footed Wolf, *canis pallipes,* which is the least ferocious of all the wolves; but others believe it to be related to the European wolf.

THE ORIGINS OF
THE DIFFERENT BREEDS

It would be impossible to mention, however briefly, all the theories that have been

MAXIMILIEN BRUGGMANN

BAVARIA VERLAG

A wolf resting.

advanced on this delicate topic. Scholars are agreed only on this point: that there was first a fairly long period of fixity. The skeletons deriving from this period do manifest a few variations, but these are minimal. Then, from what seems to be a second period, there appears an inexplicable variety of form and size in the remains of dogs—a variety which anticipates the extreme diversity of the modern dog. Bourguignat brought to light, in the caves at Calmette, near Vence (Alpes-Maritimes), the skeletons of some very different dogs. Some observers have claimed to recognize among them a basset hound, two greyhounds, a wolf-like sheep dog, several large mountain dogs, and even the precursor of the pointer.

How was it that the first dog evolved to produce in the end these innumerable breeds? Was it through rapid mutation which became fixed? Was it through gradual hereditary adaptation to the environment? The mystery remains. Striking though this phenomenon of polymorphism is in the canine species, it is also to be found, though to a lesser degree, among the equine, bovine, ovine, and porcine species.

Becker, though, has advanced an interesting hypothesis based on the development of the cranium of the sheep dog.

He established that the skull of the newborn sheep dog is of a globular shape which is also to be found, for instance, in the Chihuahua and the King Charles Spaniel.

A little later, when the pup is about four months old, this globular shape has disappeared and the brainpan has lengthened. It is then like that of a Fox-terrier, Airedale, or Schnauzer.

At the end of six months, when all the teeth are out, the sheep dog's skull is more like the Great Dane's.

Later still and up to the time when adulthood is well established, the skull has a contrary, slight tendency to become shorter, while the jaws become longer. The type then resembles more the morphology of the Greyhound.

European wolf.

Jackals in the African desert.

Starting from this case study, it is possible to develop a theory according to which some types of dog developed because of circumstances, while the evolution of others was arrested, and yet others evolved in quite a different direction in their struggle for life.

On these two specific problems, the origin of the dog and its polymorphism, there remain many essential questions which modern science cannot answer with any degree of certainty.

Are the variations between dogs due solely to domestication, or do they result from exceptional mutations?

Was the first ancestor of the domesticated dog a primitive dog, or another morphologically related canine, such as a jackal or a wolf?

Must we, as Cuvier maintained, conclude that the original ancestor of the domestic dog was a wild species which is now extinct? Or are there, among the wild dogs alive today, some which have faithfully maintained the characteristics of this first ancestor?

WILD DOGS

Some of these little known canines are still living. They are to be found all over the world; in the Southern Himalayas, in the Sunda Isles, in India, in Sumatra, in Zanzibar, in South America on the vast savannah which stretches from the Amazonian forests to the Argentinian pampas, in Africa, in Uganda and Tanzania, and finally in Europe, around the Mediterranean. They are called pariahs because, unlike wild cats, they are not formerly domesticated creatures which have reverted to a state of freedom and wildness. They are not particularly hostile to man. They will not attack him and can be kept at a distance from him only by force.

Even zoologists experience some difficulty in classifying them. For instance, Brehm thinks that the Abyssinian Kaberu (*canis simensis*) is a dog, while Trouessart believes it to be a wolf, and Grey, a fox.

However, with the exception of the foxes, these wild dogs all over the world have many common characteristics. They belong to the dog family not only by reason of their dentition, size, habits, and interfertility, but also because it is possible to tame them. The astonishing thing is that they have always been spoken of as unimportant creatures. They have been so little studied that no attempt has been made to compare them with the domestic dog in order to study their lineage.

With a few differences, the wild dogs are all alike, whether they be dholes of Indonesia, *Buansnah* of the Far East, Abyssinian Kaberus, Cape hunting dogs of Africa, or dingos of Australia. They have always lived in packs. They all have wide, quite short but erect ears, which are located on the sides of their heads, and though mobile are less so than those of the wolf or the jackal. All except the Cape hunting dog are monochromous—red, black, yellow, or cream in coloring. This quality of coloration is at present disappearing among the domesticated breeds. It is now found only in a Chinese dog which arrived in Europe at the beginning of this century at the earliest, a newcomer to towns and therefore closer to its original purity. The Chow Chow is perhaps the only breed that can today bear black, red, white, or cream pups in one litter. But it never produces pups with yellow or white markings.

It is a remarkable fact that almost all wild dogs choose to live near man, often feeding on his garbage and keeping their distance only in order to safeguard the possibility of flight. Even then they rarely wander far.

Are they humble aspirants for future friendship, or, on the contrary, are they the descendents of old servants who have regained their independence?

We will examine in greater detail one of these pariah dogs, the dingo, whose bones

*Australian aborigine
and his dogs, descendants of dingos.*

J. ET P. VILLEMINOT

Voyage au Brésil *(Journey to Brazil)*
by S.A.S. Maximilien.
Les cabanes des Puris
(The huts of the Puri) (1815-1817).
(Bibliothéque Nationale, Paris)

The Australian dingo.

MacCoy claims to have discovered mingled with those of the *nototherium* (a species long extinct) in the Tertiary layers of the Province of Victoria.

THE DINGO

Did the dingo originate in Australia? Certainly, this very beautiful, intelligent, and brave, but little liked, dog is only to be found in Australia. Skeletal remains of dingos have been found beside the bones of large quadruped marsupials, but the presence of the dingo in Australia is especially surprising as it is the only higher mammal (apart from rats and bats, who easily come to land on all insular shores) in a continent inhabited exclusively by aplacental mammals.

It is more tempting to believe that the dingo is descended from the Phu Quoc dogs of eastern Asia and that it was brought to Australia by sea-faring men. Ill adapted, decimated by disease, or simply overcome once again by their nomadic instincts, these men disappeared. But the dog remained behind and, in order to survive, returned to the wild.

Explorers who went to Australia to study the habits of the native tribes around the River Herbert noticed that these primitive people liked very young dingos. They reared them patiently, caring for them as for their children, and kept the pups with them when they pitched camp. When the young dingos were fully grown, the natives used them, without schooling, to flush game and bring it out into the open.

The Australian government has established reservations for the protection of these half savage men, survivors of prehistoric times. Some photographs were taken very recently which show these people with red dogs, undoubtedly of the dingo type, beside them, but prudently chained up. Because of its hunting instinct, the dingo willingly cooperates with man, but it never becomes irrevocably attached to him. As soon as the mating season starts, the dingo leaves the human family which has cared for it (but into which it was not born), never to return. This then, as Ménégaux has written, is only semi-domestication.

The adult dingo keeps to his own territory; he marks it by urinating on "his" bushes and at the foot of "his" trees. He hides his pups in holes in the rocks or in the trunks of dead trees; they remain in the family group until they reach the age of two or three years, sometimes longer, when they feel strong enough to fight, hunt, and procreate.

Have they any masters? Only the very primitive aborigines (who still light their fires by friction, just as their distant ancestors did) show any interest in them, and perhaps have some fondness for them. The white men who have built modern Australia regard this killer dog as a fearful enemy! It cannot bark, it tracks its prey in silence, and its terrible jaws can break clean through the spine of a kangaroo.

Are the dingos responsible for the complete disappearance of the Tasmanian Wolf, a marsupial wolf? Some authors are convinced that this is so. In any case, for a long time the dingos enjoyed an easy life; game was plentiful and their own packs were few. But their food supplies were dwindling when the colonists introduced sheep into Australia. This innovation of the newly arrived white farmers was a providential blessing for the dingos. They had less trouble in killing sheep than in catching smaller game.

Unfortunately the dingo has developed a taste for killing. It disembowels sheep with a kind of rage, either because of hostility towards the intruder, or because, faced with flocks of fleeing sheep driven mad with fear at its approach, it no longer knows where to sink its teeth. It no longer chooses its victim, and within a few minutes a pack of dingos slaughters the sheep wholesale.

In Australia, the farms are very extensive,

J. ET P. VILLEMINOT

J. ET P. VILLEMINOT

Canadian sledge dogs (17th century).
(Bibliothéque Nationale, Paris)

Malaysia: intimacy.

and the distance between flocks is great, but the dingo would find his prey in the desert. It is not afraid to walk for days without rest.

In winter it emigrates to the east coast where it goes to ground. At the first fine weather the packs reform, and there follow massacres of sheep counted in the thousands.

It is easy to understand why the sheep farmers wage a fierce battle against these incursions into their flocks. "A tooth for a tooth"—and each year thousands of dingos are killed in unmerciful roundups encouraged by the government. For each "killer" killed a bounty is paid, ranging from three to fifty pounds and even more in the case of a well-known killer dog. But the dingos are so numerous that nothing can stop them. To guard the flocks, Queensland has been forced to build an immense surrounding fence almost two meters high.

In spite of its misdeeds, however, this strange dog should not be annihilated, if only because of its scientific interest. It is perhaps, as Thévenin thinks, "the animal that today can best teach us how the domestication of a species is accomplished." The dingo could be left to go free in the reservations set aside for the primitive people of the continent, who are among the last representatives of prehistoric man. It could also be allowed into the national parks for animals, where it could wander in complete liberty without having to fight man in the search for food.

Such is the hope of John Sidney, who has so well observed these wild dogs. It is through him and a few isolated shepherds that we know what little we do about this dog, which is still shrouded in mystery.

THE POOR RELATIONS OF THE DOG FAMILY

Before we return to the domestic dog, let us say a few words about the numerous Canidae scattered all over the world and to whom the name of dog cannot be given,

because of some morphological differences (in the dentition, the number of toes, etc.).

Up to now these pariahs have been thought to be either intermediate types between the four officially classified Canidae, or else rare or little known varieties of wolves, jackels, or foxes.

In tropical Asia lives the famous jackal *(canis aureus),* which is smaller than the wolf but larger than the fox. It has spread to the Sahara, Southern Africa, Arabia, and Northern Russia.

In India lives the Arctic fox *(vulpes leucopus),* which is quite rare, and the Pale-footed Wolf *(canis pellipes).*

In Malaysia and Indonesia there is no fox, but the dhole *(cuon alpinus),* which is a little larger than the jackal, with a short, tight coat, red in color, and tall, erect ears. One would willingly give the name of dog to this canine if its dentition was not different in several respects from that of the dog. There is also a variety of Indian Wild Dog which is stockier, with a wider skull, a heavier nose, and looks like a cross between a Chow Chow and a Belgian sheep dog, the Malinois.

North America has its own prairie wolf *(canis latrans),* better known as the coyote. Nowadays officially protected, the coyote has spread to the East and North, though the common wolf *(canis lupus)* has virtually disappeared from the United States, though it still persists in Mexico and Canada. Also to be found in America are the following wild carnivores: the American red fox *(vulpes fulva),* and its cousins, the Eastern grey fox *(urocyon cinereoargenteus),* the black fox, and in more temperate regions, the American kit fox *(vulpes velox).*

South America has the Maned Wolf *(chrysocyon jubatus)* which, until it is weaned, looks very like the fox and whose legs then get longer and longer from month to month, until it has almost become a quadruped wader!

AFRIQUE PHOTO — BONNOTTE

In the Far East, China, Korea, and Japan can boast of the racoon-like dog *(nyctereute)*. This is a short-legged wild dog, with a thick fleecy coat, brownish-grey in coloring with black markings on the shoulders, stomach, and above the eyes. This nocturnal animal has gradually spread into Europe. It can be found today in Russia, Sweden, and Finland, where its fur is marketed under the name Japanese fox.

The strange Cape hunting dog *(lycaon pictus)* lives in Africa. This is the hyena dog which, it is believed, the Assyrians and Egyptians used for hunting (from the 5th to the 12th dynasty) and which they then abandoned for a dog resembling the present-day Fox-terrier.[1] It was perfectly described

[1] "Study of Domestication." A. Condoret. Veterinarian thesis. Toulouse.

by the commandant Hubert, of the Parc Albert, and could therefore not have been a wild dog.

The Cape hunting dogs wander over the African savannah, from the Oubangui to Kilimanjaro, living in packs, just like the dingos. Not knowing what to call this hyena-like dog, which reaches a height of 25 inches at the shoulder, the first Europeans who came across it gave it various names. The Boers called it "wildhound," the French *"cynhyéne"* or even African wolf, the English "hunting dog," etc. The Cape hunting dog is something between the hyena and the dog. It looks like an Alsatian (i.e. German Shepherd), but its ears are twice as wide and it is curiously speckled with yellow, white, or black. With this excellent camouflage, they hunt in packs of fifteen to twenty. As

soon as they spot a solitary antelope or cheetah they approach noiselessly and lie in wait among the tall grasses. Then they hurl themselves upon the victim, uttering their very harsh, sharp attacking bark, quite different from their playful yaps or gentle murmurs of affection. They are skinny creatures with matted coats, covered with ticks. They hunt alongside their friends, the hyenas.

What are their habits? They are the habits of the other wild dogs, those of all the poor relations of the dog family. The females gestate for four weeks, and bear four or five young which they lay in burrows, dug (rarely) by themselves or, more often, simply commandeered from the rightful owners.

Like the strange maned wolves of Brazil,

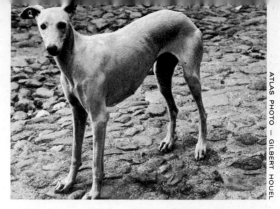

Voyage au Brésil
pittoresque et historique,
by J.-B. Debret (19th century).
The family of a Camaca chieftain
prepares for a feast.

Female Majorcan dog.

the Cape hunting dogs are victims of man's love of shooting, and their numbers are steadily diminishing. But though they are no more friendly to man than these wolves, they too do not attack him.

All these Canidae, except for the foxes, are without doubt related to the Alsatian, the Malinois, and even perhaps the Nordic dog as we know them. Are they, or are they not, dogs? Science still hesitates to commit itself.

But let us return to prehistoric times.

MAN AND DOG ADAPT TO EACH OTHER

It can be taken as certain that prehistoric man knew these dogs, which came of their own accord to prowl in packs around his caves or huts, living off his leftovers and doing a little pilfering, but never attacking him. On the other hand, as will be shown further on, only rarely do we find cave drawings of the dog, while there are numerous representations of deer, bison, and horses. Should we conclude from this that in the first ages the dog was unknown? No, it is more likely that the dog had no place in the motivation (doubtless magical) of the painters of the rock drawings.

The first men probably considered the dog as a negligible source of food. They did not hunt it and had come to believe that they could count on its good-will and neutrality. Nor did they feel any need to protect themselves by magic from this friendly parasite, or feel any need to waste their talents drawing and carving its image when there were so many other creatures which they wished to kill or to honor in some fashion by their art.

It seems then that man never had to fight the dog or subjugate it by force; if he had, we should find in the rock drawings the graphic representation of his battles, defeats, and victories. Instead, there was a longstanding, almost daily pattern of co-existence,

which was graduallly transformed into domestication. Man and dog adopted each other (one might almost say it was a process of mutual domestication) through their association and alliance.

How long was this period of reciprocal tolerance and peaceful coexistence, during which the canine creatures realized that life with man was to their advantage? We simply do not know. Perhaps it was just as long as that very long period during which the dog type remained more or less stable and showed hardly any variations in shape or size. We know how, in the course of the following millenia, the morphology of the dog was to become extraordinarily diversified. The definitive domestication of the dog seems to have been the fruit of a very slow evolution in the habits of dogs and men.

One thing is certain: In order to domesticate any other kind of animal except the dog, man has, always and in all lands, first had to capture him. Reindeer, horses, buffalo, and elephants, all have been overcome and made prisoners. Because of this they have retained an innate dissatisfaction which facilitates their return to the wild.

The dog alone has never had to be taken by force. The prehistoric dog followed man from afar, just as the domesticated dog has always followed armies on the march. It became accustomed to living nearer and nearer to this being who did not hunt it. Finding with him security and stability, and being able to feed off the remains of man's prey, for a long time it stayed near his dwellings, whether they were caves or huts. One day the dog crossed the threshold. Man did not chase him out. The treaty of alliance had been signed.

While we are on this subject, why should we not imagine a scene less inconceivable than the legend of the she-wolf giving suck to Romulus and Remus? A dog bitch dies after giving birth. In the neighboring cave a woman has just given birth to an infant which lived only a few hours. Obeying the maternal instinct, or conscious only of the

painful congestion of her breasts caused by the pressure of milk, the woman takes the pups and suckles them. (This is known to happen even today in Paraguay and Peru and in some of the lost villages of the mountainous regions of Europe.) These pups, reared by a woman, share the life and games of her children. Having no other family to protect and guide them, they would be obeying the most natural of the social instincts by integrating themselves into what is, after all, their pack. Growing up at the heart of this pack and responding to the same instincts, they will defend this, their territory. Those that do not regain their independence when they become adult, will cling to the people who surround them. From generation to generation, the links forged by this single act of dependence will become stronger and stronger, more and more durable.

THE FRIENDSHIP BETWEEN MAN AND DOG

This is of course a symbolic tale, but it does place the emphasis clearly on the "affectionate" aspect of the relationship between man and dog, and underlines the psychological aspect, to which no one before Conrad Lorenz paid much attention. This is an aspect which we will return to, for it is truly important.

On the spiritual plane there is no lack of evidence to instruct us about the magic, the rites, and the various cults which were born and developed in prehistoric times. The motivation of all these was fear, hunger, and anxiety about the future. Dealings between man and dog, however, were not determined by these sentiments. Through the remains of communal burials dating from the end of prehistoric times, we have learned that the links between man and dog were no longer those of fear but of friendship.

Once welcomed, adopted, and integrated into the life of man, the dog behaved towards

Hunting wild oxen.
(Oued Djerat. Tassili-n-Ajjer)

Bronze Age hunter
with his dogs.
(Discovered at Hultane, France)

of the confrontation. The animal had to yield to this ultimate submission, which cannot have been accomplished without difficulty, and which even today arises whenever man is unable, either by strength or cunning, to impose his superiority and domination. But since that time, the dog has literally become an integral part of man, his master, and will go to his defense when it sees him in danger.

Thus hunting man became gradually a stock-rearing man. The pastoral era began. Life was easier and the captured animals in their turn became accustomed to the domination of this two-legged creature who fed and protected them. The dog became the guardian of cattle and horses. The band now had living reserves of food at its disposal. Women and children had less reason to fear for their sleep, even for their lives.

In Europe the climate gradually became less severe. Forests stretched forth everywhere; the melting of the glaciers flooded the plains and valleys, swelling streams and rivers, forming lakes, changing the structure of the continents. The wild creatures travelled en masse to the North. The heaviest and the worst adapted did not survive. The mammoth, the lion and the Woolly Rhinoceros became extinct. For a long time to come the hunters were still to follow these slow migrations of the fauna, for hunting was still the most important human activity.

But already some tribes were becoming settled. Besides hunting, they took to fishing. Until then the reindeer had been the most important prey, but in the southern regions it was replaced by the stag. In Norway and along the shores of the Baltic, the seal and the cormorant begin to appear in pictures of the daily hunt.

These men hunted with bows and pointed arrows; they hurled harpoons made from the antlers of stags; they cooked their food and cured it with ashes. They expressed their spiritual life through drawing and magic; they honored their dead. How different they were from the dull-witted people of the

other animals, and to men who were not of his clan, as any canine behaves in the defense of its pack. It barked, as was its habit, to alert its brothers. Its barking warned its two-legged companions and also helped to frighten off the undesirable and the enemy. Man quickly came to realize the value of the dog's help. He used it to further his own interests and at the same time instinctively became more attached to this animal which had taken the defense of his family and goods so much to heart.

For the first time man lived alongside an animal without provoking it to aggressiveness or flight. He began to look after it, to

touch it, to stroke it in order to calm it or perhaps because he already loved it.

Later, this friendly companion came to share in man's work. At first it carried man's own burden (game, animal skins, or branches). Later the dog was harnessed to the first sledge; then it began to learn the disciplines of hunting. With its keen sense of smell, the dog was able to seek out the wild boar in its wallow, the deer trembling under the foliage. Its speed forced them to run; its aggressiveness held their respect or kept them rooted to the spot until man intervened to finish off the prey or catch it.

This was no doubt the most difficult part

*Cinerary urn
of the necropolis of Gela.
Beginning of the 5th century B.C.
(Museum of Syracuse)*

Mousterian Age and the skilled people of the Magdalenian Age. Neolithic civilization began, and with it came stock-rearing, and later, agriculture. Domestication was near.

At the same time as these peoples of the cultures of Maglemosia, Fonsa, and Kosna became sedentary, so in their turn did the dogs which had followed their lengthy migrations, and shared their life and occupations.

RECORDS OF THE PREHISTORIC DOG

It is impossible to be too careful in interpreting the records of prehistoric dogs, especially when it comes to the most ancient of them.

Can the dog be recognized in the shape of the little earless quadruped with its long upright tail, represented on a badly preserved rock-painting of the Cueva de la Vieja at Alpera (Spain) 10,000 years ago?

A golden knife sheath in the Cairo Museum, and an ivory sheath from Abousedan, dating from 6,000 B.C., are both decorated with canines. Can these be dogs?

On an ivory knife from Djebel-El-Arak, dating from the fourth millennium, are shown two dogs of the Nordic type, with erect ears, heavy, medium-sized bodies, and curled tails. One of these dogs appears to be wearing a collar. Is it correct to conclude that these are domesticated dogs?

It is so easy to confuse things. Déchembre relates that some reputable Egyptologists have confused the ostrich with the flamingo, the hog-fish with the aardvark. Someone even thought that what is in fact a hedgehog on a Persian vase in the Louvre was a hog! In spite of all we think we know, for example, about ancient Egypt, no one can say for certain whether Anubis, the god of the dead, was a jackal or a dog.

This shows how much paleontology requires the assistance of the other scientific disciplines: classification, genetics, zootechny, anatomy, and even comparative psychology.

But to return to the records of prehistory.

LÉONARD VON MATT

27

HASSIA

Lid of pyxis,
Minoan art. Necropolis of Mochlos,
circa 2,500-2,200 B.C.
(Museum of Heraklion, Crete).

In France, a country very rich in prehistoric records, it is fruitless to search for the dog in the bestiaries, whether they were drawn, painted, carved, or in relief, and which are still the most faithful witnesses to the fauna of banished ages.

Does this mean that the men of those times had no domesticated dogs? Or can one conclude that because they were hunters they must have had many dogs? It is conceivable that a dogless civilization may have existed, and even hunting without dogs. The example of the American Indians is a proof of this.

From the time of the Bronze Age, though, we do possess some records, like the boar-hunting scene from Hultane (in the Gothenburg museum), which clearly shows the presence in this period of domesticated dogs surrounding the hunter. However, though all prehistoric men had recourse to hunting for their livelihood, they did not all use dogs.

In Spain, the southeast of the Iberian Peninsula is even richer in prehistoric records. Joléaud and Alimen have drawn attention to several rock paintings of hunters out with their dogs. Unfortunately these records of the past are far from having the graphic purity of the Lascaux drawings. So there has been no agreement in interpreting the age of these works, which some have ascribed to the end of the Paleolithic Age.

Any discussion of the caves of northwest Spain must be just as guarded. Here the animals of the last glacial period are represented with greater fidelity. A few drawings (attributed to the Caspian culture by Abbé Breuil), represent canines which the hunters seem to be holding by the neck, as if to restrain them.

Are the remains of bones exhumed in other parts of Europe any more enlightening?

In 1936 Mertens and Baas brought to light, near Frankfurt am Main, Germany, the complete skeleton of what was indisputably a domestic dog. Unfortunately the age of this skeleton also cannot be determined with any certainty.

In Russia, the plain of Moscow has yielded a canine skeleton of the Neolithic Age, which seems to be very like the dingo both as regards the head and the body as a whole.

In Scandinavia, there is at Massleberg the famous rock painting depicting a scene in which a stag is being assailed by a whole pack. It can be dated from the Bronze Age.

But it is definitely in Denmark that the greatest number of remains of domestic dogs in Europe are concentrated. Numerous dogs have been exhumed at Maglemose, Mullerup, Svaerdbog, and Lundby. This time it seems possible to attribute their presence to that of the Maglemosian hunting peoples who settled in the region more than 7,000 years ago. (The better preserved ones have been dated chronologically by the carbon 14 method.)

These remains already show some degree of variability. Two breeds seem to have been clearly established. One is about the size of a wolf, the other is smaller and more like the Peat dog. These correspond to the two types, still osteologically alike, which will be found later in the Neolithic Age.

The records, it is clear, are not over-abundant. Who would dare to assert with any degree of certainty that these are the traces of the most distant ancestors of all domestic dogs?

Does the rock art of Africa throw any more light on the subject? In Ain-Tazina there is a scene which depicts an African hartebeest beset by two men and face to face with an aggressive canine. Is this a dog or a jackal?

There is a rock drawing in the Atlas mountains, in the region of Tiout, which shows a hunter armed with a bow; his dogs are behind him and he is aiming at some ostriches. This composition, which dates from the beginning of the Neolithic Age, seems to confirm that the dog was indeed used for hunting at that time.

In the Tassili mountains (halfway between Tripoli and Gao, between Garama and the Adrar of the Iforas, bordering the western part of the Tassili-n-Ajjar) the finest collection of rock drawings and paintings in the world has come to light. Like an open book it unveils for us the past glory of the Sahara, now a desert but at that time fertile grasslands teeming with animals and at the same time an important migration route for animals and man.

These Tassili paintings show us the dog engaged in the two activities which made it useful to man—hunting and war. There are two distinct breeds. First is the perfect greyhound type, with its long delicate head, slender long legs, sinewy thighs, and the same tail as can be seen in many representations of the greyhound of Egypt. The other type was not so well set up. The legs were shorter, the bodies quite large, with wider heads, shorter noses, powerful jaws, and tails covered with heavy coat and held halfway down.

It was from Africa and the Near East that stock-rearing and agriculture were introduced into Europe, and with them, the earliest civilizations which spread over the Iberian Peninsula, taking with them the greyhound. . . . From this greyhound are descended the present-day greyhounds of the Mediterranean countries: the Ibizan Hound of the Balearics, the Spanish greyhound (or *galgo*), and the *charnigues* of Provence.

It was also by way of Africa and the Orient that the heavy Tibetan and Assyrian mastiffs, ancestors of the mountain dogs, arrived in Europe. In the Cantabrian Mountains, these powerful dogs were the ancestors of the large Pyrenean sheep dogs which are alive today, but also of the unforgettable *Perros de Sangre* (dogs of blood), which were later used by the Conquistadores for a more dramatic sort of hunting.

From this wide and rapid survey of the origins of the dog in prehistoric times, we would like to pick out three breeds which we can without a doubt consider primitive: the great dog of the Maglemosians (of the wolf type), the Peat dog (which is like the jackal), and . . . the Greyhound.

*Is this bronze
an early representation of a canine?
(Paleolithic, from Sardinia)*

2 FROM THE EGYPTIAN TO THE CHRISTIAN ERA

Hunting, and war. . . .

From the beginning of history, the dog has been associated with man in these two activities. The dog became more and more involved in man's life in the Metal Ages, which saw the construction of towns and temples, the discovery of writing, and the growth of civilization. Soon it was valued for more than its usefulness—man took it as a totem and then as a friend.

EGYPT

About the year 4240 B.C., two deities divided between them the allegiance of all the straggling villages which formed Egypt. They were: Set, the greyhound with the forked tail (in Upper Egypt), and Horus, the falcon (in Lower Egypt and the delta of the Nile). From the time of the IVth dynasty (3,000 years B.C.) each clan had a sacred animal for its protection, and a canine creature appears regularly throughout Egyptian iconography.

Is this animal the dog, the wolf, or the jackal? Undoubtedly the men of the Cheops dynasty and the other builders of the great pyramids must have tried to establish a clear distinction between these three very similar-looking canines.

Going back to the Vth dynasty (2600 B.C.), a very brilliant period in the history of ancient Egypt, we find some dogs for the first time in the tomb of Tiy, represented only in hunting scenes. These domestic dogs are of various types, ranging from the greyhound to the Great Spitz.

The stele of Antefaa II (Xth dynasty) shows the pharoah escorted by four very different types of dog; a greyhound of the Nubian type, another dog quite like an Australian dingo, a heavily built mastiff, and a rather curious, very small dog.

In the Middle Empire (2100 to 1850 B.C.) a dog somewhat similar to today's basset hound appears for the first time (during the XIIth dynasty of the Sesostris). This long dog, with pointed muzzle, and short legs looks very much like the present-day dachshund. Is it the result of some unexpected mutation of the greyhound? This is a possibility. Indeed this basset-like dog appears to have had only a short lineage. It is not to be found on any later Egyptian relics.

For about a thousand years the Middle Empire enjoyed a long period of peace and prosperity, and during this time the Egyptian dog left no historical traces. Succeeding pharoahs preferred their cats (for hunting in the marshes), while the erect-eared greydogs were used to hunt the antelope. At about this time a running dog with pendulous ears and a white coat widely patched and speckled with black was introduced. Little by little it was to take the place of the greyhound of the primitive dynasties, during that period of tranquillity which was soon to be disturbed by war and invasion.

For a century and a half, Egypt was in the power of the Hyksos. The true origins of this people are still obscure. They introduced bronze and the horse into the Nile valley. But where did they come from? Who were they? The Egyptians carefully obliterated every trace of these intelligent and artistic strangers to whom they owed a great deal. As Paul Balta has written, the Hyksos not only changed the face of Egypt, they were also the leaven from which sprang a new Egypt—that of the XIVth dynasty, which saw the glorification of the god Set, whose animal form was the greyhound of the distant past, with its large, curiously docked ears and its forked tail. Images of this creature, however, are scanty.

Did these small, strapping Hyksos, with their chariots, horses, and dogs, come from the steppes of Central Asia? Like all Egypt's invaders (Hourrites, Hittites, or Semites) they brought a great deal to Egypt, but they allowed themselves to be assimilated by her.

Did they bring the mastiff to Egypt? It is

Head of Anubis in bronze, with moveable jaws; used by the divine priests. Egypt, 19th century. (Louvre, Paris)

ED. TEL — VIGNEAU

The god Anubis symbolized
both the dog and the jackal.
(Louvre, Paris)

Scene of a lion hunt.
9th century B.C. (Hittite art)

Persian shield, ▶
decorated with hunting scenes.
(1265, corresponding
with our year 1868.)
(Wallace Collection, London)

quite likely that they did. In any case, before them there are no documents to be found in Egypt representing this formidable, hefty, and powerful dog, which would have been of no use in hunting water-fowl or antelope.

The Egyptians freed themselves from the Hyksos, but they kept the mastiff (without, however, abandoning other dogs). Queen Hatshepsut (XVIIIth dynasty) sent emissaries to the Land of Punt to give that ruler some of the finest and fleetest of her greyhounds. The Egyptian dog was now invested with a new role. The newcomer, the mastiff, became the soldier's dog, or, more exactly, the "devouring dog" which was set

on the fleeing enemy. In the Cairo museum there is a wooden casket, as richly decorated as a Persian miniature, which shows the pharoah Tutankhamen (XVIIIth dynasty, 1352 B.C.) standing upright in his chariot, shooting arrows at routed Nubian soldiers, who are being harried by his Assyrian dogs.

Whether or not these powerful cream-colored mastiffs, wearing wide collars armed with wrought-iron spikes, were imported by the Hyksos is of very little importance. They were the ancestors of those fierce sheep dogs still so numerous in the Taurus region and the Anatolian plateau, which are still used by the Turks to guard their flocks.

With the coming of the New Empire (1500 to 1100 B.C.) the dog appears to be closer to the heart of man. Thothmes III and Amenhotep II had him portrayed on their tombs, as a prefiguration of the "dead." On the tomb of Antef, King of Thebes, he is shown surrounded by his four favorite dogs, among which is the "Abaker" greyhound, which was to give its name to the Saluki of the Berbers.

Certainly, of all the animals, the cat remained the most beloved of the Egyptians, but from this time on the dog too had its rights. After its death it was embalmed and its remains placed in a sarcophagus. The

Incantation to the god Anubis.
Egyptian stele.
(Musée Borely, Marseilles)

Since the time of the Hittites
the people of Catal-Huyuk have continued
even to this day
to cast spells against bad luck,
using the skull of a sheep-dog
and a few grains of colza (coleseed).

Egyptions wept for it, they mourned it by shaving their heads. Anyone who killed a dog was punished by death.

Probably from this late date came the fine limestone dog in the Louvre, which was found at Assiout (the ancient Lycopolis). It is the god Oupouaout who is thus represented under the form of a watch dog.

The dogs of Egypt were hunting dogs or war dogs, or even temple guards, but they were never subordinates. In the innumerable scenes of inspection, transfer, or census of livestock to be found on tomb paintings or temple frescos, the dog is never portrayed as guardian of the flock. Only black slaves or children were given the task of watching over and protecting the domestic animals, whether these were cattle, donkeys, or geese.

THE NEAR EAST

It is recounted in the Bible that according to Eliezer, the servant of Abraham, the body of Abel was preserved from the vultures and hyenas by sheep dogs. But the dog is not tolerated in Israel.

Although for a long time the Hebrews were to look back nostalgically to their nomadic lives as shepherds, their hate for the Egyptians brought them nonetheless to regard the "kaleb" (which was later to become "clebs") as an unclean beast.

From the VIIIth century B.C., the Hittites had the dog in their service, as is shown by a sculptured fresco from Malacya (in the museum of Istanbul). From his chariot the royal archer aims his arrow at a lion, while a medium-sized dog, ears bent forward, runs along at the side of his horse.

Recent excavations have brought to light, at Catal-Huyuk, a veritable sanctuary of ritual hunting scenes dating from about 6000 years B.C.[1] On the west wall there are some bearded men surrounding and harrying a

stag, while a woman and a large dog with delicate muzzle and very erect ears keep their distance from the fray. On the north wall, under a frieze of wild asses, an enormous bull dominates a large number of gesticulating huntsmen, escorted by two similar dogs. One cannot help but remember a similar scene at Lascaux, but at Lascaux the dogs were absent.

These polychrome records of Hittite rock painting are particularly interesting because they are obvious proof that the domestic dog was certainly associated with the activities of Neolithic huntsmen all over the Near East.

In 1966 the film-makers of the expedition, Réné Dazy and Jean Vidal, returned to Kucuk Koy to film the modern equivalent of these scenes. There, the legends have not changed. Here and there on the walls of the dwelling places you can still find the marks of hands impregnated with reddish mud, just as they were more than twenty centuries ago.[2] But the legends of the animal painters have become less rich as the diversity of zoological species is impoverished. No longer are there any heads of the god-bull, nor horns of the wild ox at Catal-Huyuk. As for the great black vultures of Turkey, each day they give way a little more before the advance of the storks. But magic does not die just because of this. In the interior courtyard of the dwellings of some of the villages, the people still try to ward off bad luck. The skull of a sheep dog, laid on the ground between an old plate and a little colza (coleseed), has simply become the present-day equivalent of the dried out skull of the protective bull.

PERSIA

In Persia, the dog was very early considered to be the best of the animals because, as the texts say, it is "the guardian of the flock and the defender of man."

[1] J. Mellaart. "A Neolithic Town in Anatolia." Archaeologia, August, 1967.

[2] "Kucuk Koy," by Réné Dazy. Archeologia, August, 1967.

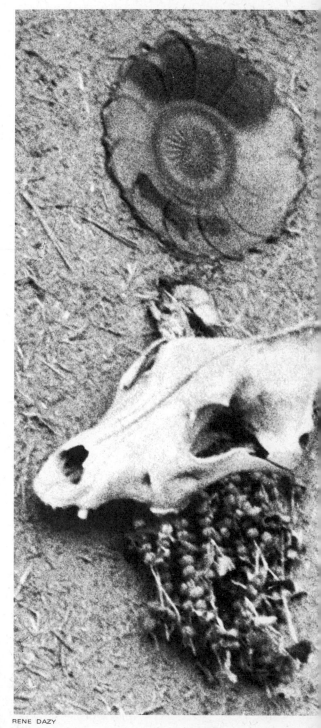

*Assyrian mastiffs
and servants carrying hunting nets.
12 century B.C.
(British Museum)*

Persian bronze: man with dogs.

Although it was allowable to destroy lizards, worms, and harmful insects, to kill a dog was a crime and to cherish it a duty. So decreed Ormuzd, the Son of Fire. That is why the ancients did not hesitate to give their great and wise men the name of Chan ("the dog"), symbolic appellation of the spirit of gentleness and wisdom. This did not prevent these same great men—the kings in particular—from using the most ferocious dogs in war. Cyrus the Great, in the course of his campaigns, exempted four towns in Babylon from all taxes, charging them with the breeding and training of the most cruel combat mastiffs for his armies. These dogs were also savagely set upon prisoners and traitors.

The Persians had the custom of never burying the bodies of the close relations of their seers without having them first torn to shreds by wild beasts. For the common people, says Cicero (in Book One of *The Tusculan Disputations*), dogs sufficed, and poor people used for this purpose the village's stray dogs, while richer people used their household dogs.

The Indo-Europeans, semi-pastoral peoples, came from these regions. From the time of the second millennium they emigrated towards western and southern Europe. As soon as they had the horse, they became fearsome warriors, and with their ravening mastiffs they invaded the Fertile Crescent from Babylon to Egypt.

CHALDEA AND ASSYRIA

In Chaldea and Assyria, each town had from the first its own animal-god (fish-god, lion-god, etc.), but there was no dog-god, as Calvet and Cruppe have noted. It is however from Assyria that we have inherited the impressive brachycephalic dogs which originated in Tibet and from which are descended the Newfoundland, the Saint Bernard, and all the mountain dogs. As for the mastiffs (of which we have spoken in connection with the Hyksos), they were already known to the Sumerians. Cuneiform inscriptions enable us to trace them back to 2000 years B.C. This is a remarkable fact. It is obvious proof that man had indeed domesticated these frightening dogs: the same ideogram is used to denote the dog, the servant, the valet, and the slave.

On the other hand, there is no trace of the greyhound in Chaldea. The famous dogs of Mesopotamia spread over the entire world, but none are to be found today either on the banks of the Tigris or the Euphrates.

In the Berlin Museum, as in the British Museum and the Louvre, one can get a good idea of the descendants of these great dogs, so swift and fierce, from the admirable bas-reliefs of Assurbanipal (900 B.C.) Also in the British Museum is the famous Sumerian bowl which has engraved on its sides a wild boar hunt with dogs in the marshes of Babylon (3000 B.C.)

When the Assyrian Empire crumbled, the Medes and the Persians, and all the huntsmen kings of the Orient, paid enormous sums for these magnificent dogs whose role seems to have been as important as that of the greyhound in the history of the canine race.

PHOENICIA

Too taken up with the things of the sea, which fascinated her people, Phoenicia did not evolve a land-based mythology in which the dog could have played a role. However, Baal, the cruel god of this great people, is often represented by a dog's head. It is no doubt more nearly correct to see in this symbol the classic image of the "devouring dog" than that of generosity and gentleness.

EASTERN ASIA

Did Eastern Asia have aboriginal domesticated dogs, originating, for instance, in China? We lack the records which would enable us to judge. According to Pauthier, who translated the sacred book of Chou-King, the Chinese imported all their dogs. However, about 3468 B.C., the kind Fo-Hi was already encouraging the breeding of little "sleeve dogs," just as later (2188 to 2160 B.C.) the kind Tai-Kang, also a great dog-lover, was to do.

Detail
on the bas-relief of Assurbanipal:
hunting wild horses 900 B.C.
(British Museum)

A thousand years before Christ, Chinese emperors were using tall dogs of the mastiff type for hunting . . . man! Five hundred years later, according to the story told by Chen-Mou-Yu about the sacrifice of king Ling on Mount Kang, the dog was part of the animal offering. Dog was served up at royal banquets, as were also joints of roast beef, pork, or ram.

Japan seems to have venerated the domestic dog, called *Omisto,* in rather curious conditions. According to the legend, Omisto, the god of suicide, with the body of a man and the head of a dog who rode a charger with seven heads, promised eternal joy to any man who killed himself in his honor. Whenever a dog died, recounts Barat, it was buried standing up, with the head above ground, and for several days people regularly continued to lay its food beside it.

AMERICA

The dog seems always to have been known to the inhabitants of ancient Mexico. Together with the turkey, it was the only domesticated animal. Symbol of the "fire from heaven," that is, of lightning (which when it hurls itself upon the earth opens the way to hell), the dog had a role identical with that of Anubis the Egyptian. Its task was to guide the dead to their last dwelling place. So the domestic dog was killed on the death of its master and its body placed beside him so that the dead man could reach the other world under the most favorable conditions.

Two very different types of dogs have been thought to have been aboriginal. The first, of medium size and with brown markings, recalls some of the dogs of Egypt and Greece, and also the modern Dalmatian. Reared in flocks, they were sold at market by the hundreds, either to be eaten, or to be sacrificed at funerary rites. The second type, smaller, with a fine, close coat, was the ancestor of the present-day minute Chihuahua with its globular head. They were beloved, tender companions long before the arrival of the Conquistadores. So, the indigenous peoples of America had already domesticated the dog. They were terrified, though, by the fierce mastiffs of the Conquistadores, these

BRITISH MUSEUM

Mexican dog.
Aztec civilization.
(Valley of Mexico)

"dogs of blood" (or "devouring dogs," of the first civilizations), so different from the smallish breeds with which they were familiar. The stylized dog which came from the museums of Tempoal (Musée de l'Homme, Paris) is obviously nearer to the modern Chihuahua than to the great Tibetan mastiff. Moreover, the Quichuas peoples did not use the same word to denote the dogs of the Conquistadores and their own dogs.

We must also mention the existence of those strange Maned Dogs *(chrysocion jubatus)* which are still the wild canines of South America and whose gait, coat, and voice are more like those of the wolf and the fox than of the domestic dog.

Like most southerly countries of America, ancient Peru also had its domestic dog. The natives of the Straits of Magellan, just like the inhabitants of the islands of Wager and Chloe, used them as fishing auxiliaries.

According to Tschudi, all these dogs of the American continent belonged either to *canis caraibicus,* a type of small, practically hairless canine with a single tuft of hair on the top of its head—which is also found in China—or to the *canis ingoe,* which is even smaller, with erect, pointed ears.

INDIA

Several centuries before the Christian era, India certainly knew and used the dog. The arch of a door of the Buddhist sanctuary of Sanchi-Tope is sculptured with several dogs which belonged to king Asoka (280 B.C.). Here again are the terrible mastiffs with floppy ears probably imported from Tibet and which Alexander the Great was to introduce into Greece on his return.

ANCIENT GREECE

In ancient Greece the dog was guardian of the flock and of the house, but it was not an object of contempt. However, the word

Chinese dog.
Han epoch. 3rd century B.C.
(Cernuschi museum)

Hercules with Cerberus in chains.
Painting of the crater of the underworld.
300 B.C.
(Museum of Munich)

"cynicism" (from *kuon, kunos:* dog) was coined to denote shamelessness, scorn for the conventions and morals. Later, through exaggerated anthropomorphism, the poets attributed to the dog all the virtues and the faults of men. But these legends do prove how well the dog had conquered the hearts of its masters. Homer moves us with his story of "Argus," the faithful dog which Ulysses had fed from his hand and which he had loved. Thin, ravenous, covered with vermin, abandoned by its master's friends and even by Penelope (the wife of the hero loved so well), Argus dragged through the streets, unhappy and pathetic. Twenty years later the great warrior returned to Ithaca, and Argus died of happiness at finding Ulysses again, in the presence of Eumaeus, the old herdsman who, himself, had not recognized his old master.

From whence came the first dog which barked in the land of Attica? Let us again listen to Homer. Vulcan, the god of Hades not only forged the shield of the impetuous Achilles; he also forged a dog, a bronze dog which came slowly to life under his divine breath and had a thousand adventures. Vulcan first gave it to Zeus, who in turn offered it to the beautiful Europa, in exchange for a single kiss . . . but a kiss so long that from it was born a son who was to be judge of the underworld and king of Crete. Menos in his turn became separated from the dog. But such an animal cannot die. It was from it that was born Cerberus, the three-headed dog, terrible guardian of the underworld, whom the dead had to placate by offering him money laid in their tomb . . . Cerberus, even more terrible on earth, and whom Orpheus calmed with the strains of his lute . . . Cerberus whom Hercules managed to put in chains, and drag behind him to Trezene and throw back into the underworld, to help his friend Theseus and to have Alomene.

And there are so many other stories of the dog playing an important role in Greek mythology! That of Actaeon the hunter, who was changed into a stag for watching Diana at her bath, and who was hungrily devoured by his own dogs. . . . The one about Nimrod, also called Cephalus, whose best Bloodhounds were suddenly turned to stone just as he was about to strangle a fox. . . . That of the greyhound of Artemis, represented on the shaft of a column, which with its slender form and erect ears is the same type as the great greyhound of Upper Egypt.

In more historic times, ancient Greece had other dogs which have remained just as famous, among them the celebrated dog of Alcibiades. This dog came down to posterity, not because it got the better of four or five brigands bent on seizing the wide golden collar it carried round its neck (with its own name and its master's on it), but because of an eccentric prank of Alcibiades.

*Attic amphora
from the necropolis of Gela.
5th century B.C.
(Museum of Gela)*

*Fine example of Greek ceramic art,
already prefiguring present-day hounds.
Attic rhyton from Falerii.
(Villa Giulia, Rome.)*

Towards the year 430 B.C., this disciple of Pericles and Socrates, who was as clever as he was handsome and brave, was both the favorite and the *enfant terrible* of Athens. The women had eyes only for him; as for the people, in gratitude for the victories he had won, they turned a blind eye to all his pranks.

When, in spite of his extravagant behavior, he was officially elevated to the rank of *strategus,* he decided to celebrate in a manner befitting this wonderful promotion.

So on the eve of his departure for his new post, during a night of frenzied feasting with his friends, he amused himself by multilating, one after the other, the most beautiful statues of Hermes that he could find. At dawn the crime (for such vandalism committed against the gods was a crime) was discovered, but the culprit was no longer there. He had enlisted in the service of Sparta.

Time passed. When Alcibiades did return, triumphant and pardoned, he was more full of eccentricities than ever. And so one fine morning he bought the finest dog he could find, paid 7,500 drachmas (more than two million old francs) for it, had its tail docked to the coccyx, and walked it through the town!

Things were going badly for Athens, but this was enough to distract the people from their troubles for a whole week. Since no dogs were tolerated in Athens (as Plutarch

A "companion dog,"
taking part in a feast.
(Corinthian vase of the 6th century)

tells us), no one talked of anything but this caprice, of the poor mutilated dog and its crazy master. When Athens returned to more serious matters, Alcibiades had again departed. Some time later he was to die, assassinated in Thrace by order of the ungrateful town of Sparta, which he had served so well his whole life long.

On the whole the Greeks were never very concerned about the fate of the canine species. Hippocrates (460-377 B.C.), who claimed he was unable to heal during the month of August (when the sun and the Dog-star arise at the same time), had, it is said, a lively interest in dogs. His statues, like those of the god Mithra, often show him with a snake under his feet and a dog at his side. Doubtless this should be seen as a symbol of the two great scourges which were then inevitably fatal—rabies and poison—and for which the medicine of those days had no antidotes.

The Greeks kept large numbers of watch dogs and relied on them for the guarding of their fortresses. Thus the citadel of Corinth, guarded outside by fifty dogs, was one night the object of a surprise attack while the soldiers slept. The fifty dogs alone defended the town and were killed to the last but one. The sole survivor ran to the gates of the town and succeeded in giving the alarm. The attack was repulsed.

Touched by this unexpected devotion, the citizens decided to erect a marble monument to the memory of the forty-nine brave creatures. As for "Soter" (that was the name of the surviving dog), it was given a pension for life and a heavy collar of solid silver engraved with the following inscription: "To Soter, defender and savior of Corinth, placed under the protection of his friends."

We have little in the way of records of the dogs used for hunting in Greece between the 7th and the 5th centuries B.C.

Xenophon (487-433 B.C.) recommends: "Do not take the first dog that comes along for hunting wild boar; and for hunting hare, the Celtic dogs are preferable to all others."

*Detail from
the Triumph of Neptune
and the Four Seasons,
5th century. La Chelbo.
(Musée du Bardo, Tunisia)*

*Attic amphora: Pollux and Leda.
(Musée Etrusque)*

However, the keen olfactory qualities of some dogs were for a long time put to use in very curious circumstances. When a man collapsed and no one round him could tell whether he was gravely injured or dead, a little dog with a well-developed sense of smell was brought into his presence. If the man were in a death-trance or simply unconscious, the dog would wag its tail, utter two or three little cries, and claim its reward. If, on the other hand, the dog was silent, immobile, and rooted to the spot, then the man was indeed judged dead.

Other friendly and gentle dogs were certainly valued for their tender companionship, as is shown by the images of Pollux, the protector of the hunt, represented on numerous amphora (dating from the 6th century B.C.) with his greyhound. On some frescoes of the classical age there are also representations of rich Athenians lying on individual couches for communal drinking bouts. Under each couch is tied a dog, usually a small greyhound, carrying a wide ornate collar. Towards 350 B.C. Aristotle enumerated the most useful of the known breeds, among them the Epirotic dog, the Laconian, and the Molossian, but he does not bother to describe them. We have few details of these breeds, but Aristotle does discuss the Laconian bitches, which were, he tells us, much more delicate than the males, and he advises crossing them with Molossian dogs in order to procure pups "which have both the grace of their mothers and the courage of their sires."

At that time, many other dogs of foreign (Cyrenian, Egyptian, or Hindu) origin were represented on coins or on the shafts of columns.

At quite a late date, heavy powerful dogs were introduced into Greece by Xerxes. Later, Alexander the Great, on his return from India, brought back a very similar type of dog. They were to be the ancestors of the dogs of Macedonia and Epirus.

Alexander was so fond of one of these dogs that he had a whole town built in its mem-ory. It was, it is true, an exceptional dog, and here is its story.

Alexander the Great had already had a similar dog which was the gift of an Albanian king. Because of all he had been told about this dog, he wanted to set it against a wild boar, and then a bear; but when the dog paid no attention to them, Alexander, annoyed, had it killed. When the Albanian king heard of this, he was stung, and sent Alexander a second dog, stating, "Bears and wild boar are no match for such dogs as these. Bestow on this one that I send you at least an elephant or a lion!" The second dog arrived; the next day it disembowelled the lion and killed the elephant. Filled with admiration, Alexander was ever after to hold this dog in fraternal affection.

ANCIENT ROME

In Rome, too, these terrible dogs, ferocious guards and fierce combatants, were adored. Their image is often found on oil lamps.

From the 5th century on, Rome sent some of these dogs into the province of Vindossia (today Brugg), in Switzerland, where recently the complete and perfectly preserved skeleton of one of them was discovered. Later, these dogs accompanied the Roman expeditions into Germania, as Monsieur Fraas has established as a result of excavations in Würtemberg.

It is difficult to distinguish precisely between what was Roman and what was Greek in everything which concerns the science of the dog (cynegenics). The Romans and the Greeks were both equally fond of hunting and consequently of the dog. The most famous authors dedicated part of their works to the selection and breeding of dogs, and to the best way of training them. As far as Greece is concerned, we have already cited Xenophon and Aristotle. For Rome, we will cite the principal authors:

Varro (116-27 B.C.) advises, in *Rerum rusticarum libri*, that one should buy sheep dogs from shepherds, and never from huntsmen or butchers, "because butcher's dogs often attack livestock, and huntsmen's dogs, at the sight of a hare or a fox, too easily remember that they were once hunting dogs."

Ovid (43 B.C.-16 A.D.) talks of the different dogs it is good to possess, of the most prized coats, of the most highly recommended cross-breeds, and he tells where to buy dogs in the best condition ". . . with the keenest sense of smell and the most lively character."

All along the dog remains a privilege of the leisured classes. It becomes fashionable to have one's own dogs in one's own house. Those who cannot afford the expense of this luxury keep geese to guard their houses. In fact geese have this advantage, that they proved themselves, on the Capitol, more vigilant than the dog . . . and besides, nothing they eat is wasted!

Pliny the Elder (43 B.C.-16 A.D.) pays particular attention to the psychic qualities of the dog and agrees with Cassius in singing the praises of canine fidelity.

Columella (1st century A.D.) was chiefly interested in fierce watchdogs.

Polyen (in the 2nd century) talks of "hefty fighting dogs responsible for preventing all contact between besiegers and besieged, by intercepting all messengers and uncovering all messages."

Oppian (200 A.D.) whose work, *Cynegetics,* was to earn him payment of twenty thousand pieces of gold from two emperors, favors the smaller dog that can run small game to earth. The "vestigator," he says, has not the speed of the "vertagus" (little greyhound), but it will serve the average huntsman nobly.

Finally, Arrian (2nd century) compares the shrewd bloodhounds, the "segusii," to swifter but less reliable dogs. He wrote an admirable work, which was to be regarded as an authority for centuries, on the thousand secrets of hunting with dogs.

The Romans were a soldierly people. They were able to appreciate the military qualities

"Cave canem."
"Beware the dog."
Mosaic from the house of the poet.
(Pompeii)

Gallo-Roman bed in earthenware.
(Museum of Saint-Germain-en-Laye)

The cauldron of Gundestrup.
Around the bull which he has overcome,
Smertellus is seen killing the three dogs
sent by Taranis.
The cauldron is of chased silver,
and of Celtic origin. (1st century B.C.)
(National Museum, Copenhagen)

of the dog and made him an integral part of their triumphant expeditions. They had watchdogs, attacking dogs, and dogs used for communications. Sometimes the latter were made to swallow secret messages enclosed in metal tubes. When the unfortunate creatures arrived at their destinations, they were sacrificed so that the messages might be recovered. Finally, Rome, like Greece, had her "devouring" dogs which were starved for several days before the combat. She also used dogs to carry "Greek fire," and had other dogs of war armed with iron collars and carrying cutting points and sharp blades fixed on their sides and backs.

GAUL

The war dogs of Gaul were no less fearful. It is related that after the defeat of the Celts and the Cimbri, the Romans had to do battle for two whole days against the dogs of the enemy, who alone defended their chariots and baggage. As for hunting dogs, from the time of the *canis palustris* (Peat dog) of their origins, the Gauls had never ceased to treat them with understanding, gratitude, and friendship.

The descendants of these dogs of the pile dwellers were in large part the original ancestors of our hunting dogs.

The Celts, who settled in Gaul in the 5th century B.C., even made a place for the dog in their mythology.

Curious though it may seem to us, there was a Gallic religion which has remained little known, and which has recently been the object of some interesting discoveries. This is how Professor J. J. Hatt, of the University of Strasbourg, working from a few rediscovered texts, has reconstructed the rite of the burning wheel *"rota flavissima circumsepta."*[3]

On certain days of the year, this wheel was brought down from a sanctuary situated at the top of a hill and passed along the

LÉONARD VON MATT

bed of a river where the fire was extinguished; then, soothed, the wheel ascended once more by an ingenious system of pulleys and ropes to its home within the temple walls. This was the symbol of the "fire from heaven" which the Gauls held in intense awe.

But on this strange mechanism (dating from about 500 B.C.) there figured some dogs. They are found reproduced on the plaques of the celtic cauldron of Gundestrap (in the Copenhagen museum) where the Gallic god Taranis is hurling fire from heaven. To left and right, two monstrous mastiffs symbolize this "devouring" fire of lightning, and the devastating power of the god Taranis. Further off, the mother goddess in majesty holds in check some elephants (symbols of danger at war), and thanks to the griffins of Belemus (Apollo) she overcomes Smertulus, the "devouring dog" of Taranis, symbol of destruction in death.

Another raised plaque shows some bulls being harassed by aggressive dogs. These dogs are of medium size and recall the Nordic dogs of today. Finally there is another plaque which represents a soldier of Gaul and his dog struck down by lightning, lying on the ground side by side.

After this, the Gauls' dogs became very highly prized, and Julius Caesar himself set a high value on them.

Gaul became Roman. Life under its sky was sweet and easy. Rome gave the men of Gaul a taste for luxury and good food, and the wealthy owners of vineyards enjoyed all the refinements of their conquerors. The house dog also tasted of these delights, and in winter it shared its master's couch, if the master considered it a good hunting dog.

Indubitably, the Gauls were masters of what may be called "the canine sport." What else could one call this almost daily game, which no longer had the quest for meat as its only aim, and which all Celts pursued

only for pleasure? To hunt the stag until it is exhausted, to capture the hare by setting at its heels two greyhounds let loose at the same moment, these were favorite pastimes, without it being thought at all useful or necessary that any single day's sport should be fatal to the game.

"The Gauls," wrote Arrian, "do not hunt in order to capture the game, but to watch their dogs perform with ability and speed. If the hare should escape their pursuit, they recall their dogs and rejoice sincerely in the luck or superiority of the adversary."

If one adds that the chieftains of Gaul took pains to send to their conquerors the best examples from their packs (for instance Bituit, king of Arverne, offered his own dogs as gifts to the consul Domitius, in 122 B.C.), no one could deny that ancient Gaul had that spirit of generosity and pride in sport that she has taught the entire world, and that—fifteen hundred years later—the hunters and hunstmen of France still continue this tradition.

[3]J. J. Hatt. "In Search of the Religion of Gaul." Archeologia, April, 1966.

MAZEL

3 THE CHRISTIAN ERA AND THE MIDDLE AGES

Between the civilizations of antiquity and modern times lie the Middle Ages, which began with the fall of the Roman Empire in the West (476) and ended with the destruction of the Roman Empire in the East and the capture of Constantinople by the Turks (1453). This much-debated millennium can be divided into three phases: the eastern or Byzantine phase, which, with the contribution of the Roman culture, flowered in Constantinople, and Byzantium became the world's center of thought; the Arab phase, which was centered round Cordoba, where the Caliphate of Baghdad had its seat and which was to be the source of European thought; the Christian phase which—once Islam was discarded—was the time when Christianity was supreme in all lands and the Pope had authority over all sovereigns.

What became of the animal world, and more particularly the dog world, during these ten centuries of slow, human evolution?

THE DOG, A SCORNED ANIMAL

In the first years of the disintegration of the Roman Empire in the West, dogs were free in many places, almost as free as they were in those far-off days of prehistoric times.

There were innumerable dogs which had followed the barbarians in their invasions and had been abandoned by them all along their routes. There were ownerless dogs which wandered around large cities in the East, living on garbage dumps, feeding on the rubbish. There were bands of dogs in the villages of Europe, living by scavenging, indulging in rough battles among themselves, and deprived of the easy relationship which they had enjoyed, until then, with man. Once they reverted to a semi-wild state, all quickly rediscovered their ancient instinct for digging up corpses on which to feed themselves. How can we forget that our ancestors protected their dead with a stone against tomb plunderers? The poet Martial

(about the year 80) was already writing this epitaph:

Sit tibi terra levis, mollique tegeris arena,
Nec tua non possint eruere ossa canes . . .

In these difficult times when violence and pillage dominated, only those people who themselves could find enough to eat and lead some kind of secure life in such uncertainty owned dogs. These privileged people were in the minority. But for others, the terrifying, scavenging packs of dogs were the objects of fear and superstition.

In the Near East some Moslems considered the dog guilty of devouring the body of Mohammed, and, over the years, tradition demanded that dogs should be hanged in the streets as a punishment for their crime.

In Europe, the defenseless peasant, the victim of constant plundering, who lived in fear of invaders passing through and laying waste to everything, readily believed the legends of fantastic animals: werewolves, devil dogs, and monstrous dragons which the Church was to depict in gargoyles on cathedrals.

Most often the dogs were represented with pendulous lips pulled back, menacing fangs, and ferocious eyes. The word "dog" became an insult and all thieves or murderers were described as "curs."

This feeling of terror for the dog owed its origin to the legend of the Cynocephalus. In the tenth sermon of St. Gregory of Nazianze on the "Mysteries of the Gentiles" there is mention of these monster-men who worshipped Hecate, the goddess who knew how to pacify the cruellest of dogs.

A naive iconography depicts a then-unknown tribe of the Black Sea as bloodthirsty "devil-dogs." In the 10th century the monks of Cappadocia, who are at that time hermits, but later assembled in a monastery in Anatolia, evoked in their paintings these disquieting Cynocephali, to which St. Andrew, usually considered the Apostle of

Stone gargoyle.
(Church of Saint-Maixent)
MARC GARANGER

St. Christopher, the Cynocephalus.
(Byzantine Museum, Athens)

BOUDOT-LAMOTTE

(Toros Roslin, 1287). The religious authorities, without setting credence by such legends, did not try to conceal their hate for the dog. The Second Council of Mâcon (585) forbade priests from having dogs, even for guarding their houses "as much because of the noise and salacious behavior of these animals, as because of the poison which is transmitted in their bite."

But the dog did not suffer the condemnation reserved for the cat, which was guilty of having been deified in Egypt. In fact, in order to exorcise the cat, the son of Beelzebub, prince of demons, the monks of Anatolia forgot their superstitious fear of the "devouring dogs," and the faithful docile animal, and good servant, was reinstated.

The nobility, the landowners, and the huntsmen rediscovered the dog. It was again to become their companion in life, and a precious auxiliary of their favorite sport: hunting.

THE REINSTATEMENT OF THE DOG: HUNTING

Some Frankish noblemen already maintained small packs of hounds for stag, wolf, or boar hunting. Very rapidly, they imposed their *droit de chasse* (right to hunt) as landowners, not without some harshness.

From the middle of the 5th century the texts of some laws already foreshadow the importance of the hunt and of the dog by way of consequence. In 490, Clovis stipulated: If anyone kills a dog, the owner has no right of indemnity if the said dog is mad; but, if the owner denies that his dog has caught rabies, it falls to the man who has killed the animal to prove that he has seen the said dog attack animals and humans, and that he has seen it bite its tongue."

In 630 it was laid down: "Whosoever kills the leader of a pack of hounds will pay a fine of six sous, the said penalty being reduced to three sous for the second dog and any others."

ARCH. R. LAFFONT

Scythia and Georgia, had been instructed to preach the gospel. At Vézélay, the same men with heads of dogs appear about 1125 on a tympanum showing the mission of the Apostles. Here it is no longer to St. Andrew, but to St. Thomas—Apostle of India?—that is attributed the much-discussed conversion to God of these imaginary tribes. We again find these Cynocephali in some rare manuscripts of the 11th century, and they were also used to illustrate some Armenian miniatures

In 789 the same offences were thenceforth punishable by fines of up to 40 to 50 sous. Had silver been devalued or was the dog more highly valued and in greater demand?

In fact the population became more and more interested in all that concerned the dog, in its breeding and in the selection of the best. Dogs were brought at inflated prices because they were thought capable of transmitting to their descendants the best hunting qualities.

At the same time, to pander to this passion of the nobility, and to make a profit out of them, the monasteries began to apply themselves to creating new specialized breeds for each kind of prey.

THE FIRST "GREAT DOGS" OF FRANCE

Their first big success was the creation of the Saint Hubert Hound by the monks of the Abbey of Saint-Hubert at Mouzon (in the Ardennes), whose patron was the celebrated repentant huntsman.

This large dog easily reached over 2 feet at the shoulder; it was at the same time powerful and fast, with an excellent nose and eager to hunt all animals. Its dark coat, its fine, dense hair, its wide, pendulous ears, its head marked with furrows and folds of skin all gave it a distinctive appearance.

It was to be the first great breed of Hainaut, Lorraine, and Burgundy, and thenceforward the good monks instituted a clever and paying tradition: that of sending six young dogs every year to the King of France, who offered them to his noble friends. There could not have been better publicity for the spreading of these valuable Bloodhounds. Their descendants were to proliferate, in less than a quarter of a century, from the eastern marches to as far as the Pyrenees and England.

For the first time, dogs other than the princely Greyhounds were the objects of great care, solicitude, and affection. For the first time also their masters began to take some care for their health.

Until then, only the Arabs had devoted themselves to giving ill or wounded dogs any medical assistance, even going as far as operating on them in cases of disembowelment or serious wounds.

As far as the Christian world was concerned, medicine was no longer an art: to ease pain and to cure with God's aid had become a ministry. A thousand years earlier, it is true, Hippocrates agreed to give of his

ARCHIVES PHOTOS

ARCH. R. LAFFONT

The Book of Hours
of the Duke de Berry:
Death at Vincennes.
(Bibliothèque de Chantilly)

(ARCH. R. LAFFONT.)

*A dog licks
the pustules of a dying man.
Detail from the portal.
(St. Pierre de Moissac)*

*—Overleaf:
Scene of an interior
from the Grimani Breviary (1515).
(St Mark's Library, Venice)*

J. RIBIÈRE

their Greyhounds at their feet! The hunters reacted. They were forbidden to enter the church with their dogs? Then they would listen to Mass outside—all doors were open —without being separated from their four-legged companions! The only thing left for the priests, wary of entering into a struggle with their patrons and protectors, was to come as far as the square in front of the church to bless them!

Thus was born out of the Third Capitulary the custom, which is still preserved, of giving the blessing in front of the church door, before a "laying on of the pack," to the animals in general, and above all to dogs.

In the ensuing centuries the attachment of the nobles for their dogs went even further. Lisoire de Montmorency, first baron of France, created "the order of the dog," in symbolic homage to its loyalty and courage. It is in this same period that the following, incredible story took place, which the inhabitants of the Oplaud Valley have passed down from century to century, the subject of which is *a dog which became their king!*

King Eystein (son of Magnus) who reigned from 1001 to 1023 over Norway, was hounded from his native land and took refuge abroad. Patiently he assembled an army of revenge. When he was ready to attack, he marched on his own frontiers, subdued his enemies, and recovered his kingdom in a few hours. Nevertheless, he harbored a justified grudge: "His subjects had no want of him? He would impose on them a king of their sort." And he therefore gave them the choice between a slave . . . and a dog!

The people preferred the dog. Thus an impressive dog called "Suening" or "Saur" was put on the throne; and this Suening-Saur, on his accession, took the title or Majesty. From that day forth he lived nobly, exactly as had his master. He had his court, his counsellors, his guard, his officers, and his household. Someone even said that the soul of a great lord of the past had been reincarnated in the body of this dog. Another,

knowledge to a suffering dog only if man's health was going to be endangered. The Church, in her turn, was to heap Platonic scorn on animals, and dogs were to remain at the church doors. She was to make medicine (or more exactly the power of healing) a mystic, religious knowledge which had its own clerics and solemn oaths. . . .

One can get an idea of the medicinal and veterinary ignorance of the time by reading the directions in an English manuscript of the 11th century: In the case of a bite from a dog suspected of rabies, it is indicated to "take the worm which is found under the animal's tongue, cut it into sections and bury it in a fig." A curious confusion between the "string of the tongue" and a worm! This did not prevent this astonishing prescription being followed in country districts until the 19th century.

In such a society, it was not possible for a true animal medicine which concerned itself with dogs or even horses to have a place.

And yet, the horse became the symbol of chivalry, which was to give the day to the nobility. The hunt became the passion and privilege of these untiring knights who, from dawn to dusk with their horse and their hounds, chased the stag, the wolf, and the wild-boar.

A PASSION WHICH UPSET THE CHURCH

Whatever may have been the desire of the clergy not to oppose the harmless pleasure of princes—even though insects were dedicated to the Gemonies and "guilty" pigs and goats were hanged, it was impossible to institute proceedings agains dogs—the passion for hunting ended up disquieting the Church. Charlemagne was the first to be upset.

Already an order prohibiting priests and abbots from owning dogs had been decreed. The Emperor reproached the nobles for presenting themselves at Divine Service with

48

Boar hunting with a pike (10th century).
(Chest in the Cathedral of Troyes)

The King's grand, white dogs.
Treatise on hunting by Gaston Phébus
(15th century).
(Bibliothèque Nationale, Paris)

going one better, discovered that "the king," in a fit of anger, could distinctly articulate two current words in Norwegian and could bark a third! When the dog-king went out to greet his people, his zealous valets escorted him. When the snow or the rain dared to wet him, his coutiers carried him under their arms.

"Saur" reigned thus for three years, which were neither better nor worse than any other reign and during which he signed (with his paw) decrees and orders which the best of his counsellors impassively submitted to him. And the people, who had first felt hurt and humiliated, ended up by taking his part. After all, the dog was less deceitful than many men, and he at least had an appreciable advantage over some powerful men at court: For one thing he could not talk, and for another, it was difficult to buy his support with money and indulgence.

But as Aesop and later La Fontaine said: "What's bred in the bone will come out in the flesh!" One day when the dog-king was daydreaming near a meadow in which some sheep were passing, a wolf suddenly appeared and leaped at the nearest lamb. It was close to killing it when His Majesty, throwing dignity to the winds, jumped upon it with fangs bared. None of the spectators present made the least attempt to put an end to this fight. A terrible struggle ensued and the dog-king died, his throat torn open by the wild wolf's teeth. He was given a state funeral. A mausoleum was erected in his memory; and since then, the region bears the name (as marvelous as the story) of "Hill of Sorrow."

The Norwegians were not the only people to be governed in this way. There is another very similar story, which took place in Hungary. The Hungarians wanted King Henry to pay them tribute money. He, under the pretence of complying, sent them a dog with no ears or tail; a dog covered in mange, but endowed with all the powers and credentials of a royal delegate. This dog, states Aventinus, was called "Hungari,"

History of Alexander the Great (15th century).
(Petit Palais)

The hunt for the thief.
Treatise on hunting by Gaston Phébus
(15th century).
(Bibliothèque Nationale, Paris)

Louis XI and his premier knights
of the order of St. Michael.
Miniature attributed to Jean Fouquet
(15th century).
(Bibliothèque Nationale, Paris)

from which are derived the words "Hungary" and naturally "Hungarian."[1]

There is also the story that Gunnard, King of Sweden, after he had conquered Reginald, governed the country through his envoys, administering from then on through a dog, to which everyone was obliged to render the honors accustomed to princes.[2]

DOGS AND CHIVALRY

The reign of Charlemagne was marked by his unswerving desire to instill order in the empire and to increase learning. But from the end of the 9th century, the Christian West returned to chaos.

In the 10th century, families lived grouped together in fortified enclosures, called *"mottes,"* in order to protect themselves and their herds from plundering.

In the 11th century, with the coming of the "manors," a kind of federation of connected families, a certain social order was established.

In the 12th century, the "manor" became the feudal castle. The lord protected and defended his vassals and serfs. Unfortunately the life of the working people and of the poor remained precarious, because of plunder, epidemic, and famine. As for the lord, he was often less troubled with protecting his subjects than he was with his intoxication with hunting and with the kill.

These men were contemptuous of learning and culture; they were men of nature; their best friends were their horses and their dogs.

The horse had far and away pride of place in the noble knight's mind in Germany, England, and France. But the dog won its way to the knight's heart by its faithfulness and the interest which it seemed to take in

[1] Aventinus "Annalium Boiorum," Book VII, 1554, infolio, p. 488.
[2] Pontanas, "Rerum danicarum historia," Book X, Amsterdam, 1631, p. 120.

his amusements. The dog to come to the fore was the Bloodhound; none other was its match in seizing the boar by the ears or forcing the hind from its cover.

The Christian knights who went to the Holy Land were matched against the Arabs, who were passionately fond of hunting and horses. The Crusaders took their inseparable companions with them, and set off with their horses and dogs. This led to exchanges of dogs between noblemen of various European countries and also to some often felicitous cross-breeding. Through this a new dog was born—the spaniel—which is not Spanish, and whose origins go back to the first crosses between the Greyhounds of the East and our pack hounds.

In 1291, the fall of Acre marked the end of the Crusades. For two centuries the knights had fought with fluctuating fortunes, but they had not become less ardent or less passionately fond of hunting.

History will demonstrate that.

THE CANINE BREEDS CHANGE

King Louis IX, the very devout Saint Louis, was no less a huntsman. It was he who introduced to Europe the grey dogs (gaze-hounds) with which he had hunted gazelle in the Holy Land. Some historians say that these hounds combined the keenness of scent of bird dogs with the strength of a mastiff and the speed of a greyhound, but others relate that Charles IX always took them for "stupid, noisy dogs, as lazy as they were unintelligent." It does not matter! Thenceforth, through subsequent cross-breedings, often by rule of thumb, several breeds of dogs changed, and each was utilized for a definite form of hunting.

Thus they used Alan dogs, descended from mastiffs, for hunting bears or more often wild boar. They needed bird dogs, of smaller statute, to put up the grouse and partridge on which the falcon swooped.

The setters knew how to "set," how to

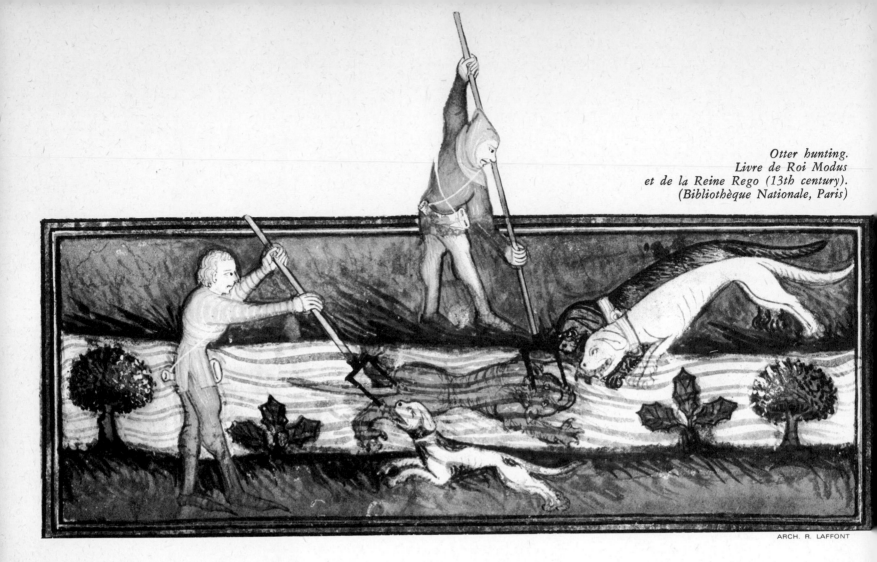

Otter hunting.
Livre de Roi Modus
et de la Reine Rego (13th century).
(Bibliothèque Nationale, Paris)

flatten themselves against the ground so as not to get in the way of the man who casts the net; the hounds harried the resisting stag for hours and could hold their own against the black boar.

And, dominating them all, there were the Greyhounds, who were fast and deadly as arrows, classic Greyhounds of "good breeding" which are still found in the 20th century in every country, and are always the same. Whether they were Greyhounds of medium height, quivering thoroughbreds, of Arab stock, quiet Greyhounds of the great tents of the East, taller Greyhounds, with silky, rippling coats, of the Khans of Tartary, or hirsute and powerful Scottish Greyhounds, all were equally capable of running more swiftly than an adult wolf and breaking its back with their powerful jaws, almost without halting their impetus.

However, up until the end of the Middle Ages, hounds (which were later to provide the stock of the pack-hounds we know today) were still not very numerous. In 1282, Philippe le Bel possessed no more than 12, whereas for stag hunting alone, Louis XV had several packs, each comprising up to 600 or 620 members!

HUNTING BECOMES ORGANIZED

Up to the 12th century, people had hunted with the same arms and by the same means as at the start of the Middle Ages. One of the oldest documents of the 9th century that we possess is a manuscript drawing which resides in the British Museum. The picture represents an Anglo-Saxon chief hunting boar in a forest, accompanied by a lone servant who is blowing his horn. A couple of dogs of medium height, with straight ears and erect tails, are behind him, held on a leash by the servant. The huntsman is on foot, but doubly armed: a heavy sword swings against his left leg, while he holds ready to throw a long, iron hunting spear in his right hand.

In the 13th century, the use of hedges and fences developed. This procedure came about at the same time in Germany, France, and England, and was to insure the success of what is called today, the "bag" of dead game.

This system of enclosures (we would call them "shoots" today) was to last a long time in Germany, but was quickly abandoned in France and England. More merit was attached to running the animal to earth by following the "tracks" that it left in its wake. These tracks (or signs) each huntsman was proud to recognize, to deduce their exact significance, and to find out more if possible from them. The dogs' attitudes, the observation of their behavior, and their spirited participation enriched the enjoyment.

Moreover, French and English writers speak much more often of the dog than of the horse. Each knight was, by definition, a good horseman, yet he had to have an innate feeling and a long period of study to get to know the dog, in order to train it and

Sea dogs.
Hortus sanitas *(Mayence 1491).*
(Bibliothèque Doucet)

Charles the Bold and his scribe.
(Royal Brussels Library)

interpret its reactions. The spirit of hunting had changed. A radical change was to be made in "laying on the pack." Thenceforward it was no longer just what the huntsman wanted.

Some wonderfully illustrated and judiciously composed works constitute a veritable handbook of hunting; they teach the best way to use dogs and how to care for them to the best advantage.

About the year 1400, the *Mayster of the Game* (whose only equivalent in France is the *Miroir de Phébus,* by Gaston de Foix), specifies that the kennels should be situated in a sunny place, be cleaned each day, and be provided with abundant fresh straw. A heated room should be provided for the dogs to rest in after the hunt. Their protection should be assured night and day. They should be fed with meat and bread; they should be rubbed down and bathed each evening. Then, for some illnesses, notably rabies (always that!), the English book prescribes sending the dogs . . . for a bathe in the sea!

From the middle of the 14th century, the huntsmen of Souabe prided themselves in being able to say, at the first sight of the "tracks," whether the game was male or female, its approximate age, and its weight. In this growing education of the huntsman *La Chace dou cerf* (stag hunting), which appears to be one of the oldest French works on this subject, was to give, among other advice, this basic rule: "If you want to become a master, it is necessary to hunt stag for a long time with a Bloodhound, and you will see that it will teach you many things."

Small dogs had no place in hunting, but they were highly valued as ratters. They were used everywhere where the presence of rodents was a danger to public health. At the beginning of the 15th century, cartoons showed these dogs chasing rats both in the back of an apothecary's shop and under the furniture and medical apparatus in a hospital ward.

THE ROYAL PREROGATIVE

The right to hunt was gradually universally confirmed as a privilege reserved for the nobility. The aim of hunting was no longer that of providing food; it was a game, the noblest game of all. For their companion in this game—the dog—sovereigns and princes committed acts of extravagance, but they were often cruel to dogs belonging to others.

William the Conqueror, Duke of Normandy, future king of England, demanded that every dog foreign to his packs and living on his lands should have three toes amputated, in order to slow its speed.

Louis XI even ordered for "Cherami," his favorite greyhound, an enormous gold collar studded with rubies. He sent to Saint-Martin-de-Tours a votive offering in the form of a wax dog, weighing 20 pounds, in order to thank God for having cured "Artus."

Charles VIII would allow his dogs which had behaved well in the forest to sleep in his bed in turns.

Nevertheless, as hunting developed, the extent of the lands, the depth of the forests, the distance of one castle from another, and the great distances which were covered (up to 50 miles!) posed many problems. Often carried away by the fever of pursuit, huntsmen, horses, and dogs, all dead-tired, found themselves separated by many leagues from their homes, and it was necessary to have recourse to another's hospitality. This kind of forced lodging soon became more than just that. Gradually it became the pretext for long stays, feasts of drinking, and revelry. Soon the huntsmen could no longer count on the welcome of their peers and friends. So they turned to the monasteries and convents; but there also, the hunters abused their hosts' welcome and the clergy in their turn complained.

From then on a custom grew up which for a long time had the force of law throughout almost the whole of Europe. The kind of services to hunters to be expected, and their duration, were codified and defined; the bailiffs, farmers, and foresters kept to these established figures.

Thus the *Livre de Salle* by the Great Hunter of Ingolstadt, in 1418 in Bavaria, gives a complete list of convents, abbeys, or religious domiciles which, from such a date to such a date, were under the obligation to receive and to meet all expenses of entertaining and food, and to know that a duke's hunt would contain, for example: 3 huntsmen of the nobility, 10 servants or grooms, 5 horses, and 45 dogs.

The Middle Ages came to an end. With its hunting qualities, the dog had conquered the hearts of the great; it was already privileged among all the other animals.

With the Renaissance it gradually became man's assistant and friend.

4 FROM THE RENAISSANCE TO THE FRENCH REVOLUTION

With the Renaissance a marked change took place in the relationship between man and dog. Certainly in the preceding centuries the dog had been man's companion: St. Roch was always depicted with his dog at his side, licking his wounds. A 14th century Abyssinian painting shows the Virgin Mary giving a drink to a dog. Also there were sheep dogs, watch dogs, and hunting dogs. But in the 15th and 16th centuries a "new man," enamored of art and science, appeared on the scene. He was to take an interest in the dog in a new sense and conceive a passion for anything involving his old, ever-faithful companion.

This new infatuation that noblemen, artisans, and commoners experienced for their dogs manifested itself in many ways. In the 12th century, an English Franciscan monk, Bartholomew Glanville, had published a book on animal medicine which was not immediately widely read. With the invention of printing, this work (which was powerfully realistic in the chapter on rabies, for example) was to be re-edited several times and translated into 17 different languages before the year 1500! It was the same in France, in 1561, with *La Vénérie* (The Science of Hunting) by Jacques du Fouilloux, which was translated into German and then into Italian.

From the beginning of the 15th century, the art of tending animals was still a matter of trial and error; but soon indications of renewed interest appeared in numerous publications. In 1492, by order of Charles VIII, Guillaume Tardif, of the college of Navarre, published the *Livre des Chiens pour la Chasse* (Book of Hunting Dogs). In 1590, in England, George Turberville published a serious treatise: *The Selection, Hygiene and Illnesses of the Dog.* The following year Arcussia published an important book in France on the same subject.

Commerce and business prospered, and Europe displayed her wealth. Dogs of all shapes and sizes had their part in this fling. Stable or farm dogs were at every village fair and at every feast, creeping under the tables and seizing a bone or a cake whenever the opportunity presented itself.

In Italy, it was in Florence where, whenever the sun shone, every wealthy citizen repaired to his farms on horseback with his servants, javelin in hand, his mastiffs beside him, in the hope of encountering some game en route.[1]

In Venice, on the green canals glided decorated gondolas, on which could be seen standing erect, like a figurehead on the bows, a small hairy, white lap dog (either a Maltese or Teneriffe), or a pale-colored Pom (called Florentine), tenderly watched over by its mistress, who was returning to her palace.

FIGHTING DOGS

Unfortunately not all dogs were dedicated to the pleasures of the hunt and to the luxuries of castle life. Man also liked to watch dogs fighting each other and made them participate in his own battles.

The English (from the 13th century onwards) more than ever were passionately fond of watching bulldogs bait bulls, bears, or even lions.

Nearly everywhere, large sinewy Mastiffs continued to be set against men. At the end of the 14th century the Alans, about which Suretimus Ducensis in 1360 spoke at length, were "cased in leather for two reasons: the first, in order that the fire that they carried on their back in a bronze vessel did not hurt them or burn them; second, in order that they might be less exposed to the fierce blows of the men at arms, when their horses, burned or cruelly bitten by them, were goaded into fleeing at such pain.

For these dogs nothing had changed. Even in the 16th century Henry VIII, King of

[1] *Cent Mille ans de vie quotidienne* (One Hundred Thousand Years of Everyday Life). Ed. Pont-Royal Del Duca R. Laffont, 1960, p. 126.

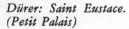

*Dürer: Saint Eustace.
(Petit Palais)*

GIRAUDON

England, triumphed over Charles the Fifth (of Germany) by hurling more than 500 starving dogs against the enemy. Have these customs fallen into disuse? Alas, no. We all know the terror that the Nazi police dogs struck in the hearts of the inmates of concentration camps.

But in the 16th century not all dogs met such a tragic fate: there were those which turned spits or became performing dogs; some remained true to the tradition of guarding the flocks; while others, by virtue of their sweetness and fragility, won the hearts of ladies. However, for the majority of dogs it was definitely hunting which represented the reason for their existence and the justification for their happiness. Patiently, men applied themselves to research into the development of the dog's natural aptitudes, its sense of smell, and its quality of endurance.

The charters of the German people (which applied not only to Germania but also to large parts of the kingdom of France and Spain) already classified them according to their respective work: the *pointer* for flushing big game, the *beater* for rounding it up, the *chaser* for pursuing it, the *castor* for hunting underground, the *netting dog* for game birds, etc.

THE GREYHOUND, PRINCE OF DOGS

As in the Middle Ages, French and English books continued to place first the different types of Greyhounds ("*leporarius*," or "*lévrier*" in French). According to some the name Greyhound was derived from the old Celtic word "grech" or "greg" which meant dog. According to others it was connected with "grey," which was the most common color of this breed.

At all times, Greyhounds had been the dogs of princes. With the development of the "laying on of the pack," they were more than ever to the fore, the prince of dogs! They shared all of life's great moments with their masters: they ate in their sight

The Emperor Maximilian hunting bears.
Drawing by Bren.
(Bibliothèque Nationale, Paris)

Stag-hunting (detail).
Florentine School (15th century).
(Musee des Augustins, Toulouse)

and slept in their bedrooms. They manifested in their behavior, a sort of pride, a distinction, a dignity which even the antiquity of their lineage did not explain. Three thousand years ago, Solomon said of this dog, that it was "one of the rare creatures that knows how to walk gracefully.") The distance that Greyhounds instinctively put between themselves and all other beings can already be found in one of the *Tales of Eurtapel* in which it is said ". . . As the mongrel never loves the Greyhound, the villain has never loved the gentleman. . . ."

The Greyhound was so bound up with the quiet and even sad hours of the nobility and such privileged people, that the wife of Robert Bruce, a prisoner of Edward I in 1304, had to be incarcerated with the indispensable ". . . three Greyhounds and a sober and wise servant to make her bed."

One can only wonder at the extraordinary vogue which Greyhounds in France and England then enjoyed. At the end of the 15th

century, three types could be distinguished: the large dogs which originated in Brittany, the small Greyhounds (which were often descendants of Italian greyhounds or Eastern ones), and the properly called Greyhounds.

THE ENGLISH
GREYHOUND AND COURSING

"If I had to make rules for hunting in France," said J. Oberthur, "I would abolish daily hunting. I would decree that apart from the rabbit, all other four-legged game could not be hunted or run down by hounds, or caught by Greyhounds. . . ." And he goes on to explain that there would thus be more interest in the sport and less interest in the victim.

J. Oberthur's proposal had at least the great interest at heart of saving from extinction a breed of dogs which was dying out: *coursing* Greyhounds.

Coursing was not born yesterday. Two

centuries before Christ, Arrian had already spoken of it, and throughout the Renaissance it was greatly in favor. It was in the 15th century that a dog, which in England had been considered good for hunting the bear or the wolf, had been crossed with the "gaze-hound" (gazelle-dog) in order to arrive at this canine masterpiece. Juliana Barnes, Abbess of Saint Albans, had said that a true Grey-hound should have ". . . the head of a snake, the neck of a drake, the sides of a bream, the felt of a cat, the tail of a rat."

What does coursing consist of? We can make a summary of the principles without entering too much into the detail of the rules. In open country, a man presents himself holding two Greyhounds on a lead. He runs across country until a hare bolts from its cover (i.e. takes to flight). He lets the hare get a start of 30 or 40 yards, then he lets the Greyhounds off the leash. They fly like arrows towards the hare, overtake it at great speed . . . and kill it. The winner

*Treatise on hunting
by Gaston Phébus (15th century).
(Bibliothèque Nationale, Paris)*

*The Battle of Pavia (detail).
Flemish tapestry.
(Naples, Pinacoteca del Museo Nazionale)*

is not necessarily the one which overtakes and kills the hare, but the one which makes the hare take the most sudden turns in a battle not only of speed, but of reflexes, deception, and skill.

From the beginning of the 16th century, smooth-haired English Greyhounds were to be in great demand for this sport. People became passionately fond of "coursing," and it was taken up in other countries, particularly Spain. The French adopted it quickly. In 1689, twenty thousand Greyhounds had been sent to France with some Irish regiments attached to King James, their master, which caused such great slaughter of hares that the question arose of regulating and even abolishing this form of canine sport in open country. Today it is an accomplished fact.

In England, the first competitions accompanied by the first form of betting began with Henry VIII, and these very quickly won the complete support of the English nobility. During the reign of Elizabeth I the Duke of Norfolk established a code for coursing, laying down the tests, the attitude of the dogs, and the very strict rules under which they could be admitted to compete. From this time coursing became the supreme right of the Greyhound, a specialized activity which no other dog could later take away from him.

THE GREAT, WHITE, ROYAL DOGS

The glory of the English Greyhound however could not obliterate the magnificent destiny, in France, of a breed of dogs, which were called: the *grands, chiens blancs du Roy."* Their blood still flows through the veins of all great packhounds, both French and English.

These great, white dogs, which Gaston Phébus, Comte de Foix, called *les bauds* (from the old French *baud* = bold, from which comes the verb *s'esbaudir*, i.e., to be delighted—at seeing them so bold in their

work) were the ancestors of a trusty dog from Poitou called "Souillard."

This was a wonderful animal about which Jean du Fouilloux related this story: However fine they were at scenting, running swiftly, and biting, these white-coated dogs were just not appreciated by the princes, because they would only hunt stag. When he got "Souillard" as a present from a provincial nobleman, the king, Louis XI, therefore was not over-excited. The Grand Seneschal of Normandy who knew all about these noble and brave animals, pleaded with the king to part with this dog, which he would give, he said, to the wisest lady in the kingdom, "who is," stated the Seneschal, "Anne of Bourbon (of Beaujeu), your daughter. . . ."

"I take you up on the point of calling her wise," replied the King, "for there is no wise woman in this world. . . ."

Then, amused, he gave him the dog. The Seneschal entrusted it to Jacques de Brézé, the famous huntsman, and "Souillard," doing the honors to numerous bitches, created the Tabbot, a variety of the breed. In the following year, Anne of Bourbon, angry that she had not taken him, sent one of her bitches called "Baude" to him, which— says the chronicle—was mated three times, from which issued fifteen beautiful dogs, six of them excellent. . . .

These and their descendants were such beautiful animals that, in the reign of Francis I, Mary Queen of Scots wanted to own some identical ones. For this, she sent "Baraud," a white St. Hubert Hound, to France, which procreated with the same success as "Souillard."

Subsequently, over the centuries, exchanges of French and English blood increased the breed for the greater good of venery.

There is another version of the origin of these famous dogs, according to which a hound bitch from Italy belonging to Lord Greffier (secretary of King Louis XII) was crossed with a white St. Hubert Hound

The family of King Charles I.
Van Dyck (detail). (Windsor Castle)

(i.e. a Talbot, later known as the Southern Hound), and gave rise to a perfect dog, as big as a Greyhound, with a beautiful hound's head, and was called after the name of his master. "Greffier" immediately became popular, and mated with bitches of various colors (grey, fawn, and black), he contributed to begetting the most popular classic hounds in Europe.

KINGS' DOGS AND VILLAGERS' DOGS

Francis I, and all the kings of France after him, took pride in owning the most beautiful packs and in showing them off with as much care as a threatre production. To keep the pure-bred dogs from defilement, certain restrictive measures were taken against stray dogs.

Mongrels still continued to multiply. They existed everywhere. In towns there were dogs round shops and stalls; in the country, farmers not only could but "ought to have on their property hounds and Water Spaniels to search for whatever occasionally entered their fields."

Unfortunately, these children of chance passion were no less susceptible to hunting in secret for themselves. Francis I, more taken with chasing girls than hinds and more of a huntsman than a real dog-lover (in spite of the famous little spaniel "Citron," which it is said, used to sleep on his couch), issued a cruel decree against them. It was obligatory that: "All dogs belonging to peasant or farmer must wear, attached to their necks, a heavy block of wood, the weight and bulkiness of which will stem their ardor, whenever they move away from their homes. If despite this precaution they take to hunting on royal land they will be punished in situ immediately by pure and simple hamstringing . . ."

These mongrel dogs however had been very useful, for wolves were still numerous

GIRAUDON — ANDERSON

*Acteon changed into a stag
is devoured by his own dogs
for having seen Diana at her bath (17th century).
(Bibliothèque Nationale, Paris)*

*Philippe IV of Spain
boar-hunting.
Velasquez (detail).
(National Gallery, London)*

in France. It was in order to do away with them completely that Francis I encouraged hunting of wolves with strong mastiffs. He created at the same time the new appointments of "Master of the Wolf-hunt" and "Official responsible for extermination of wolves."

At court and in castles, the ladies found a new interest in dogs, especially in dogs which were pretty and gentle, whether they looked like miniature Greyhounds, or whether in their bushy appearance they had that look sometimes furious or sometimes suppliant which made the ladies laugh or disarmed them, because it conveys genuine feeling better than human words or expressions.

In England many colorful legends form backdrops for various breeds, but none is more so endowed than the English Toy Spaniel. It has been said that Charles I started the fashion for these tiny dogs (probably because he had some in the palace) and subsequently his name was given to one variety (the black and tan) and it is inferred that the breed goes back to dogs brought back from the Crusades. The fact is that the last of the Crusades took place in 1270. Charles I ruled England from 1625 to 1649 when he was beheaded. After the decade in which England was ruled by the Cromwells, the son of Charles I, Charles II, ascended the throne. Another of the four varieties, a tri-color of white, black, and tan, was named the Prince Charles to honor Charles II, who cherished the breed highly.

The coat of the English Toy Spaniel looks somewhat like that on early specimens of the sporting spaniels, but there all similarity ends. There is little doubt that it stems from the same Oriental sources that gave us the Japanese Spaniel, the Pekingese, the Pug, the Lhasa Apso, and the Shih Tzu.

One of the legends that is believeable is that a Captain Saris, a British naval officer, brought specimens of the Toy Spaniel as presents from the Emperor of Japan in

1613 and presented them to King Charles I. However, Dr. Johannes Caius, physician to Queen Elizabeth I, conclusively identified these dogs in his famous *Of Englishe Dogges,* written some forty years before the time of Charles I.

The Tudors and Stuarts jealously raised their different dogs, whether they were pets or working dogs. The best examples of their kennels (Harriers, Beagles or Foxhounds, Scottish terriers, and Irish terriers) formed royal gifts which were exchanged with those from Italy, Hungary, or France.

The two Griffons of Henry II are also bound up in history. Just like the little spaniels of King Charles I of England, *"Haleine douce"* and *"Coeur gentil"* took refuge, whimpering, under the bed of the wounded Henry II when Ambroise Paré attempted the trepanning operation on him. They did not come out until three or four days later, after the death of their sovereign.

History has also told us of the attachment of Charles IX for his famous *chiens blancs du roi,* "white dogs of the king," about which he said[2] in *La Chasse Royale* that the house and park of the Hunting Lodge of Saint-Germain had been "made just for the feeding and rearing of white Griffons," i.e. water retrievers. Furthermore, Charles IX had a particular affection for two of them: "Courte" and "Caron." "Courte" was so spoiled that the king let her eat from his plate, and so dear to him that when she died he had a pair of gloves made from the hide of this lamented companion. . . . Whence the conclusion of Ronsard: "Courte, thus, dead or alive has given to her king perfect service." "Caron" was such a highly valued hunting dog that at death the Court officially went into mourning for a day!

With Henry III the passion for dogs became a ridiculous craze. The king did not hesitate to turn up at the most grave royal councils wearing around his neck a small, open basket, trimmed with ribbons, full of

[2]*La Chasse Royale,* by Charles IX. Paris, 1652, in 12.

little dogs, called "Papillons," a sort of miniature French spaniel, with which he launched the fashion which is still with us today. With pointed noses, their expressive eyes framed by wide, erect ears planted obliquely on their heads, they reminded one of the wings of a butterfly. Henry III himself used to go to choose and buy them at Lyons at a ransom price. In 1576, the annual budget for royal dogs reached the sum of 100,000 gold crowns. This same Henry III, in 1578, published an edict barring the use of hounds and water spaniels and according to which "every commoner caught in the act of hunting would be subject to pain of death."

Henry IV was more a falconer, warrior, and lover than admirer of pure-bred dogs, but he was, in deference to tradition, a keeper of Bloodhounds with glittering pedigrees, which he paraded with pride. He was very proud of his spaniels from Guyenne, marvelous big, black dogs. But he was not at all fond of them, and Agrippa d'Aubigné tells in his *Memoirs* of the little value the king set on dogs which were faithful to him. D'Aubigné had acquired a big spaniel that Henry IV had kept by him for several years and then abandoned. He took care of it, returned it to full health and sent it back to his master accompanied by a strange sonnet of admonishment, which ended with this verse:

"Courtiers who hurl scornful looks at this abandoned dog, dying of hunger in the streets . . . Wait for the wages of its loyalty! . . ."

POINTING AND HUNTING DOGS

Was it Henry IV or Louis XIII who, in exchange for Anglo-French mongrels, offered to James I of England that famous dozen pointing dogs which are mentioned in all text-books? It doesn't matter. The consignment marks a new departure in the training of dogs for hunting.

Wild duck-hunting.
Oudry (1686–1755).
(Wallace Collection, London)

Essentially French, hounds, from which pointers were descended, sprang not only from the *chien d'oysel* (bird dog), a hawking and netting dog of the Middle Ages, but had yet more distant origins: They are related to that old French dog (*"brache,"* *"brachet,"* *"braquet"* [pointer]) which was already being talked about under Charles V (". . . and the Dauphin gave him two very beautiful *Braches* with collars of gold and valuable leashes . . .") at a time when poaching was nothing dishonourable, since it was the poacher's job to destroy harmful animals.

These dogs got themselves in the "down" position, as we say today, to avoid being wounded by the large casting net weighed by pieces of lead. Later, with the coming of shooting, the reign of the great pure-bred dogs, which until then had been undisputed, was broken. The large English mongrels which were gifts from England were then much more highly valued because they had "a finer track" and because they were less awkward and yet resilient and fast.

HUNTING BECOMES AN ART AND A SCIENCE

We can get an idea of the importance of hunting—and of dogs—in the life and budget of the nobility by noting that on the death of Louis XIII the people in the employ of the king solely for his hunting numbered: four lieutenants, four sub-lieutenants, 40 noble huntsmen, two hunting pages, four knights of the kennels, 17 masters of the kennels on foot, 18 bloodhound guides, four dog servants, etc.

In the 17th century, three official methods of hunting were practiced: stalking (or the German method), coursing (or the French method), and hawking (or the Dutch method). As to the education of the huntsmen and the specialized personnel associated with them, quite a hierarchy existed of kennel lads, servants, and masters of the packs.

The conditions of entry to these jobs were strictly codified: the apprentice must be of a good family, of good health, must drink in moderation, fear God, and be unassuming. If he was admitted, he wore the special livery, but he wore only the belt, without cross-belt or hunting knife. The apprenticeship lasted three years. The first year consisted of grooming, daily cleaning of designated dogs of the pack, and preparation of the dog's food. In the second year the apprentice wore the cross belt; he learned to guide the dogs and was no longer to associate with apprentices in their first year. In the third year he worked every day with an appointed Bloodhound, and learned the language of venery and the practical knowledge of the different kinds of game. It was then, and only then, with a noble ceremony copied from the guilds, the master instructor awarded him his knife.

Louis XIV laid down the rules of hunting. While maintaining the exclusive right of hunting for noblemen, he put an end to the death penalty for commoners caught in the act of hunting.

In the drawing rooms, lap-dogs became all the rage. Their hair was cropped or crimped, dressed in the style of the day, perfumed, fondled; and men sighed or laughed at the idea that Pugs, Papillons, and Maltese dogs, those living toys so fawned upon, could run like mad things after a scornful "royal" stag, or could mingle their yapping with the deafening baying of hounds.

The distant and aristocratic Greyhound was in less demand. The king preferred shooting to the chase. According to registers of royal buildings, R. Vaultier counted that when His Majesty went out to "kill," four pages of the Great Stables followed him, carrying his dogs on cushions.

Mme. de Pompadour's dog.
French School (18th century).
(Collection of Dr. Mèry)

Wild boar seized by the dogs.
School of F. Desportes.

On the other hand, in stag-hunting (over which thence forth the blare of the hunting-horn was to resound) the number of hunting pages was limitless. The expenses of training and keeping the dogs became ridiculous. The Master of the Royal Hunt (Duke François de la Rochefoucauld) paid out 17,587 francs, 10 sous for the maintenance of the packs. In 1685, the construction of the great kennels (which were built on the actual site of today's Versailles Prefecture) cost 200,000 crowns. The buildings could house thenceforward all the packs. There was a special pack of Scottish dogs for roe-deer, a pack of dogs from Champagne for hares, a pack of powerful, Anglo-French boar-hunting dogs for large game. Against wolves (which it was reported were still quite numerous in the country), the Marquis of Hendicourt, Grand Master of the Wolf Hunt, was to utilize the white Pyrenean Mountain dogs (Great Pyrenees) that Madame de Maintenon had brought with her to Versailles.

In 1698, the King's Dogs, together with the famous packs belonging to the Dauphin, the Duke of Vendôme, the Grand Prior, and the Duke of Maine, made a total of more than 1,000 dogs, which was considered the most beautiful collection in Europe. The dogs of the Master of the Royal Hunt were nicknamed "merciless" because they pursued with the same eagerness every kind of game that they could "start." Foreigners came to admire these marvelous beasts, and the envoys of the king of Siam made enthusiastic compliments about them to the King.

However, despite all the interest shown in it, the dog knew some disfavor. Formerly as Jacques Debu-Bridel wrote, at the Louve, at the Luxembourg, at the Conde family's house, or the Longueville's mansion, the royal family and noble families used to live more or less on top of the stables and cattle-sheds; an incessant coming and going of dogs, cats, and other animals gave a rural character to the Parisian life of the nobility. With Louis XIV, etiquette forbade dogs from entering the temple of royalty that was the Palace of Versailles. Perhaps it is possible to see from this distant attitude some of the influence of Descartes's philosophy.

Louis XV was a dog-lover. He played with them in the forest of Saint-Germain where he had perfected a clever method of attracting their good favors. Servants, perched in trees, threw small stones to madden the dogs which came within reach, while the king, posted in a nearby square, called them by name, reassured them, and rewarded them. Madame de Pompadour came to share this love for these most beautiful, white and orange Braques (Pointers) that King George II of England had given to him. Later, the Marquis of Montemboeuf, to whom Louis XV had given several, made a great hunting breed from them. These are the same dogs which will one day bear the name of *Braque Saint Germain* (Saint Germain Pointer).

Braques were more and more fashionable. The smooth-coated Italian Braque (Bracco), which kept the shape of these hounds, was in vogue. The painter Oudry immortalized these beautiful, white Braques. In Italy a rough-coated variety, the "Spinone" was developed, and in France, the Braques de L'Ariège. This was also the beginnings of the smaller Braque du Bourbonnais. This active and robust trotting dog, clipped to look like a cob, roan-colored with brown markings, later became unpopular, especially in France, but the type, which was well fixed, continues down to our day.

Louis XVI was neither huntsman nor dog-lover. With him vanished a past in which the dog was closely associated with the history and life of man.

The fall of the monarchy in France carried with it the proclamation of the Republic, the abolition of privilege, and, first and foremost, the abolition of hunting; thenceforward it became the privilege of peasants and townsmen, who had longed for it for centuries. For the dog, who knew neither rank, privilege, nor riches, a new chapter was opening in its history.

5 FROM THE FRENCH REVOLUTION TO THE PRESENT

In France, on the fourth day of August, 1789, it was declared: "All citizens are equal before the law." The abolition of privilege was to have its effect on the dog, whose life was always so closely bound up with that of man.

Along with all other privileges, that of hunting was also suspended. Thenceforth all Frenchmen, commoners and peasants alike, had the right to roam the forests and the open country, shotgun in hand. Their dream had come true; they could now take their revenge on the nobleman and know at last the thrills and joys of hunting.

IT WOULD BE IMPOSSIBLE
TO HUNT WITHOUT THE DOG

The common man, now that he could go shooting, needed a dog. Because it was impossible for him to buy a pedigree dog, he was in part responsible for the proliferation of the most unwonted mongrels which was to take place.

At the same time, with a few exceptions, all the princely packs of hunting hounds disappeared in the revolutionary turmoil. They were dispersed with no thought for the preservation of the purity of the breed, decimated by lack of care.

Besides, these great delicate dogs, whose upkeep was ruinous and who had been schooled for hunting, were of no use to the humble huntsman who went on foot and shot his game.

Little by little many of these novices wearied of the hunt, and their passion for shooting subsided. Thousands of pups, crosses between the mastiff and the hound, were born of chance matings. They, and their progeny, had little talent for the hunt. So the true huntsmen began to want dogs that were good setters with known qualities.

The day of the hound had come. At the end of the 18th and the beginning of the 19th century these dogs (most of whom were of French origin, though some were Italian, German, or Spanish) were accorded

the respect they merited all over Europe, while on both sides of the English Channel the evolution of the Spaniel continued.

The first Breton Spaniels appeared in Normandy, Artois, and Picardy. Among them was the short-lived "Pont-Audemer," probably the result of a cross with the Irish Water Spaniel. Meanwhile, in England, a system of rigorous selection was gradually bringing to perfection a whole range of Setters which the French were to adopt twenty years later.

The Napoleonic wars and the new social unrest which followed them were not favorable to the French kennels. English breeding profited from this.

The English were indifferent to the ephemeral vogue for lap dogs (among them the Pug and the Maltese dog). They concentrated on perfecting a gun-dog with long, sturdy limbs, a deep chest, a fine silky coat, and a keen nose. The Setter was the successful result.

A NEW ENGLISH CREATION:
THE POINTER

Having obtained this fine result, the British were still not satisfied. They bent their efforts to producing a smooth-haired gun-dog. Probably by dint of crossing the Greyhound with the various French Braques, they created a dog which was three-quarters French, and of which they could justly be proud: the Pointer.

The beautiful examples of this breed shown for the first time in France, in 1860, were an immediate success. They excited both the admiration of huntsmen for their cynegetic qualities, and the admiration of artists for the elegance and nobility of their lines.

For a long time it was thought that the pointer was the result of the clever but simple crossing of the English Greyhound and French Braque. However, R. Dommanget, the modern authority on these matters, is sceptical. He writes: "In the course of half a century of observation and experience, I

Golden Cocker Spaniel.

Irish Setter.

have formed an opinion on the subject of the crossing of smooth-haired gun-dog bitches which the English landed gentry might (deliberately or otherwise) have accomplished in their kennels. The Greyhound contributed to the length of the head and the tail, which increased speed by making the body slighter; it diminished the keenness of the nose and the desire to work for the master. The bloodhound gave body to the whole, diminished the density of the tissues, lengthened and folded the ears, augmented the soundness of the scent and the soberness of the character. The foxhound ameliorated the skeleton by making it bigger, but rectified the shoulder and gave the characteristic cat-like track. The setter made the gait more sloping and contributed the slightly fringed tail (a cross between a Pointer and a Setter is called a 'Dropper'; there were certainly more of these dogs than is usually believed . . .)."

He adds (probably because the stop of the pointer has always been very marked and its nose is raised as high as possible): "The boxer too, has no doubt played its part; the heads of some pointers are too like the Boxer's for there to be any doubt. Besides, a few of the pups in a litter sometimes have 'squashed' heads, and tails bearing characteristic nodules."

Whatever the truth of the matter, the Pointer must take its place among the finest dogs of the past. Today it is without a doubt the greatest of the shooting dogs, the magnificent result of scientific breeding which has created the dog the modern hunter needed, uniting in one animal perfect beauty an amiable disposition, and very great hunting qualities.

However, the average French hunter has not shared the enthusiasm of his English counterpart for the Pointer.

So the fine French Braques were not abandoned. They adapted, the Braque Saint-Germain more than the others. This dog of royal descent can be divided into two distinct varieties, one of which was, in the words of

DIM

A GHOST: THE BASSET HOUND

the Marquis de Chaville, "the pretty cadet branch, to which the 20th century owes so many of its intelligent and stylish dogs, which were so adorable that many men were just as happy to make their way to the kennel as to the boudoir." Certainly the huntsmen of the Second Empire were very taken with the white and chestnut pointers "which can flush game even at distances up to two hundred yards." A great variety of pointing dogs was developed in France—rough-haired, woolly, silky, or smooth-haired. Many of these varieties have disappeared, while others, such as the Poodle and the Cocker Spaniel, tended to become house dogs. English dogmen claim England's pointer traces back to 1650 and limit his ancestors to Greyhound, Foxhound, Bloodhound, and spaniel; they say the suggestion of Boxer blood is ridiculous. The Boxer did not become a distinct and separate breed until the 19th century.

It was now, at this time of renewed interest in the breeding of dogs, that there arose, on the fringe of the known and protected breeds, dogs similar in every way to the great hunting dogs of the past, but whose development had been, as it were, arrested. These were the Basset Hounds, whose legs, more often bandy than straight, were not even a third as long as those of the ordinary dog.

Far from being unknown, these dogs appeared to be the ghosts of very ancient breeds. Some claim Egypt had had her Basset Hounds, unwonted sons of the greyhound, and there are numerous documents, from this or that foreign land, which record the existence of these dogs which suffer from achondroplasia. Why were there so many of them in Europe at this time (the end of the 19th century) when the great pack dogs were little more than a memory?

"Bassetism" is even today not fully explained. This natural mutation has been artificially reproduced by scientists by undernourishing one half of a litter of normal hounds. The other half of the litter, well fed, grew up to be the same size as their parents. This does not explain the curious proliferation of these natural mutations which gave birth to so many Basset Hounds, with the heads and bodies of St. Hubert Hounds, Bloodhounds, etc., and who in spite of their dwarfish stature have preserved the courage and spirit of the great breeds whose descendants they are. The astonishing thing is that these dogs did not appear until relatively recently, so much so that they were still unknown in England until after the 1870's. It is also astonishing that there is no appreciable trace of the Basset Hound in the Middle Ages, when all except princely dogs suffered so much hunger and misery. . . . What is even more extraordinary is that at

Greyhound.

Pembroke Welsh Corgis (Cattle dogs).

the same time, still at the end of the 19th century, on both sides of the English Channel, so many different Scottish terriers, just like the French dogs, appeared.

THE SMALL BRITISH TERRIERS

It was about 1880 that the Skye Terrier first appeared. [However, England's Dr. Caius wrote of them three centuries before that.] Originating on the Isle of Skye, on the northwest coast of Scotland, they were at that time "normal" Skye Terriers, whose coats lay flat and were long and quite wiry, and whose legs were of normal length. A few years later, the Skye Terrier had become a heavy basset-like dog, with erect feathered ears, steely jaws, muscles of iron, and fearless courage. Dragging along its pathetic stumpy little legs under its silvery coat, almost shuffling along, it seems to be afflicted with the inferiority complex of the small person.

After this came a multitude of ill-defined varieties, also Scottish and very closely related to the Skye Terrier. Within a few years this confusing situation was to become clarified, and the Scottish terrier family rapidly became fixed. There were now Cairn Terriers (brindled or fawn), Scottish Terriers (dark, wheaten, or black), immaculate West Highland White Terriers, Dandie Dinmont Terriers ("pepper" or "mustard"), white Sealyham Terriers, etc. All of these dogs, on their little short legs, are very proud, all have a varminty expression, dazzling teeth, and, finally, they are all (whatever their fate, for most are today pet dogs) only too willing to burrow under the ground to pursue their prey, either rabbit, fox, mole, or rat!

Slightly different but just as popular are the Yorkshire Terrier and the two Welsh Corgi breeds.

It is said that, before it became a lap dog with a coat as silky as a woman's hair, the fragile little Yorkshire Terrier was the fierce ratting companion of artisans and miners, who have the same lyrical fondness for this

Mastiff. (Korean painting)

Boxer having a rest.

dog as the miners of Northern France still retain for their beloved carrier-pigeons.

Is it reasonable to suppose that the Welsh Corgi[1] is a basset? This is not important. The Welsh Corgi has short legs, it is true, but its history is just as confused as that of the natural basset. It was in Wales, in the 10th century, that this amusing creature was born, a mixture, perhaps, of fox and farm dog. In the 12th century it became a cattle-dog; in later centuries it was to become a "dog of kings," the companion of many English sovereigns, among them Henry II, Richard I (Coeur de Lion), George VI, and, at the present day, of Queen Elizabeth. All the same it is astonishing that this aggressive little Welsh dog (so ready to bite one's ankles) remained, until 1925, so little known outside its country of origin.

Today, English breeders continue to create (or to bring back into fashion) all sorts of dogs, new or forgotten, most of them terriers, of all sorts and breeds: the Bedlington Terrier of Northumberland, as curly as a lamb; the minute English Toy Terrier, black and tan; the Smooth-haired Fox Terrier and the Wire-haired Fox Terrier; the red Irish Terrier and the Kerry Blue Terrier; the Airedale Terrier, confident of its own strength; the Boston Terrier, which is often mistaken for a Bulldog; the Bull Terrier which is mistaken for a Fox Terrier; and the traditional Bulldog, set so solidly on its well-muscled legs, so calm and tenacious that it has become a national symbol of the resistance of "Old England."

It is well known that no dog is allowed into England without first submitting to six months' quarantine. This rule is doubly wise. It closes the door to rabies, and also to for-

[1]The Cardigan Welsh Corgi, found in Cardiganshire, was brought to Wales in 1200 B.C. by the Celts; the Pembroke Welsh Corgi (Pembrokeshire) come to Wales in A.D. 1107 with the Flemish weavers who were induced by Henry I of England to make their home in Wales. In modern times there was some inter-breeding between the two breeds, but they are raised against different standards of perfection.

69

Pekingese.

eign competition, to the benefit of the exclusively British market in dogs.

CYNEGETICS: THE SCIENCE OF THE DOG

Over the centuries huntsmen passed down their ever-richer experience, in the traditional manner, from father to son. Some published excellent treatises. In the present century all this knowledge has been assembled and collated into a science of the dog, both theoretic and practical; cynegetics has become a branch of zootechny.

It is to Professor Baron that we owe the strict definition of the "breed." This was to rescue breeding from the empiricism of the 19th century, which was too much guided by the shape of the subjects' bodies and a utilitarian interest in the types to be fixed.

At the same time the interest of the public was stimulated by the growth of dog competitions and shows. It is not difficult to appreciate the value of a fixed variety, capable of transmitting its own special qualities of usefulness and beauty. So, since then, very high prices and stud fees have been paid for recognized sires and dams. The need arose for close communication between breeders and amateurs, who, quickly warming to the game, became breeders in their turn. The heartfelt wish of these amateurs was to produce ever better dogs, dogs which would carry their name, sometimes into foreign lands, and it was to their own advantage to take their dogs to meetings of amateurs or to the great dog shows which are open to the public.

THE DOG-SHOWS

England's first dog show was organized in 1859, its Kennel Club in 1873. In 1863, 1865 and regularly up to 1873, France followed her example, under the aegis of the *Société d'Acclimation*. From year to year the success of these shows grew, and a new, more

Chow Chows.

Smooth-haired Dachshund, unicolored.

German Shepherd Dog

specialized organization was formed in 1884, the *Société Centrale pour l'Amélioration des Races de Chiens en France*. It was not long before this body split up into more and more specialized clubs where amateurs of specific breeds could get together. These clubs led to an enormous growth in the number of occasions on which they could compare their results, exchange advice and organize important competitions, to which the *Société Centrale* contributed expenses and prizes

Which breeds benefited from this rivalry? First of all the great hunting dogs who were already listed in the classic "records of the packs" and so many other stud-books. Then the other breeds captured more and more of the limelight. First gun-dogs, then watch-dogs and sheep dogs, and finally, more than all the others, pet dogs. Thus the public was in a position to know precisely what were the characteristics of each breed and to appreciate its qualities.

DOG AND MAN TODAY

During the first World War several German

HOLMÈS-LEBEL — HUET

Japanese Spaniel

Appenzell Mountain Dog.

breeds, until then almost unknown in France, were introduced into that country. Among these were the Schnauzer, the Doberman (a fine-looking, courageous dog which is nevertheless quite vulnerable), the Boxer (which was to prove itself just as good a watchdog and guard dog as a companion dog), and the Alsatian, improperly called a wolf-dog, which used to be called the German Shepherd Dog, as it is today throughout much of the world.

In the category of shepherd dogs—for thenceforward dogs were sometimes classified according to their use—the Briard (a French sheep dog), the Beauçeron (a French herding dog), and the little Pyrenean sheep dog vied with the Belgian sheep dogs; the Malinois, the Groenendael, and the Belgian Cattle Dog; while the great heavy mastiff-type dogs, the Great Dane, the St. Bernard, the Newfoundland, the Mastiff, the Old English Sheepdog, and the Dogue de Bordeaux, saw their numbers diminish until by the end of the first half of this century they had become curiosities seen only at shows.

Then came the Second World War, distinguished by so much cruelty and suffering. At the start of the hostilities, and then throughout that catastrophic time, thousands of dogs of all ages and value were necessarily sacrificed. In spite of this slaughter, neither the exigencies of the occupation, nor privation, nor danger could sever the pact of friendship between man and dog. With the return of peace it took only two years for the number of dogs in all villages to be trebled.

What kind of dogs? They were mostly small dogs, whether pet dogs or otherwise, because they were easier to house. Among them there was an amusing little short-legged hound, from the far-off Vallée des Rois, which the post-war generations adopted because it felt at home everywhere, in the kitchen and the drawing room, at the feet of its master and in the arms of its mistress, under the eider-down and in the deepest of burrows. This was the Dachshund, or badger-dog, which could even then pride itself on

its rare claim to zootechnic fame. No British breeder has so far succeeded in imitating it. The English Basset·will never be as fast, willowy, or sinewy as this German basset.

But the Dachshund has other successes it can be proud of. Within a quarter of a century it has become the most popular of the pet dogs. It has cast back into oblivion the Griffon Bruxellois, the Brabançon, and the black Schipperke (to mention only Belgian dogs). It has made mincemeat of the infatuation people used to feel for the little French Bulldog, for the intelligent Poodle, and the amusing French cross-breed Fox Terriers. It had a tussle with the most lovable of the Chinese dogs, the voluptuous Pekingese and the grave, solitary Chow Chow. It has barred the way to the Lhasa Terrier, which was rapidly gaining in popularity, and it is also responsible for the present loss of interest in that other dog from beyond the Rhine, the Pomeranian.

In the meantime the pug has reappeared. This dog originally stood in the same relationship to the ancient Assyrian dog as the ferreting Dachshund does to the great Egyptian Greyhound. Which of them will win the battle for popular affection?

Long live the present-day Dachshund, if it really is the dog we hoped for, which we wanted to be at once a good sporting dog and watch dog, and very affectionate, but also to be small and easy to house, to keep clean, and to feed. But let us hope that the little pug, so gentle and affectionate, the refuge of the heart in this time of selfishness and violence, does not die out.

Let us also hope that of all the other dogs which in the future will be called upon to share our life, there will be none which are valued only for their usefulness. Army dogs, sledge dogs and harness dogs, hunting dogs, police dogs, dogs for the blind, truffle-dogs and mountain rescue dogs, racing dogs, shepherds' dogs, ratters and scavenging dogs, circus dogs and cinema dogs, and—can we mention them without a shudder?—dogs for experiments, and even, alas, edible dogs.

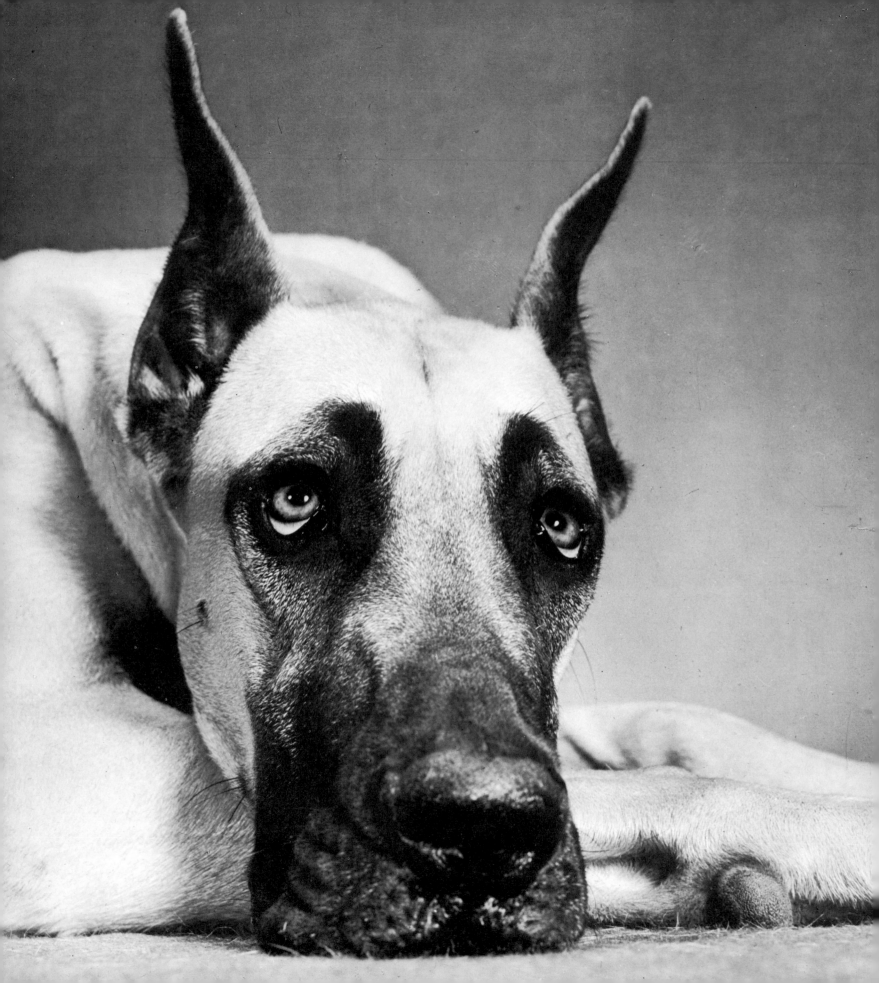

6 CLASSIFICATION OF THE BREEDS

It is virtually impossible to establish an exact and complete genealogy of the domestic dog.

Starting with the sheep dog, Buffon thought of a *Table of the Origin of the Breeds* which followed the geographical regions reputed to be the places of origin of certain breeds.

He explained it as follows: "The animals which stayed independent of man so that each might choose its climate and food are those which best keep their original shape. The result of this is that the first dog, *i.e.* the most ancient, is today still reasonably faithfully represented by its descendants."

Where man has intervened and changed their environment and their food, dogs have evolved until they show the diversity we know today.

Since then, various attempts at classification have been made, in a completely different way, *but classification is not genealogy.*

CLASSIFICATION IS DIFFICULT

Two great dog experts of our time, M. de Kermadec and Dr. Oberthur, envisaged in their own way a classification based on the cynegetic behavior of dogs, according to how they hunt: 1) *by surprise* (such as the jackal and pointing dogs); 2) *by speed* (such as Greyhounds and their various, indirect descendants); 3) *in noisy packs* (such as the Cape hunting dog); 4) *in silent packs* (such as wolves).

Other experts have tried to draw up a family tree by pruning the number of branches, so as to leave only the principal ones and thus provide a practical reference for the amateur dog-lover, as much as for the experienced breeder. Genealogical classification of this kind always remains questionable, for nothing can confirm the exact affiliation between breeds which have disappeared and those which exist today.

What dog expert would agree to passing without transition from the *canis matris*

optimae to its direct descendant represented by the "Persian sheep dog" or from *canis familiaris intermedius* to the no less strange "Lhasa terrier"?

In all scientific exactitude we must therefore admit that it is impossible today to resolve the enigma of the dog in a satisfactory manner. Many questions remain unresolved concerning its origin, its variation of form, the nature of the breeds, and, because of this, their classification.

Therefore we are led, in the light of today's knowledge, to propose the classification of breeds by criteria which are without doubt conventional, but which at least have the merit of some clarity.

First, there is the criterion of *resemblance*. But what do we mean by resemblance?

There is a "physical resemblance," but there is also a "psychic resemblance." It appears that we have never given the latter the importance it deserves. Nevertheless we know to what extent psychic qualities can be linked to the development of skull and brain. There is then a parallel between the morphological characteristics and the psychological characteristics, and the study of behavior is teaching us every day how to recognize them better.

Starting from these two elements, it is perfectly logical to think of a classification, such as was established by Jean-Pierre Megnin, which sets out four major groups to which are linked either directly or indirectly almost all representatives of the canine species.

1. The GREYHOUND FAMILY *(GRAIOIDES).* Of all domesticated dogs the Greyhounds have best preserved the characteristics of the type: elongated line; narrow, long, cone-shaped head; pointed bony nose, which overshoots the mouth; thin, short, set lips; small, more or less flat ears. The narrow chest is deep, the stomach tucked up, its bone structure long and fragile, its musculature lean, well-developed and very conspicuous.

Psychically all Greyhounds are high-

Ulmer Mastiff (Great Dane).
HOLMÈS-LEBEL

75

strung, despite their calm appearance, and can change very rapidly from a state of indifference to one of excitement.

2. The MASTIFF FAMILY *(MOLOS-SOIDES)*. They have round, solid craniums; small, pendulous ears; wide, deep chests; a uniform musculature which is scarcely visible; and a solid bone structure varying in length according to breed. They are the ancestors of the majority of mountain dogs, fighting dogs and probably mastiffs *(chiens allants)*, and pugs. Their character is generally placid and docile.

2. The WOLF FAMILY *(LUPOIDES)*. Morphologically, the Alsatians and Malinois are often—wrongly—considered to belong to this group. The "dog-wolf" does not necessarily have wolf's blood in its veins. Among the true "dog-wolves" which are nearest to the wolf we can class the Chow Chow, all sledge dogs, and the Spitzes.

Members of the wolf family have a horizontal, pyramidal cranium; a more or less pointed muzzle; small, slanting eyes; and short, erect ears which are pricked at the least signal. Their tails either hang down or are carried upright, and are always tufted.

Their character is marked by a natural defiance to man, but on the other hand an innate attachment to the person who has reared it and fed it. Faithful in the extreme, these dogs nevertheless do not know servile obedience and remain independent.

4. The HOUND FAMILY *(BRAC-COIDES)*. The majority of hunting dogs, and also the Pekingese and the Japanese can be grouped under this heading. All hounds have slightly oval craniums, which are lightly curved but never round. Their pendulous lips hang well down and are rather creased at the corners. Their noses are of medium length, with a wide truffle, well-open; the well-developed eyes have a tendency to protrude (exorbitism). Their skeletons are well-balanced, their bone structure strong, their chests fairly open and deep, their hindquarters slightly curved, and they have an upright stance.

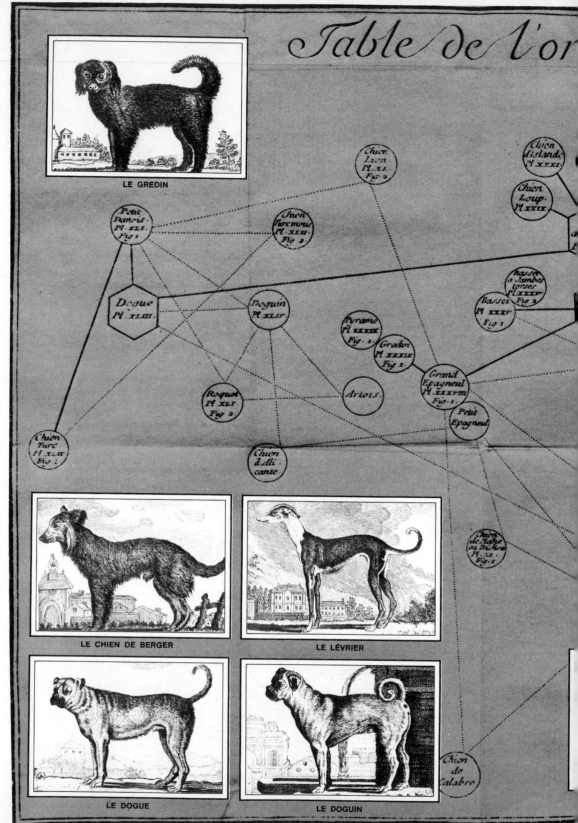

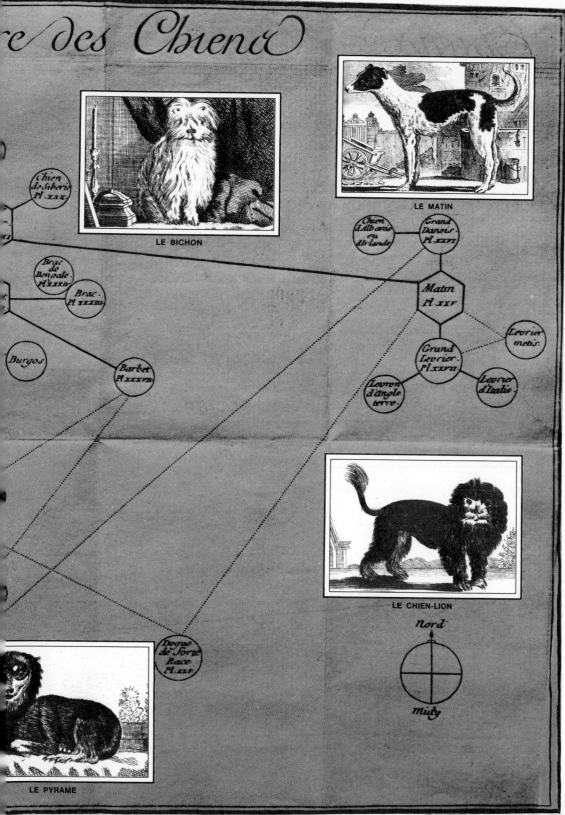

re des Chiens

LE BICHON

Chien de Siberie Pl. XXX.

Brac de Bengale Pl. XXXIV.

Brac. Pl. XXXIII.

Burgos

Barbet Pl. XXXVIII.

LE MATIN

Chien d'Albanie ou Ir-lande

Grand Danois Pl. XXVI.

Matin Pl. XXV.

Grand Levrier Pl. XXVII.

Levrier metis.

Levron d'angle terre.

Levrier d'Italie.

LE CHIEN-LION

Nord

Midy

Dogue de sorte Race Pl. XXV.

LE PYRAME

ARCH. R. LAFFONT

Buffon.
Family tree of the dog.
Histoire Naturelle (18th century).
(Dr. Méry's Collection)

Psychologically, we can note extreme docility, an obvious desire to learn, obedience without bounds, and generally a great attachment to the master, especially if he is a huntsman and the dog has developed early on its natural qualities in training.

Is this classification perfect? No. Because in spite of its attractiveness, it remains incomplete. It does not allow for the inclusion of various types such as the many terriers.

THE USUAL CLASSIFICATION BY FUNCTION

This is why, in short—although aptitudes are not necessarily linked to the breeds—the *classification by function,* proposed by Dr. Caius and adopted by Hugh Daziel and others, now seems clearest to us. Nevertheless it neither pretends to account for the breeds of dogs being divided into three main categories, nor the fringes, nor the direct line of descent. A dog such as the Chow Chow, classified as a non-sporting dog, is a fierce guard-dog. A dog such as the Boxer, classified as a guard-dog, is nonetheless often the most docile of non-sporting dogs. Two dogs of very similar appearance, such as the Chihuahua and the English Toy-Terrier, do not necessarily share a common ancestry, although it is easy to classify both of them as non-sporting dogs.

On the whole, Dr. Caius' classification today is followed because of its almost complete grouping of sporting dogs. This divides dogs into:

1. *Hunting dogs* (including Greyhounds)
2. *Working dogs* (guard-dogs, sheep dogs, draught dogs, terriers, etc.).
3. *Non-sporting dogs* (or companion dogs).

Dog societies, in general, subdivide these three main categories into "Groups," in order to facilitate exhibiting.

GREYHOUND FAMILY
(Graioides)

GREYHOUND

WHIPPET

MASTIFF FAMILY
(Molossoides)

GREAT DANES (Ulmer Mastiff)

PUG

WOLF FAMILY
(Lupoides)

KEESHOND

GERMAN SHEPHERD DOG

HOUND FAMILY
(Braccoides)

BRITTANY SPANIEL

DALMATIAN

Included in this category are:

- The Saluki, the Ibizan Hound, the Charnique, the Galgo
- The Greyhound, the Whippet, the Italian Greyhound
- The Wolfhound, the Deerhound, the Borzoi, the Circassian
- The Persian Greyhound, the Afghan Hound,
  and morphologically by their general characteristics: the Collie and the Shetland Sheepdog

COLLIES (Rough)

As improbable as it may seem, these come into this category:

- The Pyrenean Mountain Dog, the St. Bernard, the Newfoundland, the Leonberg Dog, the Bobtail Sheepdog, the Briard
- The Bloodhound, Spanish Mastiff, the Great Dane, the Mastiff, the Boxer
- The Dogue de Bordeaux, the Bulldog, the Bull Terrier, the Boston Terrier, the French Bulldog
- The Pug, the Brabancon, the Griffon Bruxellois, the Chihuahua, the Tibetan Mastiff
- The Dobermann, the Schnauzer, the Riesenschnauzer (Giant Schnauzer), the Affenpinscher
- The Retrievers, the Labrador, etc.

FRENCH BULLDOG

In spite of its appearance the German Shepherd is not typical of this category. More closely related to the wolf are:

- The Keeshond, the Elkhound, the Husky
- The Chow Chow
- The Samoyed, the Spitz
- The Pomeranian, the Schipperke, the Corgi

CHOW CHOW

This family comprises two main divisions:

- Hounds (among which some breeds have disappeared or are becoming extinct) with: St. Hubert hounds, the Saintongeois, Normans, Poitevins, Blue Gascons, Griffons Nivernais, and the corresponding basset hounds (Norman, Artesian, Gascon) and Beagles, Foxhounds and Harriers
  Pointing dogs of which the best known are:
- The French Spaniel, the Brittany Spaniel, the Pont-Audemer, the Water Spaniel, the Braque d'Auvergne, the Braque St. Germain, the Braque du Bourbonnais, the Braque Dupuy, the Boulet
- The Pointers, the Cocker Spaniel, all spaniels and all setters
- The Korthals Griffon or Wire-haired Pointing Griffon, the Braque

(Cocker) SPANIEL

DIM

HUNTING DOGS

GREYHOUNDS

EGYPTIAN GREYHOUND

INDIAN GREYHOUND

SALUKI

AFGHAN

IRISH WOLFHOUND

SCOTTISH DEERHOUND

BORZOI OR RUSSIAN GREYHOUND

ENGLISH GREYHOUND

WHIPPET

HOUNDS

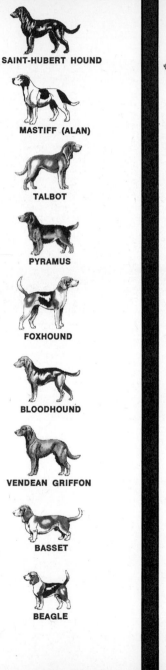

SAINT-HUBERT HOUND

MASTIFF (ALAN)

TALBOT

PYRAMUS

FOXHOUND

BLOODHOUND

VENDEAN GRIFFON

BASSET

BEAGLE

GUN DOGS

ITALIAN SPANIEL

SPANISH SPANIEL

IRISH SETTER

IRISH WATER SPANIEL

ENGLISH SETTER

GORDON SETTER

COCKER SPANIEL

SPRINGER SPANIEL

FIELD SPANIEL

NORFOLK SPANIEL

BRAQUE

WEIMARANER

POINTER

GERMAN POINTER

BLOODHOUND

GOLDEN RETRIEVER

CURLY-COATED RETRIEVER

LABRADOR

CHESAPEAKE BAY RETRIEVER

OTTERHOUND

OWTCHARKA (A RUSSIAN SHEEPDOG)

ELKHOUND

GUARD-DOGS

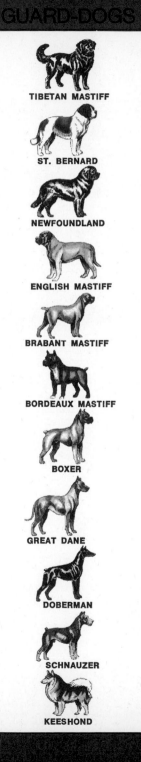

TIBETAN MASTIFF

ST. BERNARD

NEWFOUNDLAND

ENGLISH MASTIFF

BRABANT MASTIFF

BORDEAUX MASTIFF

BOXER

GREAT DANE

DOBERMAN

SCHNAUZER

KEESHOND

WORKING DOGS

PET DOGS

SHEPHERD DOGS

PYRENEAN MOUNTAIN DOG

PERSIAN SHEPHERD DOG

OLD ENGLISH SHEEPDOG

BRIARD

BOUVIER DES FLANDRES

ALSATIAN

COLLIE OR SCOTCH COLLEY DOG

SHETLAND SHEEPDOG

TERRIERS

WHITE ENGLISH TERRIER

AIREDALE TERRIER

WIRE-HAIRED FOX TERRIER

SMOOTH-HAIRED FOX TERRIER

WELSH TERRIER

IRISH TERRIER

KERRY BLUE TERRIER

BEDLINGTON TERRIER

SCOTTISH TERRIER

WEST HIGHLAND WHITE TERRIER

CAIRN TERRIER

BULL TERRIER

SKYE TERRIER

STAFFORDSHIRE BULL TERRIER

SEALYHAM TERRIER

BOSTON TERRIER

CORGI

DANDIE DINMONT TERRIER

DACHSHUND

SLED DOGS

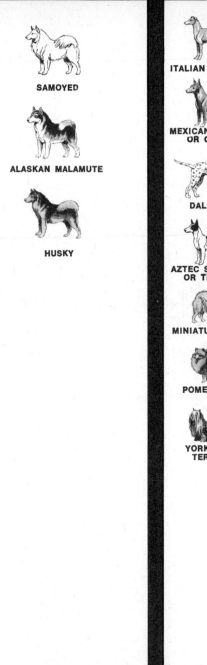

SAMOYED

ALASKAN MALAMUTE

HUSKY

PET DOGS

ITALIAN GREYHOUND

POODLE

MEXICAN DWARF DOG OR CHIHUAHUA

BULLDOG

DALMATIAN

LITTLE LION DOG

AZTEC SACRED DOG OR TEECHICHI

TIBETAN APSO

MINIATURE SPITZ

MALTESE

PEKINGESE

POMERANIAN

JAPANESE

YORKSHIRE TERRIER

PUG

SCHIPPERKE

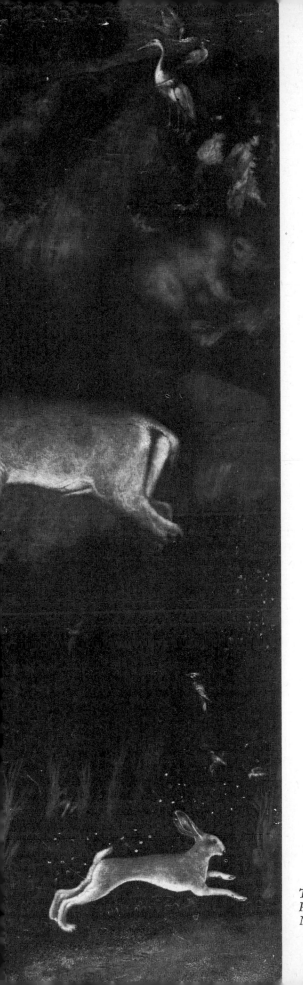

2
THE DOG
IN THE MIND
OF MAN

The vision of St. Hubert.
Pisanello (15th century).
National Gallery, London.

7 THE DOG IN LITERATURE

*"Among all the forms
of life which surround us,
none except the dog
has allied itself with us."*
MAURICE MAETERLINCK

In the chapter on "The Dog in Antiquity" we have quoted many ancient authors. We ask the reader to see in this brief repetition nothing more than the introduction to the present chapter.

After Baal of Sidon and Tyre or of Babylon, the cruel dog of mythology no longer inspires terror. **Homer** is the source of all the literary culture of the Western World. He was the first to introduce the dog into the world of letters. *The Odyssey* sings the praises of dogs by way of the faithful Argus, and the most famous Greek and Roman authors were in their turn to do the same.

Aristotle boasted of the courage of the mastiffs of Laconia.

Virgil, in the *Georgics,* recalled all that man owed to the swift bloodhounds of Sparta and the vigilant guardians of Epirus. Ovid retold the dramatic tale of Actaeon being devoured by his own dogs after he had been shorn of his human form. **Pliny** paid tribute to the affection of the dog, and well before **Arrien** he completed a work on natural history which included some cynegetic prescriptions, whose poetic qualities we value today more than their medical ones.

FRENCH LITERATURE

Through the ages there have been many French poets, fabulists, philosophers, and writers of romances whose works betoken their warm liking for the dog. Some of them are restrained by rational scepticism, but others open their hearts freely so that all may see the love they bear the dog. Very early a spiritual barrier grew up between those who loved animals and those who despised them.

Because of this we find in literature, on the one hand, the dog as miracle worker, the dog as symbol, the dog as remedy, the dog as example, the dog as judge (the finger of God)—the classic type of the latter being *"Le chien de Montargis";* and on the other hand we have the systematic, abusive tirade.

In the Middle Ages, the dog finds its place in literature not only in the *Book of Hours of the Duke de Berry.* **Marie de France** *(Le Bisclavret, Graelent)* describes the passionate fondness of the king for the sweet companion of his days; she recounts the tribulations of the wolf and how it regained the friendship of men. With the *Roman de Renart,* the fantastic animal is again consigned to the shadows: Isengrin (a real wolf) and Renard (the real fox known to terriers and open country) join battle once more with the forces that have always opposed them, before they unwittingly helped to bring the dog to our side.

Froissart, in Book IV of his *Chronicles,* told of the role played by a Greyhound in the long and bloody war caused by the succession of Jean III, Duke of Brittany. The duke was choosing a husband for his niece, Jeanne de Penthievre. Three suitors were in the running. Charles d'Evreux, son of the king of Navarre; Charles de Blois, nephew of the king of France; and John Plantagenet, brother of the king of England. The duke, more than a little hesitant, decided to leave the whole thing to chance. He called Jeanne's beautiful greyhound, Yoland, and let the dog nominate the winner. Yoland (on a discreet signal from his mistress) ran towards Charles de Blois and, having sniffed the young prince at length, tenderly licked his hand. Several years later, the winning suitor was to appreciate the qualities of this extraordinarily clairvoyant dog in quite different circumstances. Jean de Montfort, asserting his right to inherit Brittany, waged war on Charles de Blois. One day Yoland the greyhound, "deserting its master, went over to de Montfort's army, and, as if recognizing him, placed its two forefeet on de Montfort's saddle-bow, thus portending that fortune was passing from one to the other." The duke's courtiers became nervous and followed the greyhound, whose act they knew to be a portent. One hour later Charles de Blois fell mortally wounded and Jean de Montfort became Jean IV!

Lamartine and his dogs. Decaisne (1839). (Lamartine Museum)

Illustration from The Fables of Aesop:
"The dog with a yoke and a block at its neck."
(Bibliothèque Nationale, Paris)

*Combat between a dog
and a gentleman
who had killed its master, at Montargis.
About 1371.
(Bibliothèque Nationale, Paris)*

as he tears a cry of pain from a dog he is ill-treating. "It's obvious that the creature feels nothing!"

Pascal, who so often disagreed with Descartes, seems to have shared this poor opinion of dogs, but he was not so sure. The following story, which was told by the Jansenists, seems to have posed him a problem. One day the dog that turned the spit in the house of the Duke de Liancourt did not show up at the appointed hour. The servants roused its work companion, but this dog refused to go with them, and performed quite a pantomine to show that it wished them to follow it. The servants understood readily, followed it, and discovered the shirker in the loft, where it had hidden itself so that it would be left in peace to sleep. The other dog then chased it out of its hiding place and made it go downstairs to get on with its work. It is said that Antoine Arnauld, the Jensenist, was highly amused by this story, but it did not diminish the belief he held in the Cartesian theory.

Madame de Sévigné, a lady of feeling and sensitivity, held to her own convictions. She was so fond of her bitch "Marphise" that she wrote to Madame de Grignan: "At Les Rochers Madame de Tarente made me a present of an extraordinarily beautiful fragrant little dog, with silky ears, very sweet breath, as tiny as a sylph, flaxen as a fop," and who, she feared, would attract the jealousy of her bitch on her return home. On the subject of Descarte's ideas, she later said, "Machines which love, which prefer one person to another, machines which are jealous . . . come now! Descartes never thought to make us believe that!"

Scarron, the first husband of Madame de Maintenon, dedicated one of his works to his dog: "To Guillemette, my very honest and amusing dog. Although you are only an animal, I prefer nevertheless to dedicate this book to you, rather than to some great satrap whose sleep I would thereby be troubling."

Racine, in a famous scene (scene III, act III) of his play *Les Plaideurs* (The Plead-

In the *Cent Nouvelles* of **Antoine de La Salle** there is the story of the death of a clever performing dog that had been the pride and joy of its master, a parish priest. The priest wanted to give it a Christian burial. Unfortunately his bishop was angered by this and summoned him to appear before a tribunal. The priest, pleading against the charge of sacrilege, ended his speech with this plausible argument which cleared him of the charge made against him. "And you will understand, my Lord, that I was able to put this dog, who was worth much more than a good number of Christians, in a discreet position. The dog gave me many instances of its wisdom in life, and above all in its death! It even wished to leave me its

will, at the head of which is the name of the bishop of this diocese, to whom it bequeaths 150 crowns, which I have here for you now."

No less cynical, but expressing himself more gracefully, **Montaigne** claims to see a likeness between men and animals, thinks the dog is particularly like man, and generously accords it all our virtues without attributing to it any of our vices. "The friendship of a dog," he writes, "is without a doubt more intense and more constant than that of a man."

Not only does **Descartes** express nothing but scorn for the dog, but he considers it, as well as all other animals, nothing but an insensible piece of machinery. Everyone knows the celebrated phrase of Malebranche

Illustration of Rabelais.
Little Pantagruel, carrying his cradle, enters
the room where his father
is amusing himself with his friends.
(Bibliothèque Nationale, Paris)

ARCH. R. LAFFONT

Illustration in the manner of Tournai,
for "The Pleaders" by Racine.
(Bibliothèque Nationale)

GIRAUDON

ers), ridicules the pompous justice of the 17th century, but not the bewildered common people, symbolized by dogs. Under the law *"Si quis canis,"* Citron, a dog, is brought before the court charged with eating a capon. The advocate, *"l'Intimé,"* pleads comically in defense of the unfortunate little four-legged orphans, and the dogs (people) are so tearful that Dandin has them ejected from the courtroom:

> "Come now! What a din!
> They have pissed everywhere."
> "My Lord, these are our tears."

La Fontaine did not like animals, especially the dog, which he does not seem to

have understood. He readily accuses it of faults, and also of stupidity. In the fable, "The Two Dogs and the Dead Donkey," he writes:

> Then the Brutes—the dog indeed
> Stands high for duty and devotion,
> But also for stupidity and greed.

In "The Farmer, the Dog, and the Fox," he emphasizes the scorn he felt for the dog. Without a doubt

> The argument was very sound,
> And coming from a master's mouth
> Would have been lauded for its truth.
> But since the author was a hound,
> Its merit went unrecognized.

Aesop had already compared the wolf's instinct for liberty with the rational servitude of the dog. La Fontaine took up exactly the same theme in "The Wolf and the Dog." The Wolf would like to be a dog,

> But as they went, he spied his friend's bald
>   scruff.
> "What's that?" he questioned him. " 'Tis
>   naught."
> "How naught?" "Well, nothing much." "But
>   what?"
> "The collar of my chain, 'tis like enough,
> Has caused the trifling mark you see."
> "Your chain?" exclaimed the Wolf, "then
>   you're not free
> To come and go?" "Not always—but no
>   matter."
> "Indeed? It wouldn't do for me,"
> Replied the starvling. "You may be fatter,
> But I prefer my own sweet will
> To all the riches of your platter."
> Therewith he ran: I guess he's running still.

There is also the fable of "The Dog and His Master's Dinner," in which La Fontaine goes so far as to deny the fidelity of the old friend. The dog is tempted by the appetizing smell of the meal which he is carrying to

Buffon: A dwarf spaniel.
(Bibliothèque Nationale, Paris)

ARCH. R. LAFFONT

Buffon: Mountain dog.
(Bibliothèque Nationale, Paris)

ARCH. R. LAFFONT

Beagles awaiting the "laying on of the pack." ▶
(Rapho de Chatillon)

his master. On his way he meets a mastiff who picks a quarrel with him. He puts his burden down on the ground so that he can defend it better, and then three large dogs appear on the scene. Faced with overwhelming numbers, the dog cowardly decides that it would be wiser to eat the meal with them, and that an excess of devotion is not worth fighting for.

In "The Ass and the Dog," the dog is even more cruelly ridiculed. For fear of waking his master, the dog allows his friend the ass to be throttled by a wolf. Of course the fable is above all a lesson in human morality and wisdom.

"Without this element any fable is an imperfect thing,' 'said La Fontaine. The animals are not portrayed for their own sake, but it is regrettable that they are so gratuitously caricatured and misrepresented. For instance, to return to the first fable, "The Two Dogs and the Dead Donkey," how did La Fontaine dream up this unlikely situation: Two dogs on the seashore catch sight of the body of a donkey floating on the waves. How are they to reach it? They can find no other solution than that both should start drinking the salt water and so dry up the sea! This is really to put too low a premium on the intelligence of the dog, which is perhaps very different from our own but whose existence it is nevertheless difficult to deny!

A hundred years later, **Florian** was to show more consideration for man's best friend than had the Administrator of the King's Gardens. In *La Brebis et le chien* (The Sheep and the Dog), there is more understanding and kindness than in the whole of La Fontaine's work. The sheep recounts his misfortunes and disappointments to the dog, and tries to make it take part in its revolt against the cruelty and selfishness of man. The dog wisely comes to the conclusion that it is always preferable "To submit to evil rather than to do evil."

"The Cat and the Dog," again by Florian, tells of the adventures of a good dog which is sold by its master, and breaks its chain to

The Works of Florian:
Estelle *(1788)*
(Bibliothèque Nationale, Paris)

Rousseau
examining herbs in his room
at the Ile Saint-Pierre (1765).
(Bibliothèque Nationale, Paris)

return to him. The unfortunate creature is beaten with a stick when it comes home and is sent back to its new owner:

> His companion, an old cat,
> Seeing the dog's astonishment,
> Says as it passes,
> You poor fool, did you really think
> That they love us for ourselves?

This sympathy for the dog which Florian shows in his verse is quite typical of the 18th century, during which man became more and more fond of the dog and made a friend of the animal.

Buffon had read Montaigne, but he was too much of a scientist to accept the morality which gives the dog "virtues"; he had read Descartes, but because of his experience as a naturalist he was unable to accept Descartes' system which reduced the animal to a piece of machinery. He wrote: "The dog has, above all, all the interior qualities which can attract man's liking. Its nature, which is spirited, bad-tempered, even ferocious and bloodthirsty, makes the wild dog feared by all animals, but in the domesticated dog this nature changes, it becomes very gentle, takes pleasure in loving and desires to please." Like all zoologists, Buffon was struck not only by the variations of form and color found in the different breeds of dogs, but he also acknowledged a psychic evolution peculiar to the species: "Of all the animals, the dog is the one whose nature is most impressionable and which is most susceptible to character-training. . . . But what is difficult to discover in the midst of this great variety, are the characteristics of the primitive race." And, further on: "These animals are farther from their origins than are those which live longer. Man is today eight times nearer to Adam than the dog is to the first dog, because a man lives for eighty years, while a dog only lives for ten. . . . So if for any reason whatsoever these two species tended to degenerate at an equal rate, the change

89

*The dog
that returns to the tomb
of its master.*

ARCH. R. LAFFONT

and friend of the Duke of Montmorency, when he gave it the more discreet name of "Turk." When the dog died he was inconsolable: "My poor Turk was only a dog, but he loved me. He was sensitive, disinterested. . . . As you yourself said to me, how many so-called friends were not worth this one!" This was his reply to Madame de Luxembourg, who had written him this friendly note: "I arrived from the country last night. What bad news greeted me! I am in despair. . . . Poor Turk! Monsieur de Luxembourg has not heard the bad news yet." A few days later the Marshal, Monsieur de Luxembourg, wrote him several pages in which he showed himself as moved and sympathetic as the Duchess of Montmorency. It is impossible to think of Madame de Luxembourg without remembering that however sensitive she may have been, she sometimes had a cruel tongue. Everyone knows the epigram she dedicated to both "Tonton," Madame du Deffon's dog, and to Voltaire:

> You will find them both charming,
> You will find them both biting,
> That is their point of resemblance.
> One bites only your enemies,
> The other bites all your friends. . . .
> That's the difference!

With the coming of Romanticism, sensibility is more freely expressed and is not limited to the bonds between men and women or to the beauties of nature. A profound feeling of love for animals moves writers of prose and poetry alike.

"It is really with Romanticism that the dog makes its triumphal entrance into literature," according to Calvert and Cruppi. Was it Victor Hugo or Lamartine who lit the flame?

The portrait of **Lamartine** by Decaisne is enough to show the place his dogs held in the heart of the poet. He gave their offspring as gifts to his best friends, but only after making careful enquiries and with a thousand scruples. Witness this note: "Mon-

sieur Lamartine has the honor of sending to Madame the Countess of Boigne the friend she wished for and which he has reared for her. It is the most sentient and intelligent animal he has ever known. . . ." Then follows his practical advice concerning the care that this delicate greyhound requires, and, at the end, this strange remark: "If he should cough, give him a little mallow. Nothing else. The doctors kill them all because these are not dogs, but four-legged birds. . . ."

Fido was one of the best loved, if one is to believe this tender poem *"Le chien du solitaire"* (The Lonely Man's Dog) in which Lamartine confides in us:

> Never have I kicked you in scorn,
> Never with a brutal word saddened your
>   tender love,
> My heart has never repulsed your touching
>   caress
> But always . . . Ah, always in you I honor
> The ineffable goodness of your Master and
>   mine.

The poem ends with this invitation;

> Like my damp eyes, place your heart next
>   to mine
> And alone, let us love one another, poor
>   dog!

Could **Victor Hugo,** with his immense heart, have failed to love dogs? He devoted many pages to those which had shared his trials. To "Ponto," who followed him into exile;

> My dog Ponto follows me. The dog is virtue
> Which unable to make itself man, became
>   beast,
> And Ponto looks at me with his honest
>   air . . .

To "Chougna," in *"La Dernière Gerbe"* (The Last Straw), he says in an amusing tone, and a familiar rhythm:

would today be ten times more marked in the dog than in man." Buffon, after talking as if with precognition of "the almost continual sleep of the dog cut off from dreams," concludes by saying that the climates, environments, and circumstances in which dogs have lived have had a great influence on the variability of the species, and that one should "consider the sheep dog to be the true, natural dog."

Meanwhile, love for dogs had become in many cases sentimentality, and people were not ashamed to display their grief on the death of a dog which they loved.

Jean-Jacques Rousseau talked at length, in his *Confessions,* of the good and beautiful dog which he was given at the Hermitage, and which, he said, had this peculiarity, "that it never obeyed me." He called this dog "Duke" until he became the protégé

Illustration
for Paul et Virginie,
by Bernardin de Saint-Pierre: Paul at the tomb
of Virginie.
(Bibliothèque Nationale)

CI-GÎT L'INFORTUNÉE
ET VERTUEUSE VIRGINIE

Why . . .

Do you behave badly, Chougna, in front of
people?
Why, when we go out (I must give you a
row)
Do you run, yapping, through the bushes
After young dogs and little boys?
Why can you not see a cock without
chasing it?
So that I look as if I have a drunken dog?

On the subject of Victor Hugo's dogs,
according to the tittle-tattle of the day one
of them beat all records for canine intelligence. Escaping from the home in
Moscow of a diplomat to whom the poet
had given him, this poodle succeeded within
a few months in retracing his journey and
was found one morning scratching at the
door of his old master's door in Paris!

Alexander Dumas, Fils, had all his life a
horror of dogs, which he thought were
"idiotic, for they run after their own tails."
This strange prejudice earned him more cold
shoulders than handshakes at a time when
people no longer died at twenty plucking
at a camelia, but when the dog was a
trusted friend—"a good pal."

Emile Zola, in keeping with his brotherly
compassion for the unfortunate and for the
victims of society, loved the dog of the
poor man, the stray dog, the abandoned
dog, the dog that prowled around garbage
cans. "Why is it that my heart is so touched
whenever I meet a dog lost in our noisy
streets? Why do I feel such anguished pity
when I see one of these creatures coming
and going, sniffing everyone, frightened,
despairing of ever finding its master?"

Edmond Rostand immortalized the farm

dog. Patou has no need of formal proof of
his nobility:

He carries every sort of blood in his veins;
he has been them all,
That ought to make for an enormous sum
of goodness!

Unfortunately, though he is

Guardian of the house, the garden and the
fields.

Patou has also hunting dogs among his
ancestors, and besides, he has a delicate
conscience:

No, but I have several dogs in my make-up.
I fight a bit.
The spaniel part of me gets excited at the

Illustration by Beuville for
"Le chasseur au chien d'arret" by Elzear Blaze.
(Bibliothèque Nationale, Paris)
ARCH. R. LAFFONT

sound of gun-fire,
But then my memory of being a poodle
Evokes a bloody wing, the eye of a dying hind,
I remember what a rabbit puts into its last look
And I feel stirring within me my heart of a Saint Bernard.

Marcel Proust patiently observed provincial life and manners, and he liked to talk of the dogs of the rich and those of the poor in Combray, "where everybody knows everybody else." In *Du côté de chez Swann* (Swann's Way) he describes family life with these few strokes of his pen: "A dog that my aunt did not know at all? That must be Madame Sazerat's dog, said Françoise, to prevent my aunt from saying any more about it. What? As if I didn't know Madame Sazerat's dog, replied my aunt, who was not going to admit defeat as easily as that. Then in the end, Françoise said: That must be the new dog that Monsieur Galopin has brought back from Lisieux. It is a very pleasing creature, always good-tempered, always likeable. . . . It is rare for such a young dog to be so well-behaved."

Was **Anatole France** interested in animals? Such a suggestion may seem surprising. However, the Société Anatole France has published[1] a complete study on the love of animals of the author of *Le lys Rouge* (The Red Lily) whose work, says Charles Braibant, exhales a "rustic perfume."

There are many other dogs which we must leave to their fate, and get on to talk of their greatest friends.

Tristan Bernard admitted, with his delicate smile, "Yes, I love dogs; they are nearer to man than . . . to the other animals."

Maurice Maeterlink, who never liked cats, always surrounded himself with dogs, and even today the tender and faithful vestal of *Orlamonde* is surrounded with Borzois and Salukis: Ariel, Melisande, Syska, and the

[1] *Le Bestiaire d' Anatole France. (The Bestiary of Anatole France),* by Marcel Maupoint.

Pekingese Arkel, with its snub-nose like Pelleas the black bulldog, and Golaud who is also a bulldog. In *Le Double Jardin* (The Double Garden) the sensitive giant of poetry and theatre wrote: "The other day I lost a little bulldog. It had just come to the end of the sixth month of its short life. It has no story. Its intelligent eyes opened just to look at the world and to love men, then they shut again on the unjust secrets of death."

In 1948, **Jean Cocteau,** who loved cats especially, wrote and illustrated a little book which, though not widely known, is full of humor; *Un drôle de ménage* (A Strange Family). In it he amused himself by entrusting to a pet dog, so intimate a part of the human family, the task of raising the children of that too busy couple, Lord Sun and Lady Moon. Left to themselves, these children became cruel, stupid, and wicked. The dog taught them to be good, patient, and obedient, so much so that their parents, overcome by remorse, found them one of those perfect nannies "who by night make wonderful watchers," and they came to regret their paradoxical education as dog-children.

There is also a paradox in the story by **Curzio Malaparte** (who is known to have liked to bark at night) of the seige of 1870 when, after eating the last rat, the master of the house decides to sacrifice "Fido" the dog. He makes the dog into an appetizing stew, invites some relatives over, and when he sees them all enjoying their meal, sighs, weeping: "Oh! if only poor Fido were here! How happy that would make me!" Anyone who knew the extraordinary tenderness Malaparte felt for his last Dachshund cannot fail to understand him, a Latin, taking refuge in this black humor, nor this other brutal statement: "The disgust of Montherlant for dogs has always upset me. His "Chienne de Colomb Bechar" seems to me to be a work unworthy of a man and a Christian."

Should we take this quick-witted dreamer

more seriously when he declared: "Jean Giraudoux asked me one evening, 'You haven't seen my dog Puck, by any chance?' 'He must have gone out for a walk with Jean Giraudoux,' I replied. And Jean Giraudoux, entering into the game, said, 'Oh, yes, that's right; he must have gone out with Jean Giraudoux.'"

Paul Claudel, too, let his imagination carry him away to the boundary of this biological fraternity: "As I get older," he wrote, "I feel myself becoming more and more a dog, and I feel my dog becoming more and more an aristocrat."

In *Mon caniche Adour* (My Poodle, Adour) **Maurice Rat** has devoted moving pages to the good poodle which, he says, had shared his life for almost sixteen years. Maurice Rat had always had a secret preference for this breed. He spoke of "Frimousse," Jules Lemaitre's poodle, to whom the latter did not hesitate to dedicate, from time to time, a chronicle. "One loves cats perhaps as one loves gods; but in dogs there is such friendliness, such ingenuity, such loving kindness, such a way of turning to one to give one their heart, that one comes to love dogs almost as one loves men."

George Duamel has given us something much better than sentimental effusions; in *Les Fables de mon Jardin* (Tales from My Garden), he marvelously portrays canine psychology, writing of old Dick and young Castor. In *"La querelle des generations"* (The Generation Gap) he shows the tensions which arise when the wisdom and experience of the former come up against the blundering whims of the latter. In *"Les incorrigibles"* (The Hopeless Cases) we discover with Castor the monster called the motorcar; in *"Le sentiment du devoir"* (Duty) Dick appears as a brave but not very daring watchdog. These three stories are all masterpieces of truth and exactitude, presented in the pure style of this sensitive writer, and not even the most scrupulous animal psychologist could discover the least fault in them. "The

Illustration for
La Fortune des Rougons
by Zola (19th century).

Illustration,
by Toulouse-Lautrec,
for Jules Renard's Histoires Naturelles (1896).
(Bibliothèque Nationale, Paris)

car, sir?" says Dick. "How do you explain the effect that this diabolical machine has on the nerves of a fine healthy dog? It is stronger than me, sir. I just have to bark! . . . I just have to bark!" And elsewhere, there is this indisputable conditioning: "On stormy days, when the terrified dog lies shivering under the chest of drawers, and refuses to come out, we ask someone to go and open the door onto the street. As soon as he hears the bell, old Dick comes out of his hiding place, barks as usual, stretches out his neck, straightens his legs and rushes downstairs to action stations for 'what must be done must be done'; there can be no argument with the standing orders!"

Less light-hearted but even more marked in its scientific truth is the true story of Douchka, the cross-bred Alsatian bitch which her mistress Colette Audry saw die *"Derrière la baignoire"* (Behind the Bath). There is not the least literary affection in these pages, just the astonishment of a woman who questions herself before this dog, which is neuropathic, unstable, shifty, difficult to catch, but which, by these very characteristics, first rebuffed, then attracted, and finally gained the affectionate interest of her mistress. "Why, in the name of what mysterious communion, of what concordance or discordance, is it possible to become fond of a dog?" she asks herself. This was a fascinating subject for a writer. To experience at the same time pity and shame for the hardness of one's heart, to wish to perform only one's basic duty, and, through one's forced devotion at the sick-bed of an animal, to discover that one loves the creature one is tending more than anything else . . . is this egoism or altruism?

How far we are from the dog of **Ninon de Lenclos**:

I cannot offer riches
To him that finds me,
If he takes me back to my mistress
Seeing her shall be his reward.

*Illustration by
Jean Cocteau for his book*
Drôle de ménage.

Freud in his study.
(Collection of Hans Casparius)

How far we are, too, from the romantic effusions and even from the happy dogs of another Colette, Madame **Colette.** They, like happy people, would have had no story, had it not been for the incisive talent of their brilliant mistress. This is truly literature, of the best kind, and how can one fail to be spellbound: "I lie! All the animals lie to you, oh heavy two-legged people! Do you really believe that the white greyhound, when she clears the cane like a jet of flame, uses all the strength of her powerful thighs? I myself growl when I am confronted with a closed door, as if I could not, with one jump, reach and pull down the latch!" Pousette the bulldog (of bronze, or old black Chinese wood, hard and burnt, or of glazed sombre earthenware?), Pousette

with her direct glance, her erect ears "which speak of rectitude, vigilance, domestic honesty," Pousette lies! Yes, this is literature, but literature that carefully bears in mind the elements of Pavlovian theory. The parish priest had asked Colette's mother not to come into the church with her dog Domino ("which was sometimes a black and white cross between a Pomeranian and a Fox Terrier, and sometimes a yellow barbet") because it had growled at the Elevation. "But of course he growled at the Elevation . . . I would have had something to say if he had not growled at the Elevation! A dog I trained myself to be a watch dog— he should bark as soon as he hears a bell ring."

I would like to close this section here, with

this quotation from Colette, but it would be both unjust and incomplete to omit to mention several other people who were friends of dogs, and also loved them very sincerely.

Paul Léautaud was a sarcastic and bitter man, but during his life in Paris he adopted, fed, cared for, loved, and wept over nearly 165 dogs of all breeds. But did Léautaud really love animals? Was he not first and foremost disappointed in women, and did he not merely seek refuge in animals and transfer his affections to them?

Am I alone in feeling unhappy that he prefers to pour scorn on his friends rather than to waste time recounting his unhappy feelings as an animal lover? Perhaps it is the style he uses to convey this type of pain: "I am going to tell you now of the death of 'Singe.' . . . Laugh if you will . . . I don't care at all. . . . I can see again the evening he died." And later, the way in which he openly displays his despair: "Then, on my knees beside him, overcome by sobs, my face almost against his body, I called him, stroked him." Is this perhaps exhibitionism, a secret joy in posturing? I do not know, but in the course of our brief meetings, Léautaud's love for animals seemed to me to be rather irritating and a little suspect.

In *Raboliot* or in *La dernière harde* (The Last Herd), the sure, precise, familiar strokes that **Maurice Genevoix** uses to convey a feeling or to evoke a scene, ring so much more true. In *Raboliot,* man and dog are closely bound together, they rub shoulders and complement each other, they are in a sense accomplices: "What was he going to do now? Tell me, Aïcha, what are we going to do? The black bitch, lying by his side, snuggling up to his warmth, pressed her side against his thigh; little by little she relaxed, her head in the man's lap, and fell asleep, warm and sweetly heavy."

And further on: "He leant towards the little dog, and with a tender, familiar gesture took her head in his two hands. He looked

*Illustration by
Jean Cocteau for his book
Drôle de ménage.*

*Maurice Maeterlinck
with his Borzoi.
(Collection of Countess Maeterlinck)*

deeply into her russet eyes, transparent with damp love, as if to ask her advice and help. What was he trying to say?" And then one day something terrible happened to this disappointed man who had only one passion in the world, to live free of the constraint of family life, and who had only one friend, his dog. "At first he did not really take in what had happened. In a moment he realized that he had just heard a bang. Cycling on, he looked over his shoulder, and saw Bourrel standing in the road. The policeman, his head bent a little, was looking at a little dark, hairy heap that lay at his feet. From the revolver he held in his hand a thread of bluish smoke still drifted into the evening air. . . ."

The dog was dead. "The only companion left to me, a policeman has killed her with a bullet from a revolver, when my back was turned, out of pure treachery. There is nothing of her left but the vision of a small black thing which stains the road at the feet of a murderer."

The dog is dead, but Raboliot and Aïcha are immortal. Maurice Genevoix was awarded the Prix Goncourt for this work, and this he regards as a proud souvenir of his youth . . . but a dog always grows old alongside his master; a silky Pekingese is the affectionate companion of Monsieur le Secrétaire Perpetuel de l'Académie Française (the permanent secretary of the French Academy), in that palace of letters where—and this would make Richelieu turn in his grave—cats also roam at will.

The second half of the 20th century, so pragmatic, unfettered, and fanatically scientific though it may be, cannot in fact manage without poetry. The animal world we are gradually discovering astonishes us, fills us with enthusiasm, and also humiliates us, encourages us to return to the "animal origins" of man. Thanks to this we have numerous works, essays and novels, in which the main characters are dogs. These authors endeavor to express the uneasiness we feel in the face of the unknown and the unknowable,

for as Gérard de Nerval has said, "Often in the lowly creature there lurks a hidden god."

ENGLISH LITERATURE

Between the Middle Ages and the present day, many English authors have written about the dog. But few of them have abandoned themselves to the sentimentality too often found in French literature. Only the poets have given free rein to the expression of the love which the English have always, but with modest reserve, born for animals.

Thomas Hood (1799-1845) wrote a charming poem of some 20 stanzas, under the title of "Lament of a Poor Blind." This was about the best known breeds of dog,

and through the poem wander the classic examples of the canine species.

In the present day, **Robert Sward** has brought to life (in "The Poet at Nine"), Uncle Dog, an animal who is so happy in being a dog that he has no desire at all to be a man.

English novelists have given a less important role in their works to this ever-present companion, although many of them have been true dog-lovers. **Walter Scott** had a marble mausoleum built at his house, Abbotsford, to the memory of Maida, a large Scottish Deerhound. It bore the inscription *Sit tibi terra levis* (May the earth lie lightly on you).

In the work of **Byron** there is hardly a mention of the dog. However, long after the

95

p. 96
Colette and her dog,
by Dunoyer de Segonzac.
(Collection of Monsieur and Madame Hamaide)

Colette in 1905, with Toby
the dog and Willy's hat.

death of Boatswain (the Newfoundland to whom he owed his life, as this was the dog that found him when, as a child he was lost and injured), the author of "Childe Harold" consecrated to this dog these disillusioned lines: "When all is finished for the proud son of man, one sees on his tomb what he should have become, and not what he did become, but the value of the dog is forgotten and the soul he had on earth is refused him in heaven."

And he added this epitaph, destined for the anonymous passersby, "Oh you who, by chance, see this simple urn, pass on! It honors no one you would weep for. These stones have been raised on the remains of a friend. I have only known one, and he lies here!"

Charles Dickens did not content himself with weeping, too late, over a lost friend. Throughout his books he helps us to understand dogs better. Everyone knows the lines of tender admiration which he wrote about Bouncer the Pomeranian, Don the Newfoundland, and Sultan, the hunting dog, in *My Father as I Recall Him.*

Rudyard Kipling used to say, smilingly, of his Cocker Spaniel, "He is my most sincere admirer; he loves me though he has never read my work!" Unfortunately no dogs appear in *The Jungle Book.* This book is, as everyone knows, peopled entirely by wild beasts. Perhaps it was to make up for this omission that at the end of his life. towards 1931, Kipling wrote *Thy Servant a Dog.*

Today, English literature seems to have found the right tone for its dog talk, the language of humor.

John Tickner, in *The Doggies Make the Law,* brings the most delicate observation to the task of teaching us about ourselves in chapters like "You Are Bought by a Dog," "You Are Trained by a Dog," etc.

G. W. Barrington, in his epic poem for the young, "Jan, the dog on board," tells the story of Jan, with his little erect ears

*Picasso
with his boxer "Jan"
and his goat "Esmeralda."*

Willy and his French bulldog.

and his glorious tuft, and at the same time recounts the worries of Black, the Cocker Spaniel who digs up bones as presents for his large wounded friend.

Thenceforth the list of works in English grows longer and longer; works "to instruct, move and make dream," which ought to be the aims of all animal writers the world over.

AMERICAN LITERATURE

From the bloodhounds that pursue Eliza across the ice in *Uncle Tom's Cabin* to the ubiquitous hounds, or 'coon dogs, of **William Faulkner's** Yoknapatawpha County novels, the dog permeates American literature, particularly the literature of the South and the frontier, as a felt presence. He is as much a part of the background of the stories and novels of **Bret Harte** and **Mark Twain** as to be almost taken for granted, and emerges perfectly naturally from the setting to advance the action or to help define character.

As the no-doubt mythical Hollywood producer put it: "If you want to establish the character of the villian, when he gets off the stagecoach, have him kick a dog." Thus **Mark Twain**, in *Huckleberry Finn*, describes the small Arkansas town in which those immortal rascals, the duke and the dauphin, are to present their Shakespearian extravaganza: "The hogs loafed and grunted around everywhere. You'd see a muddy sow and a litter of pigs come lazying along the street and whollop herself right down in the way, where folks had to walk around her, and she'd stretch out and shut her eyes and wave her ears whilst the pigs was milking her, and look as happy as if she was on salary. And pretty soon you'd hear a loafer sing out 'Hi! *so* boy! sick him, Tige!' and away the sow would go, squealing most horrible, with a dog or two swinging to each ear, and three or four dozen more a-

Illustration, by Pierre Gaudon,
for Maurice Genevoix's book Raboliot.
(Bibliothèque Nationale, Paris)

coming; and then you would see all the loafers get up and watch the thing out of sight, and laugh at the fun and look grateful for the noise. Then they'd settle back again till there was a dog-fight. There couldn't anything wake them up all over, and make them happy all over, like a dog-fight—unless it might be putting turpentine on a stray dog and setting fire to him, or tying a tin pan to his tail and see him run himself to death." Not a very nice town, but a perfect setting for the violence to follow.

That other genius of the west, **Bret Harte,** is at his most typical in the gently ironic and amusing story, "A Yellow Dog," in which Bones, the masterless habitant of the camp at Rattlers Ridge, the companion of drunkards and incompetents, the inept hunter and the bungler of chases, achieves a certain fame and envy among the men of the gold fields by being adopted by the prettiest girl in the county. Finally, after actually *cutting* his friends from Rattlers Ridge, Bones passes away "in the odor of sanctity and respectability." The good humor that permeates the tale restores in some small measure the dog-lover's faith in the *human* occupants of those small western towns who failed to win the admiration of Mark Twain.

As a distinct genre, the dog story has had a tremendous popular success in America. The literary merit of these stories, however, is not always of the highest, but there have been a number which can be considered genuine classics. The first and greatest is **Jack London's** *Call of the Wild.* This tale of the "dominant primordial beast" that is awakened in Buck, a powerful cross between a St. Bernard and a Scotch Shepherd bitch, who is kidnapped from his California home and sold for use as a sled dog in the Alaska gold rush of 1897, has moved generations of readers throughout the world since its publication in 1903. Told entirely from Buck's point of view, the chronicle of his

p. Gaudon

From Fables for our Time,
by James Thurber.
(Harper & Row, Publishers)

adventures as a sled dog, then as companion, friend, and savior of a young prospector, and, finally, as the leader of a wolf pack, has several emotional high points which never fail to stir the reader. Not the least of these is the book's ending: "When the long winter nights come on and the wolves follow their meat into the lower valleys, he may be seen running at the head of the pack through the pale moonlight or glimmering borealis, leaping gigantic above his fellows, his great throat a-bellow as he sings of the younger world, which is the song of the pack."

There is a rightness, a completeness, in the ending of Buck's story. The tale is told, and that's the end of it; but in a sense it never ends, for Buck's blood still flows in the veins of the wolves and the wild dogs of the far northland. The same is not strictly true of that other great dog story, *Lassie Come-Home,* by the Anglo-American writer **Eric Knight,** for this odyssey of the faithful dog which returns to its young master though separated from him by more than 1,000 miles of rough country, has been somewhat cheapened by its exploitation as the basis for several motion pictures and television programs. (Incidentally, the true meaning of the book's title is seldom understood. "Come-Home" is part of Lassie's name, since in Eric Knight's native Yorkshire, dogs are trained to return to their masters, and are called "come-home" dogs. Lassie lives up to her name beyond all expectations.)

Canine courage, loyalty, and intelligence shine through the stories of **Albert Payson Terhune,** which are based on true happenings at the author's famous home at Sunnybank, New Jersey. Seventeen of his books remain in print, and many of them, particularly *The Way of a Dog* and *Lad of Sunnybank,* are deservedly considered classics in their field.

Others who have more or less successfully pursued the genre, mostly in nostalgic evocations of boyhood, have been **Mackinlay Kantor, Robert Ruark,** and **Hal Borland.**

But the man whose career seems most bound up with dogs (mostly a succession of baleful hounds) actually *wrote* very little about them. "Probably no one man should have as many dogs in his life as I have had," says **James Thurber** in "The Dog That Bit People," from *My Life and Hard Times.* This short sketch has been called, with some justification, the funniest dog story ever written. It is the tale of Muggs, the Airedale who bit everybody, friend and foe alike. He was fed at table, because he would bite the hand that lowered his food to the floor. The bane of postmen, meter readers, and salesmen, the only way Muggs could be rendered harmless was by an electrical storm, which was the only thing he was afraid of. Mrs. Thurber rigged up a "thunder" machine out of a piece of sheet iron with a wooden handle, and whenever she wanted Muggs to come inside, she shook it vigorously. "It made an excellent imitation of thunder," says Thurber, "but I suppose it was the most roundabout system for running a household that was ever devised." And yet, for some inexplicable reason never questioned by the reader, the Thurber family not only tolerated but loved Muggs. When he finally died, they buried him beneath a simple wooden marker on which Thurber had written *Cave Canem.* "Mother was quite pleased with the simple dignity of the old Latin epitaph."

SPANISH AND PORTUGUESE LITERATURE

"Un perro es un perro!" says the Spaniard, rather scornfully. In fact "a dog is only a dog" to the majority of this Catholic, Latin nation, so profoundly marked by the Arab influence. Yet in some periods the dog has held a more important place in the hearts of Spaniards than one would expect. The same Spain which created the *galgo* (which is certainly not far removed from the greyhound) as well as the famous *perros de sangre* (the direct descendants of the "devouring mastiffs"), gave birth, in the 17th century, to some masters of the art of venery. There are some excellent technical books which date

Nineteenth century illustration for a novel by Walter Scott. (Bibliothèque Nationale, Paris)

from this time, such as *Orogins and Dignity of Hunting,* by **Juan Mateos;** then, in 1634, *The Hounds,* by **Espinar,** and *La Monteria,* by **Argote de Molina.** But these are very specialized works, and it is to **Cervantes** that we owe one of the best works on canine psychology in Spanish literature.

It was in fact in 1613, before the publication of the second part of *Don Quixote,* and before his famous novel *Rinconete y Cordatillo,* that Miguel Cervantes published a curious satire, *Dialogo de dos perros* (Dialogue Between Two Dogs), which is also known by the name *The Dogs of Mahudes.* This work was to be translated and edited, at a later date, in France. An excellent edition was brought out by the publishers "A l'Enseigne du Pot Cassé," illustrated with woodcuts and preceded by a foreword of fifty pages written by Prosper Merimée. Two dogs, Scipio and Berganza, spend a whole

night chatting at the hospital of the Resurrection in Valladolid. Scipio, the simpler of the two, is at first surprised to hear his friend talking in the language of men; but Berganza assures him that the miracle is well and truly accomplished and that he ought to hurry up and talk, so that he can say all he wants to say in case tomorrow the power which "has opened his mouth, shall shut his trap." It is a philosophical, humorous dialogue, in the course of which Berganza proves to Scipio, using a hundred examples, that crime does not pay, but that wisdom always does, in the face of the folly, blindness, or stupidity of human beings. He goes as far as offering his help to thinking bipeds. Are the financial affairs of the country in difficulties? He knows what a good economist would do. He would make all His Majesty's subjects, between the ages of fourteen and sixty, fast, putting them on a diet of bread and water for one day in every month. The sum saved

would balance the exchequer. Berganza owes his experience to the fact that he has had several masters, wise men and madmen, rich men and poor. He has even lived with actors, and he does not rate them very highly. "All that I could tell you about men, is as nothing compared to the men of the theatre, of their faults and vices, their qualities and talents, their ineptitude, their pride, their baseness." However, Berganza admits that he himself has been a performing dog, an acrobat, and, in fact, a player. Never had such a hail of abuse been so cruelly heaped upon the Spaniards!

Of course, there had been fables before this. The credit for having assembled all that Spanish and Portuguese fabulists have had to say about the dog must go to **José Vidal Munne.**

There has always been, in Catalonia, a marked interest in this genre of literature, whose cradle was really Greece and which

Illustration by H. Chapront
for "The Dialogue of Two Dogs," by Cervantes.
(Bibliothèque Nationale, Paris)

quickly traveled to Rome. In Spain the fable made its first appearance in 1480, though in a form very much expurgated by the tribunal of the Spanish Inquisition. But from year to year the ever-increasing favor of the public led various Spanish authors to write, in their turn, what they knew, or what they thought they knew, about the world of animals and men, borrowing the masks of animals.

What place had the dog in this fabulous bestiary?

In *"El perro y el gato"* (The Dog and the Cat) **Concepcion Arenal** described what separates these two domestic animals, which are so often thought to be enemies.

Crespo, in his *"El perro y el gato,"* seems to be scoffing in a dialogue in which the cat tries to persuade the dog that he is a slave and an idiot to perform his duties. In *"El mastin delincuente"* he takes up the idea behind one of Florian's fables: "The Guilty Dog." A dog finds the body of a lamb which has just been killed by a wolf, and is about to eat it. The tearful mother appears on the scene, and the dog, at its wits' end, can find no better way of calming her than to throw itself on her. Just them the shepherds arrive. They put an end to this misunderstood creature in the decisive yet unjust way one would imagine.

Govantes, in "The Dog and the Cat," demonstrates the stupidity of man and the no less stupid fidelity of the dog. A dog has just lost his master; overwhelmed by grief, it leaves its home and goes off to find adventure; but everyone it meets is frightened by the way it looks. They think it has rabies, and they kill it!

Riera y Bertran (Portuguese) sets the scene of a lion receiving animals in audience. Very proud of himself, the dog wants to boast about his qualities and virtues; but very few of the animals present congratulate him or are grateful to him for his recital.

Ibanez, more proudly—like La Fontaine in "The Crow and the Fox"—has as his characters "The Dog and the Crocodile." The dog drinks from the Nile, running along the banks of the river almost without stopping. "Drink in peace," says the crocodile. "You have all the time in the world!" But the dog is no crow, he pays no attention to the crocodile's words and goes on his way.

Samaniego, in "The Master and His Dog," shows that virtue has its weaknesses. Who in fact would expect a poor starving dog to remain indifferent to his master's meal for three long days? And the dog, of course, succumbs to temptation.

Principe, finally, in "The Dog and the cat," imagines that the dog and the cat want to change places. Jupiter accepts the swap, but in spite of his miaowing, the dog never manages to eat a rat; as for the cat, his barks put all the mice to flight. Both die of starvation.

But could there be a better way of concluding these few pages on the dog literature of Spain than by recalling that great lover of animals whom our era has christened the brilliant Rector of Salamanca?

In *Niebla,* one of his best novels, **Miguel de Unamuno** puts the following bitter soliloquy into the mouth of Orfeo (the dog of the hero of the tale). *"Qué extraño animal es el hombre! Nunca esta en lo que tiene delante. Nos acaricia sin que sepamos por qué, y no cuando le acariciamos más, y cuando más a él nos rendimos, nos rechaza o nos castiga!* (What a strange animal is man! He pays no attention to what he does. He loves us we know not why, and when we are most fond of him, and when we are most attached to him he repulses us or beats us!) In *"El idiota y su perro"* (The Fool and His Dog), Unamuno also introduces us to a dog who knows nothing of the stupidity of his weak-minded master, whom he always regards as a superior brother. Throughout his writings Unamuno, who was to die a bitter and misanthropic man, shows just as clearly his tenderness for the animal world, and it is perhaps in *"Elegia en la muerte de un perro"* that his genius expresses most movingly the secret of this affection "outside men":

I have been your religion, I have been
   your glory . . .
For you my eyes have been a window into
   another world.
If only, my dog, you could know
how sad your god is at your death. . . .
The gods weep at the death of the dog,
The dog that licked their hands
And looked deep into their eyes.
The dog, that when he looked at them thus,
   asked:
Where are we going?

8 THE DOG IN ART

Whatever the artist's intentions, whether they be magical, religious, or purely aesthetic, art always has an informative value, in that through it we can learn about the life and culture of certain societies.

Thus, the paintings and sculpture of past centuries in which dogs are depicted, allow us simultaneously to follow the evolution of the different breeds, and to discover the place that the dog hed in man's life and heart.

We have already said that prehistoric man did not depict the dog side by side with bison, horses, and reindeer in the paintings on the walls of caves, as doubtless wild dogs neither constituted a frightening enemy nor a fully appreciated form of game. Over the centuries there have been the naive and clumsy graphics of Hultane, the more precise representations of Alpera, and above all the pure drawings of the Tassili; later came the evocative paintings and sculptures of the Sumerians, the Egyptians, the Assyrians, the Etruscans, and of the Bronze Age peoples.

FROM ANCIENT TIMES TO THE MIDDLE AGES

In the classical art of Greece and Rome, however, the dog figures very large. Greek and Cretan vases reproduce hunting and family scenes, and even illustrate legends. Many of the records reveal to us the existence of small and large greyhounds, guard dogs and watch dogs, and even lap dogs, as much cherished in Rome as they were in Gaul, where we find them depicted at the foot of the first recumbent figures.

There were numerous bas-reliefs in stone or bronze in which the artist brought to life powerful dogs, full of action, often called the "Segurians" or swift "vertragi."

In a "Young Satyr at Rest" (Louvre) the dog is so true to life that one can almost see it leaping at the game which its master is presenting to it.

The paintings and mosaics of the rich houses in Pompeii are of exquisite sensitivity. Here the dog takes on the new aspect of a happy, cherished animal in spite of the classical, aggressive *"Cave Canem"* (Museum of Naples).[1] In the frescoes of Herculaneum (Louvre) a decorative scene in bright red colors represents an amusing scene of two dogs harnessed together, pulling the small carriage of a musician.

Byzantine art did not forget to portray the dog as the companion of hunt and hearth, and most often depicts greyhounds around the bowls of Sassanid cups.

Pre-Columbian art did not depict the greyhound, but the animal (legendary and actual) was soon adopted in Central America, as much from a symbolical point of view as from an aesthetic point of view. The dog, symbol of fire from heaven, was to open—like Anubis—the way to the next world for its masters. More prosaically valued for culinary ends, they were depicted as tailless dogs of small stature on clay or hard stone, black and polished, to accentuate the smoothness of their skin.

ARTISTS WHO PORTRAYED THE DOG FROM THE MIDDLE AGES TO THE RENAISSANCE

In Europe, from the beginning of the Middle Ages the dog was generally allowed to be present in noble society. Its services were highly appreciated, and the more it was loved the more artists began to regard it as an interesting subject.

For a long time, however, the primitive artists did not seem to want to get to know —and even less to convey—the intelligence of the animal. To paint this animal with an

[1]Although the majority of cynologists have assumed that *Cave Canem* means simply to beware of a guard dog there is an advanced school of thought that reasons the sign's meaning was protection of the countless tiny toy dogs which often slept where they might be stepped upon. After all, Pompeii was a summer resort for the richest class in Rome and the ladies valued their lap dogs highly.

The sons of Moses
(detail) by Botticelli.
(Sistine Chapel, Rome)

The militant and triumphant church (detail). School of Giotto. (Santa Maria Novella, Florence)

Treatise on Hunting by Gaston Phébus. (Bibliothèque Nationale, Paris)

The militant and triumphant church. School of Giotto. (Santa Maria Novella, Florence)

BIBLIOTHÈQUE NATIONALE

and "natural hunting dogs," which, for several centuries, were to unite swiftness with strength and to fill all the needs of hunting.

In the same series, at the side of *"Deux lévriers pour lièvres"* (Two Greyhounds for Hares), another greyhound, much larger and more powerful, is crouching (at the bottom right) attentive and anxious. A hound is scratching its ear. Another seems to be howling into the wind, and Pierre Cuc very justly notices that the dogs' flanks are jutting out; they occupy the abdominal region as far as the umbilicus, which is indisputably pure fantasy! The breeds depicted do not seem in the least to correspond to the same type as the famous *"chiens blancs du Roi"* which today have disappeared.

The black bloodhound of the *"Départ en forêt"* evokes the black St. Hubert hounds. This is a very beautiful composition where the range of yellows enhances the green livery of the servant, who is holding an enthusiastic dog by its leash.

In *"Le Repas en forêt,"* several tawny colored dogs encircle a few of these black St. Hubert Hounds near a *"chien blanc du roi."* The vivid red color which dominates the iridescent sheen of the clothes and flowers gives this work the brilliancy of a stained-glass window. Were the *"chiens blancs du roi"* then still rare? This is very probable, because nearly always only one of these great, royal dogs is present in the midst of the pack of other animals, who have black or fawn colored coats.

The *"Recueil"* of Gaignières, a marvellous miniature, depicts a lady gravely watching the hounds devouring parts of the stag, her Maltese dog curled up in her arms. This is the recognition of the lap dog at the be-

expression, which could convey that it was capable of feeling, was thus carefully avoided for a long time in sacred and religious paintings. The dog was generally represented curled up, sitting with its back to its audience or dozing; and in the most daring paintings, with an aggressive or stupid expression.

Eventually, the dog gradually became the precious auxiliary of princely huntsmen and the companion of noble ladies, and artists ceased making it the symbol of indifference and fear and began to depict it in a more favorable and truer light.

Jean Fouquet (1415-1480) and then Pierre de Limbourg illustrated numerous hunting scenes in the famous *Book of Hours* of both Etienne Chevalier and the Duke de Berry. Forty miniatures of this genre are preserved in the Museum of Chantilly. In this same Musée de Condé, under the title of *"Les chiens,"* we can see two mastiffs with docked ears: the one is white with a halter and red collar; the other, without a halter, is brown and wears a similar collar. Out of the union of these massive dogs with swift greyhounds, were to come the "boar-hounds"

GIRAUDON — ANDERSON

Paolo Veronese
in hunting dress, by Maser.
(Villa Giacomeli, Treviso)

Charles V, by Titian.
(Prado)

ginning of the 15th century.

The dog also begins to figure in the portraits of the nobility. Often, in a curious way, whether intentional or not, the artist has given the animal a pose and an expression so obvious, that a sort of parallel can be detected between master and dog. If the prince was a bully, as Charles le Mauvais, king of Navarre (1332-1387) was, his dog is shown gnawing a bone. If the prince was a worthy sovereign, as Philippe Le Bon, duke of Burgundy (1396-1467) was, the dog was shown lying calmly and obediently at his feet. The dogs most often depicted are white, slender greyhounds, or even mastiffs; but dogs of medium height soon appeared, which were, to start with, "bird dogs" and soon became house dogs.

THE FRENCH SCHOOL

In *"Le Christ en Croix du Parlement de Paris"* (1460)—which has been attributed to numerous famous painters, but which must finally remain anonymous—we can see at the feet of Charlemagne a small dog, seated quietly, with erect ears and a round head. We are unable to define the role this vague product of chance passion played, or whether the artist felt the need merely to fill an empty corner of the canvas.

The "Portrait of Marguerite de Valois" (Chantilly Museum) and the "Portrait of the Son of Francis I" by François Clouet (1510-1572) were the first appearances of a type of dwarf spaniel (today known as the Papillon) which is later found throughout the Renaissance and up to the 18th century, and becomes the most often depicted companion dog.

In *"Le Bal à la Cour de Henri II,"* the same little spaniels, much reduced, are frisking about and playing right there on the carpet, unconscious of the dancers around them. In *"Le Bal donné à la Cour de Henri III"* (on the occasion of the marriage of the Duke of Joyeuse, 1582), again this type of

small, white dog, with silky hair, figures in the foreground (Fontainebleau School).

The same spaniels, one of which is white with yellow markings, enliven *"La Naissance de Saint Jean";* they are engaged in a playful set-to, and in the center of the canvas, the angels are caressing fondly a white Maltese dog.

THE ITALIAN SCHOOL

Dogs occupy the foreground of a large fresco in Florence attributed to Giotto (1266-1336). Black and white dogs, with erect ears and of a small greyhound type, are pursuing wolves which are about to devour some sheep. It is a symbolic painting, in which the preaching friars have refuted and confounded the heretics' arguments and the Jewish and Arab philosophers can be seen tearing up their books.

In Rome, in 1303, Pope Benoit XI valued his good relations with France, and a fresco (in the Church of Santa Maria Nova) depicts him between Edward I of England and Philippe le Bel. In the foreground, in front of the three important personages, two dogs, one black, one white, are playing, one of which is definitely of the Italian greyhound type.

In 1348, Clement VI was in Avignon. At the time he was protecting the poet Petrarch. An illuminated manuscript of this time shows the poet writing in his library, with his companion, a sort of Pug, which is probably the result of a cross-breeding.

About 1350, the fresco of the "Triumph of Death," attributed to Orcagna (the Church of Campo-Santo, Pisa) depicts a quite different type of dwarf spaniel, with wide ears falling close to the cheeks, a short muzzle, a high, curved skull, and a drooping tail.

In the Sistine Chapel, Botticelli (1447-1510) painted the wonderful fresco "Moses and the sons of Jethro," in which a smooth-haired dog with round head, bulging eyes, and enormously long nails can be seen. A

BULLOZ

*The pilgrims of Emmaus
(detail), by Veronese.
(Louvre)*

*Christ washing the Apostles' feet,
by Tintoretto.
(Prado)*

young man is holding this dog, which is without reasonable doubt a crossbred, under his arm.

Jacopo da Ponte, called Bassano (1510-1592), in the "Wedding at Cana" conveys in a rural, good-natured mood the visit of Christ to a country landowner. The bill of fare is simple, copious, and without ostentation. The naive intimacy of the scene is underlined in the foreground by a hunting dog of the "bird dog" kind, which is comfortably seated in the midst of the plates and dishes and the musical instruments, in order to take a greater part in the festivities taking place around him.

Titian (1477-1576) painted a very stately picture of Charles V, holding a sort of fly-swatter in his right hand and affectionately running two fingers of his left hand through the collar of an enormous dog, which is leaning its head on its master's doublet. This canvas, full of grandeur and majesty, is in the Prado Museum in Madrid. The dog bears

a resemblance to the boar hounds and large hunting dogs of the past, in its powerful muscles and in its Braque-like height and skull. In the "Portrait of Alphonse I d'Este" (Prado) the artist depicted a delicate tousled, matted, dull-colored dog, like a miniature Barbet, with hair falling on to its skull (which is very rare). Some dog experts see in this the beginnings of the Papillon, others the ancestor of the Teneriffe or the little Maltese.

Paolo Caliari, called Veronese (1528-1588), painted the Spaniel-Papillon more than any other dog. It was very popular at this time. It can be seen in "The Queen of Sheba" (Museum of Turin), "The Lady at the Balustrade" (Museum of Treviso), and also in "The Family" (Museum of Dresden). In "The Wedding at Cana," however, a very beautiful, short-haired hunting dog, with a chestnut-colored head, and markings on its body, looks forward to the most modern French Braques.

THE GERMAN SCHOOL

"The legend of St. Ursula" by the Master of Saint-Severin (1480-1510) shows a very beautiful, two-colored greyhound, wearing a wide collar, enriched with an engraved coat of arms (Museum of Cluny).

We should also mention Albrecht Dürer's (1471-1528) celebrated work of "Saint Hubert" showing him at the head of his horse, with his five dogs assembled around him, and his wonderful engraving of the "Knight, Death and the Devil" in which a spaniel is running between the horse's feet.

THE FLEMISH SCHOOL

In "David and Bathsheba" by Jean Matzys or Massys (1500-1570), Bathsheba in transparent veils is all charm and gentleness, but remains on her guard. She seems to be symbolized by the small lap dog which, with

The bridal procession (1623)
(detail), by Brueghel the younger.
(Private collection)

Henry the Pious and his spaniel,
by Lucas Cranach.
(Museum of Dresden)

Catherine of Mecklenburg,
wife of Henry the Pious, and her little Lion dog,
by Cranach.
(Museum of Dresden)

less reserve, is holding its own against the white greyhound companion of David. Here also, this little dog, which seems keen to defend its rights, is the beginning in Flanders of the fashion for the Spaniel-Papillon that the French School established at the same time.

Besides the tiny black dog of the "Calvary" by Breughel we must mention his picture of "The Massacre of the Innocents" (Museum of Vienna), in which a dog is attacking a woman, while a man is striving to check the ardor of a mastiff held on a leash.

Rubens (1577-1640) painted a dog in the wonderful "Raising of the Cross" (Cathedral of Antwerp). The masterpiece was completed after the priest of Sainte Walburge, while visiting Rubens in his studio, had admired the artist's dog. "A dog like that ought not to die," he said. "How can that be prevented?" asked Rubens. "By painting it into your picture!" And Rubens, soon convinced, painted his spaniel in the corner of his composition.

Van Dyck (1599-1641), his pupil, has left us in "The Family of Charles I of England" (Windsor Castle) an impressive record of a relatively enormous dog in comparison to the size of the infant princes around it. In another work in which the same sons of Charles I are also depicted, the artist has framed the young princes with a couple of medium-sized spaniels on the right and left of the canvas.

THE DUTCH SCHOOL

Hieronymus Bosch (1450-1516) in "The Conjuror" (Museum of Saint-Germain-en-Laye) has hidden behind the conjuror's table a tiny, mongrel dog, curiously wearing on its head a fool's cap. Carrying a wide belt, ornamented with bells, and its tail in a small tuft, this tiny, discreet animal seems to be playing the role of the conjuror's confederate. This is one of the first pictorial

The dog's sense of smell is apparent in this picture by Chardin, called "The Sideboard."
(Louvre)

ARCHIVES PHOTOGRAPHIQUES

examples of the performing dog. Also by Hieronymus Bosch are the naive diabolical dogs in "The Adoration of the Shepherds" and "The Temptation of St. Antony."

Antonio Moro, called Sir Anthonis Mor (1512-1576), who was the protegé of Cardinal Granvella, painted "The Dwarf" flanked by his large mastiff, which bears the arms of its master (Louvre). Mor thus inaugurated the string of dwarfs escorted by mastiffs that Velásquez took to with even more enthusiasm.

THE 17TH AND 18TH CENTURIES

On the whole, it was the dwarf spaniel which triumphed in the course of the 17th century. However, it had a slightly different appearance and was developing progressively towards the Maltese, which thenceforth we find in most paintings. Another dog also held the attention of some artists. This was the farm dog, the peasant's companion, the future sheep dog.

The three brothers Le Nain painted this newcomer in "The Return of the Hay Harvest" (Louvre) and in various country scenes full of simple good-heartedness and tranquility. It was more often than not a medium-sized dog, solid, good-natured and docile, well suited to farmworkers, those unaffected peasants whom the brothers Le Nain loved so well. In "The Meal of the Peasants" (Louvre), however, there is a small, yapping dog, which was useless to these humble men. For them it was purely a self-indulgence.

Charles Lebrun (1619-1690) exercised a tremendous influence on contemporary artists. With Fouquet and later Colbert as protectors, he was able to feel easy when he brought the dog closer to man in his attempts at analysing its physiognomy, but this aspect of his work was mysteriously underrated. Of all his paintings, in which hunting dogs appear more often than others, we have retained the set of six pictures of "Meleager and Atlanta Hunting the Wild Boar," in

Smooth-haired Maltese dog.
(Bibliothèque Nationale, Paris)

Fragonard: "The Love Letter."
The Teneriffe foreshadows the miniature Poodle.

Watteau: "Fête Galante"
(detail from the "Embarkation for the Island of Cythera").
The dwarf spaniel depicted here already looks forward to the Papillon. (Louvre).

Greuze: Portrait of the Marquise de Chauvelin with her black and tan dwarf spaniel. (Private collection)

which two breeds of dogs are at work— hounds of a size and strength unknown to us today, and mastiffs with short ears and impressive jaws, set loose on the boar. In "The Death of Meleager," three Greyhounds (two of which are fawn and brindle and until then were quite rare) are watching a large black and white mastiff, which is reminiscent of our Great Dane of today.

Pierre Mignard (1612-1695), whose style was pleasing but mannered, in "Portrait of the Great Dauphin and his Family" (Louvre) depicted a beautiful type of spaniel which has scarcely changed. This type of Breton Spaniel (Brittany Spaniel), which reached fixed type at the end of the 19th century, is curled up in the arms of the son of Louis XIV, while the small Duke of Anjou (later to become Philippe V of Spain) clasps a black Griffon lovingly in his arms.

Largillière (1656-1746) in the picture of

"Louis XIV with His Family" (Wallace Collection, London), does not shun painting the Papillon-Spaniel, which obsessed him, and which was still then evolving and was to become the *"chien-de-Cayenne."*

Watteau (1684-1721) in "The Embarkation for the Island of Cythera" (Louvre, Paris and Museum of Berlin) placed near La Desmares, his triumphant love, a Papillon-Spaniel which we shall come across again in "The Meeting in the Park"; but it was a Greyhound, an odd sort of Borzoi, that he made lie on the ground while its mistress chose some engravings in the *"Enseigne de Gersaint."*

Boucher (1703-1770) could only conjure up the *"grands chiens blancs du roi"* to be present in "Diana rising from her bath" (Louvre) and showing a light leg to her companion. The two dogs however are much smaller than those in the royal packs.

Chardin (1699-1779) who was much closer to everyday life, in the portrait of "The Busy Mother" (his wife) painted a Pug curled up at the feet of its mistress, who is tidying her linen. Yet the traditional Papillon-Spaniel is absent from his canvases.

Greuze (1725-1805) also used his wife as a model. In "The Portrait of Madame Greuze" (Louvre) she is stroking absent-mindedly with her finger a black and tan spaniel, which he painted with such realism that Diderot remarked: "If you stare at it for a few minutes you will hear it bark." In "The Two Sisters" he depicted a small, white, smooth-haired dog, which seems like a Foxhound in miniature.

Fragonard (1732-1806) remained faithful to his Papillon-Spaniels, which were to him irreplaceable. He slipped them into nearly all his works: "The Love Letter,"

*In this "Wolf-hunt"
by Oudry, the Greyhound
protected by its studded collar
joins in the fray. (Louvre)*

*In "The Music Lesson" by Terborch, in which
the lady is learning the first chords of the
theorbo, the dog has been slipped into the
picture. (National Gallery, London)*

"The Gimblette" (cake), "The Lover Crowned," "The Levee" (rising), "The Lady with a Dog," etc.

All the masters which we have just named accorded a place to the dog in their work. There are, however, two great painters of this first half of the 18th century who were strictly speaking animal painters and who put the dog in the center of their compositions. They are Desportes and Oudry.

A. F. Desportes (1661-1743) became a painter of animals after he had been portrait painter at the court of Poland. Immediately this became his success and glory. A member of the Royal Academy of Painting, and "Painter to the King," he painted a self-portrait on the occasion of this nomination, with a very beautiful Braque lying in his arms and a Greyhound standing at his side. Four of his great hunting pictures are famous: a "Stag at Bay" beset by seven or eight dogs, a "Boar Seized by the Ears by Two Greyhounds" surrounded by mastiffs, a "Return from the Hunt," in which some hounds are licking the blood of a kid, and a "Wolf Being Attacked" by six dogs, several of which have been cruelly bitten. On the subject of Desportes' work, the *Encyclopédie de Diderot et d'Alembert* states that the Greyhounds represented are of three kinds: large, medium, and small. Some have coats which are thick and either grey spotted with black, or bright red, and they serve to seize the ears of the wolf or the boar. "The Greyhounds that run at the stirrup threw themselves at the claws of the wild beast, the flanking Greyhounds attacked at the sides. As to the Greyhounds at the front, which were much faster, their mission was to bar the flight of the game." According to Diderot, the medium-sized Greyhounds, which were used for hunting hares, were replaced by Charnigues from Provence or by Ibizan hounds from Spain, which leaped on their prey silently.

Desportes' pictures confirm the two apparent lines in the evolution of the dog: the dogs of relatively short lineage which bore a resemblance to the Dogue of Bordeaux and already heralded the Boxer; and the others which in themselves were bigger and of longer lineage, and which already had the general appearance of the Great Dane. It was some time after this date, about 1758, that hunting with Setters was forbidden to all except nobles in France. Thirty years later, of the two varieties of Braque—the one light and swift in tracking, and the other heavier and closer to the spaniel type of Braque—only the latter had survived. The light Braque had disappeared. It should be pointed out that in the case of these very beautiful dogs, which are often quite difficult to distinguish from our Pointers of today, Desportes portrayed them faithfully, just as they looked at the time: with a small tuft of hair on the ends of their tails.

Desportes, nevertheless, could not escape the fashion of the day. In addition to his portraits of the favorite dogs of Louis XIV, "Bonne," "Nonne," and "Ponne," he left a remarkable study of ten drawings of the Papillon-Spaniel, which was to become the definite darling of the drawing-room.

Jean-Baptiste Oudry (1686-1755) was twenty-five years younger than Desportes. It seems that in spite of his success, the latter was secretly jealous of his young rival: "I certainly like Oudry's paintings," he said, "on condition that they are painted entirely by him. . . ." Be that as it may, Oudry entered Largillière's studio early, and he also was soon honored. Commissioned by the king to execute portraits of his favorite dogs, he had to produce annually six big pictures to serve as models for the owners of the tapestry factory of Beauvais. From his innumerable drawings, Jean Locquin drew up a catalog from which we can pick out: "fighting dogs, Bulldogs, Great Danes, grey, yellow and white Barbets, Poodles, hounds, the king's favorite Greyhounds, Spaniels, Braques, Pointers, Griffons, Bassets, Pugs and even King Charles Spaniels. . . ." The collection constitutes a dog study which has never been equalled.

THE ITALIAN SCHOOL

Here we should above all mention "The Last Supper" by Tiepolo (1696-1770). In the middle of the picture and right in the foreground, a medium-sized dog, a type of hound, with black coat and white head, is munching scraps and bones from the table. The beautifully observed stance of the dog is quite remarkable—leaning on its two front legs, its neck stretched out and its head turned to the side, to enable it to chew better with its jaws.

THE DUTCH SCHOOL

"The great strength of the Dutch Masters," said Eugène Fromentin, "lies in their capacity

In the
"Portrait of Prince Baldassare Carlo"
by Velásquez, the black and white mastiff
already resembles the St. Bernard.
(Prado)

NATIONAL GALLERY

to paint an exact portrait of their surroundings." Whence came some excellent animal portraits. However, unlike many other painters of Europe, the Dutch did not specialize. In anything that concerned the dog they knew quite simply how to look and seize the moment ". . . whether the animal was an awake and interested partner or whether it was a philosophic and submissive companion." And one can think of the modest dog of the Steen family and many others from which we must regrettably choose only a few.

Hendrick Goltzius (1558-1616) is more famous as an engraver than as a painter. "Goltzius' Dog" is a pet spaniel. It can be found in numerous studies by the Master, sometimes executed in colored crayons, and

it figures in the famous engraved portrait of his friend the painter de Vries. The same dog and the same head studies (Museum of Amsterdam and Harlem) figured in the Exhibition of Dutch Bestiary in Paris in 1960.

Rembrandt (1606-1669) has few works in which animals are represented, which is all the more reason to draw attention to a very beautiful etching (Museum Albertina of Vienna) depicting a sleeping dog; also the "Sleeping Dog" (1675), the "Hunting Dog Pointing at the Game" (École des Beaux-Arts, Paris) and the "Head of a Dog Turning to the Left" consisting of three excellent stone-engravings in black and watercolor (or India ink) that we can recognize to this day.

Terborch (1617-1681) left us the "Young Woman Playing the Theorbo" (Lute) in the presence of two men, while a black and white pet spaniel, attracted by the noise, comes in to see what is happening. But his greatest masterpiece without doubt is his "Young Boy with a Dog": a child on his knees is conscientiously cleaning his favorite dog of fleas, while the animal, half-anxious and half-resigned? closes its eyes.

It is often regretted that Paulus Potter (1625-1654), whose drawings of donkeys, goats, horses, cows, etc. are so numerous, showed no real interest in the canine race. An excellent "Seated Dog" turned to the left, is the subject of a stone-engraving in black that can be seen at the Museum of Albertina in Vienna.

Some sketches in red chalk and some black stone-engravings by Jean Le Ducq (1630-1676), such as the "Greyhound Lying Down," and by Visscher (1629-1662), such as the "Seated Small Dog" are also worthy of note.

F. Van Mieris (1635-1681) has left us numerous studies of Maltese dogs. One of these is depicted half asleep on the knees of his mistress, whose hand has been lightly sketched at the top right-hand corner of the work.

GIRAUDON — ANDERSON

Claude Monet: ▶
"Man with a Parasol."
(Kunsthaus, Zurich).

(ARCH. R. LAFFONT.)

This russet and white spaniel
with Miss Lowndes, by Gainsborough,
could be the ancestor of the
Breton (Brittany) Spaniel.
(Museum of Lisbon)

*Self-portrait by Hogarth,
with his dog. (Tate Gallery)*

TATE GALLERY

GIRAUDON

Gabriel Metsu (1629-1667), who was inspired by the intimate compositions of Terborch, painted a Dutch interior in which a woman is puzzling out a Solfeggio score in the presence of her seemingly indifferent pet spaniel.

THE SPANISH SCHOOL

Velásquez (1599-1660), "one of the greatest colorists of all time," allows us to distinguish between fighting mastiffs, in which we can still see the musculature of the Greyhound, and the large heavy bull-fighting dogs, which Van Dyck was painting at the same time. Both in the "Portrait of Philippe IV of Spain," painted between 1650 and 1660, in which the king is dressed in a doublet of black silk, with moustache and blond hair streaked with silver; and in the portrait of "Ferdinand of Austria" (Prado),

the same type of mastiff with docked ears figures. This same dog, whose external ears were cut as close as possible to the head to leave the minimum for the adversary to grab hold of, we shall find—but perhaps a little coarser—in the brindled mastiff in "Les Meninas" (The Dwarfs of Honor) (Prado); The Infantas could not wish for a fiercer and at the same time safer guardian. In the "Portrait of the Young Prince Baldassare Carlo" (Prado) the huge mastiff lying down resembles more the type of mountain dog which became the St. Bernard.

THE ENGLISH SCHOOL

William Hogarth (1697-1764) who, it is said, invented the moral caricature, painted himself in a daring self-portrait, which seems to invite the observer to make a delicate comparison between his rosy features and large eyes and the no less eloquent head of the Bullmastiff, his companion, which is badly squared. In his "Marriage a la Mode" (National Gallery, London) he depicted a pet dog which seems to be one of the first Pekingese in European painting.

Sir Joshua Reynolds (1723-1792) in his marvelous painting of "Nelly O'Brien" has shown the pretty girl holding a Maltese dog on her knees.

Thomas Gainsborough (1727-1788) gives us a newcomer: the large, white Pom of "Mrs. Robinson" (Wallace Collection, London). The Spitz type of dog had been rare until then. In the "Portrait of Mrs. Lowndes" (Museum of Lisbon) there is next to the young, pretty woman a grown-up Spaniel that is running into the picture. In "Robert Andrews and His wife" (Louvre) a dog, which looks like a cross between a small Braque and a Beagle (with a chestnut coat and white front), raises an admiring glance at the huntsman and his gun.

Sir William Beechey (1753-1839) already belonged to the following century. His painting of "Brother and Sister," which depicts

BULLOZ

two children escorted by a Cocker Spaniel (a breed still not definitely fixed), is very characteristic of the English style.

MODERN PAINTERS OF THE DOG

With the 19th century, at the same time that writers and poets were discovering and were making their readers discover an imaginary, animal psychology, we see the birth and flowering of Romanticism, which continued to the beginning of the 20th century.

Some artists were content to illustrate anecdotal scenes in which the dog had its role. There were more moving scenes, of course, scenes of such sensitivity that they were capable of making one weep or smile: the poodle which followed the poor man's hearse, the Newfoundland which saved a child from drowning, the performing Foxhound dressed up as a clown, the soldier's dog which defended the flag, etc.

FRENCH PAINTERS: Descamps (1803-1860) who lived in Fontainebleau and Paris, knew not only pack-hounds and poacher's dogs but also the fat town dogs. His "Hunting Dog" which waits stoically, with a resigned air, offering its hindquarters to the stable boy for punishment, is the result of perfect, psychological observation. Descamps also excelled at St. Bernards, which by then had become fashionable, and which in his drawings served as mounts for monkeys.

Other artists specialized in "anatomo-zoological" knowledge, painstakingly catching an expression, or certain attitude characteristic of a species (whether wild animals or domestic animals).

Dogs were among the best natural models, for hunting had ceased to be a privilege and had become democratized. Under the influence of the zoological works of Geoffrey Saint-Hilaire, they were given stricter details as to the "notion of breeds." Breeding which had been essentially empirical until then, and had been based on the vague probabilities of practical experience in conjunction

Decamps: Hunting Basset hounds. (Louvre)

In the "Arrival of the Coach" by Boilly, two hunting dogs indulge in fighting which terrifies the Pug. (Louvre)

GIRAUDON

*American primitive painting:
Two children with their pets.*

*Bonnard: Mademoiselle Bonnard
and her dogs. (Private collection)*

MUSÉES NATIONAUX

with the dogs' general conformation and the qualities of their sires, was to become a scientific study.

Boilly (1761-1845), heir to the 18th century, placed all kinds of street dogs on the pavements, in inn courtyards, or near the wheels of stagecoaches.

Isabey (1767-1855) was more interested in lap dogs and pretty girls, both of which he loved.

Horace Vernet (1789-1863) illustrated soldiers' dogs as in "The Regimental Dog," executed for the Duke de Berry. One of his pictures represents a wounded Barbet, being kindly helped by two soldiers, his brothers in arms; another conveys with emotion the dog's affection—it is seen licking the blood from the wounds of a cavalry officer about to die.

Courbet (1819-1877) had numerous hunting and pet dogs; he painted them in all different aspects, while Manet (1832-1883), who was interested in the Teneriffe (a lap dog resembling the Toy Poodle but slightly larger), left only too few portraits.

Toulouse-Lautrec's favorites (1864-1901) were the little Foxhound strays of Paris, street dogs escorting an errand-girl, dogs in the wings in the Music Hall, and dogs running at the wheels of barouches in the Bois de Boulogne.

The busy sheep dog, the anonymous Griffon, or the stocky Briard often served as models for Millet (1814-1875) who had been an artist of the peasants of old. Charles Jacque, also of the Barbizon School, gave perfect life to the same sheep dogs, which watched their flocks from a hillock above, or who busted themselves with stragglers.

Luc-Olivier Merson (1846-1920) in his "St. Francis of Assissi" preaching to the fish at the edge of a lake, placed beside the Saint a sheep dog which shared in the astonishment of the spectators of this scene. It seemed, by its similar attitude, to join the mysterious world of animals to the intelligible world of humans.

Ingres (1780-1867), a classical painter, yet also influenced by the Romanticism that he fought against, hardly looked at animals. We do not know of any study of dogs by him.

There remains a great draughtsman of dogs, who faithfully painted the last of the real hounds. He was Oliver de Penne, whose studies of the heads of porcelain dogs and whose silhouettes of large Bloodhounds and their attitudes while at rest can be considered the last records of a venery which was dying.

The Impressionist School, in effect, seems to have entirely forgotten the "subjects" of the 18th century, and reacted against the over-emotional representations of the genuine love of animals which no one was ashamed to display.

Renoir (1841-1919), Bonnard (1867-1947), and Marquet (1875-1947) were perhaps the only ones to have made the effort to observe the lives of pet dogs and to love them. We still have Bonnard's portrait of his daughter with her two dogs. Marquet found in watching his dogs "a truth that men disguise through self-interest, through distrust, through complacency"—"He did not have dogs to train or to command," wrote his companion "but to observe and to get to know better. He approached his model with caution, he did not speak to it, he moved it as little as possible, as if he feared that the least noise, the least movement might be sufficient to upset the momentary balance. . . ." We must agree that this method worked well for the artist for everything from port wines to green water. The exhibition that the Gallery Francis I dedicated to Marquet the animal painter is brilliant proof of it.

Raoul Dufy (1877-1953), Vertes, Dignimont, Touchagues, and Christian Berard introduced the dog into their works, but mostly as an accessory and usually to emphasize the sporting character on the one hand or the particularly feminine character of their models on the other. The true specialists: Tavernier, Dachin, Reboussin, Merite, Jourcin, Schnurr, etc., attached more importance to reproducing accurately the

Toulouse-Lautrec:
"The Departure for the Country."
(Private collection)

Joseph Stevens: "The Dog in the Mirror."
(Museum of Brussels)

In this drawing of a Basset on a lead,
Giacomo has perfectly conveyed
the illusion of movement.
(Private collection)

actual animal and its beauty. They stood on the fringe of dog caricaturists and behavior painters.

In short, despite the place it was beginning to have in men's hearts and minds, the dog hardly ever tempted the French artists of the 20th century to depict it, and abstract art made even its sincerest friends eschew it. Only Picasso, who has loved roughly twenty dogs in his life, was able to make it fashionable in his painting; and Picasso to our knowledge has been the only painter who has tried to give painting animals in the abstract a chance.

Modern ENGLISH ARTISTS have fortunately remained faithful to the traditional attachment of the British for all household animals.

R. Parkes Bonington (1802-1828) in his "Portrait of Francis I and the Duchess d'Etampes" set on the opposite side to the Duchess, who is sitting well back in her chair and dressed in a gown of yellow silk with wide bouffant sleeves, an elegantly and finely shaped, small Greyhound, which would now be called a Whippet.

Sir John Everett Millais (1829-1896) painted marvelous Collies, such as the famous "Lassie" which much later became familiar to all Europe. In a famous picture, "The Order of Release," he depicted a very beautiful black and white spaniel which is joyfully taking part in the emotion of a young Scotswoman, whose husband, condemned to death for taking part in the Rebellion, has been released. This association of a household pet in the joys and sorrows of the family was very soon to be exploited.

J. M. W. Turner, who is closer to the artists of the preceding century, brought to life mastiffs and mongrels in "Crossing the Brook" and a group of hunting dogs in "Venus and Adonis" (National Gallery, London).

We should also mention C. W. Furze's "Diana of the Uplands" and F. R. Lee's "The Cover Side" (Vernon Gallery), which depicts spaniels no longer with the resigned

appearance of so many little spaniels of past centuries. H. Wyatt's "Fair Slipper" (Vernon Gallery) shows a very beautiful King Charles Spaniel and a Cavalier King Charles Spaniel; and in the National Gallery, London, there are Constable's sheep dogs, full of enthusiasm in two well known pictures, "The Cornfield" and "The Hay Wain."

Out of all these works, however, we should not overlook the wonderful and often humorous paintings by Sir Edwin Landseer.

In "Two Spaniels" the artist has wisely placed a King Charles and a Blenheim next to a musketeer's hat, to show that their size is drawn to scale. In "Dignity and Impudence" it is a Bloodhound, burdened with the weight of its facial wrinkles, which is compared to the lively mischievousness of a

Cairn Terrier. Sir Edwin Landseer also displayed psychological intentions in his animal paintings, and thus under the majestic portrait of a black and white Newfoundland (later this variety was named the Landseer after him) he wrote the legend that it was a "distinguished member of the human society."

BELGIAN PAINTERS could also paint dogs as they lived. Joseph Stevens (1819-1892) devoted numerous pictures to them. *"Le Chien au miroir"* (The Dog in the Mirror) (Museum of Brussels) has as its only character a large black and white Griffon, with docked ears. This posed the irritating problem which painters before had never ceased trying to solve, however uninterested they were in the actual intelligence of the dog; this was the problem of a dog in front

Terra-cotta tombstone in the form of a dog. Han dynasty, 3rd century B.C. (Museum of Cernuschi).

The dog with the curly hair in this scene from the life of St. Martin is to become more and more rare. (Cathedral of St. Saviour, Aix-en-Provence)

St. Roch being fed by his dog. (Church of Villefranche-sur-Mer).

GIRAUDON

Burial vault of the crypt of the Basilica of St. Maximian.

The Annunciation of the shepherds. (Chartres, ancient rood-screen)

J. RIBIÈRE

J. RIBIÈRE

BULLOZ

of a mirror face to face with its double. When a monkey is placed before a mirror, it first tries to wipe the glass; then, intrigued but relatively conscious of the reflection, goes behind the mirror and tries to catch its possible brother. The dog, however, remains indifferent to this phenomenon. The stimulus sends no message to its brain.

Also in the Museum of Brussels there is an unusual composition: *"Marché aux chiens à Paris"* (Dog Market in Paris) which depicts a sort of court in which about fifteen dogs of all shapes and colors are playing, sleeping or fighting, under the disinterested eyes of the shopkeeper, who is more occupied with cleaning the fleas of his pet Fox Terrier that is lying on his knees.

It is that these animal painters enjoyed painting dogs for themselves, and not simply as secondary figures, as was the fashion in the centuries before. From then on, every knowledgeable dog-lover who was placed in front of a picture could state precisely to which breed or variety it belonged, what was its approximate age, its probable character, etc.

Photography and color films, unfortunately, have superceded painting; and the marvelous progress of color photography has already thrown the art of portrait-painting into the shade—whether it concerns men or dogs!

SCULPTURE

We have already spoken of the dog in sculpture, when we described ancient Egyptian and Assyrian carvings as the first records of its history.

A recent exhibition of Hittite Art (1700 to 1200 B.C.) in Paris gave us the opportunity to admire dogs galloping between horses' feet on the bas-reliefs devoted to hunting, and extremely rare carvings of dogs at rest.

From China we have the terra-cotta dog (Museum of Cernuschi) with its massive body, its Bulldog head, and its amusing expression, and the famous Korean dogs of

*Stele surmounting the tomb
of the brothers Appolodorus and Laocoon.
Athenian marble.
(Collection of R. Kappeli)*

*Door-knocker
of an old house in Pau.*

Fo, which guarded the temple doors up to about 550 B.C. Their appearance, akin to heavy-jowled dragons (which is reminiscent of the modern Pekingese), is curiously close to the squat mastiffs placed at intervals on the steps of the Buddhist temple at Katmandu (Nepal).

"The Marble Dog" of the Vatican Museum and "The Bronze Dog" of the Museum of Naples are famous; in Basle, the Museum of Antiquities boasts a Greek stele representing a dog sniffing and scratching at the ground on the tomb of the brothers Apollodorus and Laocoon (410 B.C.).

A sculpted stone in the crypt of Saint-Maximian (Var) came from a Gallic sarcophagus of the 4th century, on which a dog of medium height with semi-long hair can be seen between two people wearing togas.

In the Middle Ages statues of St. Roch proliferated, all with his dog licking the wound in his leg, just as in the statues of St. Hubert with his pack of hounds. The Middle Ages gave the mouth of menacing dogs to gargoyles while the silent Greyhound lay next to recumbent figures on tombs. A very beautiful Greyhound keeps watch over the body of Marguerite de Bourbon beneath the arches of Brou at Bourg-en-Bresse.

The importance of burial statuary, which is widely distributed throughout France, is well known; from the time of St. Louis to Henry II there are more than 500 statues of recumbent figures.

Let us also recall other representations of the dog which remain memorable. On an old house in Pau, a door-knocker (of no exact date) whose motif is a bronze basset hound with curled tail, could well be attributed to some contemporary artist of Santiago at Compostella. At Villefranche-sur-Mer (A-M) a many-colored piece of unpolished wood depicts St. Roch, with his inseparable companion at his side. At Aix-en-Provence (Cathedral of St. Saviour) St. Martin mounted on a horse shares his cloak with a beggar, whose left leg has been amputated, while a sort of cross between a basset and a

*The assembly
of new Freemasons,
at which the dogs are spectators.
(Bibliothèque Nationale, Paris)*

*The gentleness Saint Louis
showed towards his mother.
Engraving by the younger Moreau.
Histoire de France.
(Collection of Dr. Méry)*

*Pisanello:
drawing from the Valardi Album.
(Louvre)*

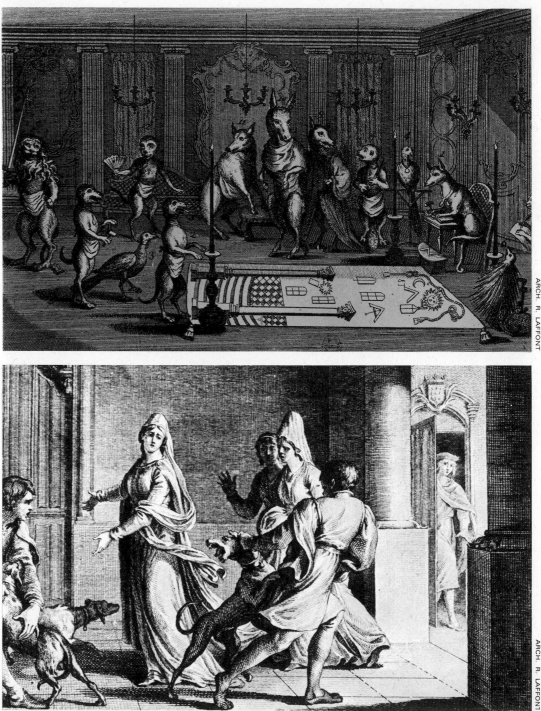

spaniel, with the wavy hair that recalls our Teneriffe dogs, looks on with interest. In the bishop's palace of Saint Maurice à Vienne (Isère) there is a gargoyle in the shape of a frightening spaniel with its front legs placed like a lion ready to leap. At Chartres, on the old rood-screen, there is a scene depicting either the shepherds of the Nativity or a shepherd with his sheep, assisted by two dogs scarcely bigger than the lambs, listening to the heavenly voices. Again at Bourg-en-Bresse, the ends of the 16th century stalls were marked by two dogs, face to face, lips curling, which are sizing each other up prior to attack. Finally, since we must limit ourselves, let us mention the Braque of the Fountain of Diana at Fontainebleau and the great mountain dogs of Oudry seated along the waterfall at Saint-Cloud.

The sculptors in hard stone and porcelain have left us some wonderful works in which the dog has been given pride of place. Mention should be made of a 17th century crystal snuff-box, and, after the style of Oudry's pictures, "hunting dogs escorted by a huntsman" in a most beautiful Sevres porcelain group, by Blondeau, and also a most beautiful "dog pursuing a swan into the reeds."

Animal sculpture of the 19th century is characterized by the care for anatomical exactitude and truth of posture. The "Great Dane Leaning on a Bowl" by Stanislas Lami is well known; copies abound in French chateaux. Antoine Barye, who was a better sculptor of the tiger or the lion than the shepherd dog, carved a marvelous bronze of a "Stag Laid Low By a Greyhound" in the Louvre. The Greyhounds and miniature Greyhounds by Mene have been known round the world. The famous terra-cotta by Charles Paillet of "The Two Friends" depicts a monkey carefully delousing a dog with the gestures of a man. Finally, Fremiet, who was the nephew and pupil of Rude, sculpted "The Wounded Hound" (Luxembourg Museum).

Closer to our day, Sandoz, Petersen, and Pompon interpreted the dog in their own

Lucas Dawson: "Tamac,"
a young pack-hound.
(Collection of Dr. Méry)

Anthropomorphic engraving by Granville
(Collection of Dr. Méry)

Hunting in the autumn.
(Bibliothèque Nationale, Paris)

way. E. M. Sandoz, between sculpting a carved jade carp and a black, marble seal, applied himself to representing his favorite Greyhounds, and they look as if they have come out of a medieval, illuminated manuscript. Pompon, whose work was also very electric, and whose artistic curiosity progressed from pigeons to white bears, and from bears to bulls, literally revolutionized this kind of animal sculpture by keeping to pure lines and stylized forms without attending to detail. Glory came to Pompon rather late in life, but he had loved dogs his whole life through. He immortalized "Nenette" (who was believed to be a Spaniel bitch). Nenette, as a mongrel with head lowered and tail in the air, occupies the place of honor in the Museum of Dijon.

ENGRAVINGS AND DRAWINGS

Engraving, which is more exacting than painting because it cannot accommodate indecision, presents us with completely truthful representations of dogs.

The men who engraved one of the first books on hunting by J. du Fouilloux have given us an exact representation of the great, powerful dogs which were unleashed in the Middle Ages.

Engraving has even rendered the famous *"Chien de Goltz"* that its master depicted with as much truth as good fortune. A child, a falcon on his wrist, prepares to bestride a dog as he would a horse. Each hair of the animal's coat can literally be seen, and the drawing of it is so pure that the prints taken from it are of inestimable value. It is a work by H. Goltzius, a Flemish engraver of the end of the 15th century.

In the 18th century, Breant engraved for *L'Histoire Naturelle* by Buffon a series of plates, the majority of which were devoted to the breeds of dogs then known. It is interesting today to compare a dog of that time with its counterpart of today.

The younger Moreau (1741-1814), who

was well versed in dogs, engraved several with excellent animation to illustrate the *Chansons de Laborde*. Here, small, anxious mongrels are seen accompanying unhappy lovers, while spaniels, quivering with excitement, are capering around marchionesses or shepherdesses. In *L'Histoire de France* which is illustrated by the same artist, there is a little known scene called *Les chiens-gardiens de Saint Louis.*" This shows a little-known side to the character of this great king, who was a respectful and gentle son. Blanche of Castille, his mother, showed serious anxiety in seeing him meet his wife too often. This maternal jealousy reached such a point that when Saint Louis wished to rejoin Marguerite of Provence, his princess, he had a devoted servant accompany him with several dogs on leashes. If Queen Blanche was found in a passage, the servant had instructions to cry out and strike the dogs. This provoked sudden barking, and Saint Louis, once alerted, disappeared immediately.

From the end of the 18th century, another anonymous engraving, but no less unique, is *"La Reception des apprentis à l'assemblée des francs-maçons"* (The Reception of Apprentices at the Free-masons' Meeting) (1785) in which the characters present are symbolized by animals: the treasurer is a hedgehog, the doctor a big donkey, the grand master an imposing dog, and the onlookers . . . all mongrels.

Artists who drew the dog are more numerous. Many of them have been—or are still, in our time—painters or sculptors whose sketches are above all studies made before attacking the final work. Such are the albums of Pisanello (1375-1455) (Louvre) and Leonardo da Vinci (1452-1519) and, in the 17th and 18th centuries, the designs of Desportes and Oudry for Gobelin and Beauvais tapestries.

Among modern artists, Vertes, Andre Lagarrigue, Gus Boffa, Simeon, R. Reboussin, Merite, Dachin, Gabrielle Bouffay in France, and, above all, Dawson in England, are the best draughtsmen of the known breeds.

"Snoopy,"
the dog hero of "Peanuts,"
which Charles Schultz made famous.
(United Features Syndicate)

"125 Reflections of Ric and Rac."
Drawings by Pol Rab.

Thurber drawing
for Men, Women and Dogs.
(Harper & Row, Publishers)

CARICATURE

Very often it is through caricature that the most able pencils have interpreted the various types of dogs in their time.

In the 19th century, incontestably the best known at this genre was Granville, who marvelously exploited the overflowing, plastic anthropomorphism of his time. The *"Contradictions d'une levrette"* (Contradictions of a Greyhound) in particular, gave him the occasion to exercise his humorous verve; he excelled in anthropomorphic caricature, from the severe bulldog in the obsequious foot-servant or inflexible door-keeper, to the bare-foot tramp with the head of a hungry wolf; from the ridiculous dress of the wealthy fashionable Poms, to the gravity of the St. Bernard judges or policemen, etc. One famous caricature is that of a guard-dog with docked ears, dressed up in a collar of horse-hair and a wide belt with a buckle, who, looking at his back in a mirror, seems terrified by the thought that his caudal appendage

LES CHIENS NE DOIVENT PAS MANGER DANS LA VAISSELLE DU RESTAURANT

is about to disappear between the blades of a large pair of scissors lying on an armchair in the foreground.

English caricaturists also excelled at drawing in the same style that made Granville famous in France. The cartoonists of Punch enjoyed themselves to the full, often with political ends in mind. The tradition is kept very much alive by their successors of today, e.g. Norman Thelwell.

We ought to set a place apart for an English woman caricaturist, Persis Kirmse, for she has had the original idea of adapting to her drawings of dogs and cats, which she draws with impeccable style, captions which in fact are extracts from Shakespeare. For example, we read under a drawing of a dog sleeping in its corner, which it prefers to leave rather than fight over with two inquisitive cats: "The better part of valor is discretion" (Henry IV, Act V, Scene 4). Further on, an enormous Greyhound finds

itself face to face with a tiny kitten: "Cry, Havoc! and let slip the dogs of war! (Julius Caesar), while a Pekingese, two small Fox Terriers and a Scottish Terrier throw themselves into the pursuit of a cat.

The Germans also did not deny themselves the enjoyment of caricaturing John Bull and his dog.

American caricaturists particularly enjoy associating the dog with scenes of modern life. The comic strip, which is so popular in the United States, has made "Snoopy," the hero of "Peanuts," drawn by Charles Schulz, into a character loved by young and old. The adventures of Sam Cobean's dog have also been very successful. Nothing illustrates in a more amusing way the excessive regulations governing dogs in large cities than these short cartoons. In one of them we see a cat in a panic pursued by a dog which has got loose. In order to escape it the cat has no other solution than to hide in a food shop,

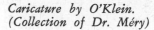

Caricature by O'Klein.
(Collection of Dr. Méry)

Walt Disney's "Pluto."
(Disney Productions)

Drawing by Eiffel:
"The Creation of the Great Dane."

Drawing by Steinberg: "All in Line."

which has a notice stuck over the door saying: "Dogs not allowed." We should also mention Steinberg, whose drawings are more bitter, Walt Kelly whose likeable "Pogo" rivals Walt Disney's "Pluto," and lastly the late James Thurber, who drew, with that cold humor which characterizes his work, *Men, Women and Dogs.* Thurber's pages eloquently show his kindly feelings towards the canine race and his sometimes cruel severity towards humans.

In 20th century France Benjamin Rabier has taken up Granville's torch, but his adaptations of the dog to the vicissitudes of men seem to reflect a good-natured joviality.

In the first quarter of this century, Pol Rab, with his unforgettable drawings dedicated to "RIC ET RAC," contributed to the launching of a real fashion: that of the wirehaired Fox Terrier and the Scottish Terrier, a couple which inevitably makes us think of that other funny pair—the clown and the funny man at the circus. The unexpected craze for the wirehaired Fox Terrier that

lasted from 1928 to 1932 is certainly not irrelevant to the nearly total disappearance today of this type of resourceful and sporting dog which was a product of its time.

O'Klein, a few years later, caricatured the sporting dog, and his illustrations of *"Avoir un chien"* as well as his innumerable color drawings of Cocker Spaniels, Dachshunds and Braques in difficulty, brought him some notoriety.

Jean Eiffel always had dogs around him. His Biquet, Rabonne, Mousse, Doudone, etc. remained in his heart, and reappear in this artist-poet's charming compositions. A few of his drawings immediately come to mind. For instance, the drawing of the prototype of the Greyhound, in which an angel is finishing ironing it out. God the Father looms up and thunders, "I told you to clean it, not to iron it!" Or again, a drawing concerning the origin of the Bulldog: Two angels are working, the one occupied with the modeling of the future donkey, while the other is trying, without much success, to model a type of ill-

— ...et comment appellera-t-on ce beau chien tout blanc?
— Le Danois !

"Superboy"
in the year 2000.

The life-saver dog.
(Le Petit Journal du dimanche,
26th April, 1914).

SNARK INTERNATIONAL

SNARK INTERNATIONAL

defined dog. When the donkey, at last finished, comes to life, its angel-creator panics and cries: "Careful, it is beginning to move!" And the result: a kick in the face of the dog, still only in contemplation, produces . . . the Bulldog! Finally another drawing of the Almighty who is explaining to a cherub, astounded to see a basset raise its leg, "You see now, why I made the tree before the dog."

Most humorous artists have had to place some dog in their drawings, because it is so bound up with day-to-day life. Consider

Tetsu's drawing of the wife whose husband, hand on the door handle, is watching the dog bring its leash to him in the hope of a walk. "You would be better saying NO to him firmly," she says, "instead of doing what he doesn't understand. He will take you for a fool!"

The perceptive eye of the psychologist we again find in Dubout, who had a smiling indulgence for cats, and who has illustrated with such talent *"Entre chiens";* in Barberousse and his mongrels, to which it is im-

possible to relate any living breed; in Coq and his amusing little Dachshund; in Schmoit and his fantasy dogs; dogs with a thousand legs, dogs bound together by a butterfly, a tailless dog joined to another tailless dog; and in Maurice Henry, who drew all his animals with such tender humor.

PHOTOGRAPHY

Whenever it is a matter of surprising an animal in its expression, its gestures, or its attitudes, or whenever we want to fix the images of the different stages of its movements, photography and the cinema have always surpassed manual, graphic processes.

Dogs do not have the speed of birds or the mobility of insects, but it took a lot of artists' and sculptors' talents in days gone by to manage to give to these models, who were incapable of keeping their poses, an image which remained true both to their anatomy and character of movement. The first daguerrotypes of dogs were achieved on the express command of Queen Victoria by a Frenchman, M. Claudet, who had already reproduced, under the best conditions, the picture of "Snowdrop," her favorite horse.

The perfection of modern optical devices allows the photographer today to take in one-hundredth of a second a Foxhound barking. Such prints are as far removed from the fuzzy, stiff photographs of the last century as the works of Oudry in their anatomical truth are from medieval paintings.

The second quarter of this century has seen several specialists take the lead in this sphere, and their works will remain classics of their genre.

With Kertez, Germaine Krull, and others, Villa, a young girl from central Europe, arrived in Paris in 1928. She had been given my address by that other aesthete and zoophile, Florent Fells, and she asked me this question shyly. "Do you think one could live in Paris by photographing dogs?" I hesitated in replying, and the young girl pulled out

Drawing by Cobean.

Dog playing, by Ylla.

of her little portfolio some beautiful photos of dogs, just as they were in life, and not necessarily lying on a cushion or balancing on a frightful white lacquered Louis XIV pedestal table. There was a stray dog yawning from boredom at the end of a chain, a Greyhound racing at nearly 50 m.p.h., a young Boxer gnawing a bone, all arranged with a perfect taste, all stressing instinctively a detail of the head or the dog's stance through which Ylla had defined not only the individual but the characteristics of the breed. I encouraged her enthusiastically. She began by covering dog shows, taking portraits of champions. She soon became, in a few years, one of the first animal photographers whose work was featured in magazines all over the wolrd. It was also in Paris, where he is considered the number one dog portraitist, that Dimont (called Dim) began his career. He was another great friend, and very experienced in all aspects of dogs. We owe to him the best collection of pedigree photographs of the last thirty years. The objectives of Scaioni, Colyann, Sally Anne Thompson, Raymond, Shafer, etc. are similar and continue to increase our knowledge of purebred dogs and to bring them to the notice of a wider public.

CINEMA AND TELEVISION

The comic strip has been called the poor relation of the cinema. Nevertheless the next episode of the adventures of Milou, the Wirehaired Fox Terrier belonging to Tintin, is always awaited impatiently, and it is only because he was originally in a comic strip that he has become a film star.

It is to Walt Disney, however, that the glory of having launched the first canine stars is due. The faithful "Lassie" has succeeded the courageous "Rin Tin Tin"; the likeable "Pluto" (who deserved to be a French Braque) continues to extricate himself from all his misadventures with the most disarming bewilderment.

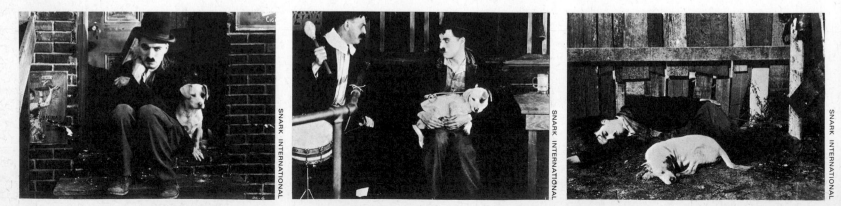

Jerry Lewis with his dogs in "Who's Minding the Store." (Paramount Pictures)

Chaplin in "A Dog's Life."

COLL. DES CAHIERS DU CINÉMA

"The Great Adventure" was also made by Walt Disney. The realization was a great technical achievement and the film itself was highly successful. It starred a Bull Terrier, a Siamese cat and a hunting dog, all of them better performers than the best comedy actors. The public, however, preferred to this film the Walt Disney productions which were entirely designed by the same specialized team that made "Snow White," such as "The Lady and the Tramp," "A Hundred and One Dalmatians," etc. The first tells of the loves of a silky Pekingese and a mongrel, whose empire is the garbage cans and the streets. The second, taken from a book by Dodie Smith (also called _A Hundred and One Dalmatians_), is through little careful touches an amusing critique of a certain category of Anglo-Saxons whose exaggerated love of dogs has quite simply led to their enslavement.

I have memories of Walt Disney's visit to the Comtesse de Quelen, who owned a set of these white and black dogs (whose markings do not appear on the puppies until after the twelfth day). After his first quick visit to her home on the outskirts of Paris, Disney returned with his technicians, filmed both big and small dogs in all their different aspects, then left and made the film that we all know. In the months which followed the filming the price of these dogs rose to as much as 300% to 400% above the price usually reserved for these beautiful Dalmatians, virtually unknown until then.

Such is the power of the cinema and television.

We deem it regrettable that the small screen is limited in presenting, often felicitously, records of the marvelous uneducated animal world. We should like television to broadcast more programs about the love and intelligent respect for animals, which would educate the public in its duties to make animals happy.

SNARK INTERNATIONAL

9 THE DOG IN SYMBOLISM

Everything has been said on the subject of the dog as a symbol. Man has endowed it now with every fault, now with every virtue, now with every vice. Happily the dog pays no attention to all this, and neither do those who love him. Partiality and logic have no place in our love for the dog.

THE NAME "CHIEN" (DOG)

Where does this name come from? From keleb (or cheleb), the Hebrew word which signifies both "lion," and "heart"? From the Chaldean "kelba," or from the Arab "keleb"? From the Persian "ag," or the Greek "kuon" (or "kunos")? From the Sanskrit "swan," or from the classical Latin word "canis" which became "chen" in 12th century French, and "chien" in the middle of the 13th century, which remained "chen" in the Walloon tongue, "kien" in Picardy, "ki" in Lower Brittany, "chi" in Lower Languedoc? Later "canis" evolved into the Provençal "cania," in which language the word "cagnard" is used metaphorically (but so eloquently) to designate the sunny corner sheltered from the Mistral, where the dog has long known that life is pleasant.

These origins are of little importance. How could the dog (in French, *chien;* in German, *hund;* in Spanish, *perro;* in Italian, *cane*) know that he is "the dog"? People of all languages whistle for him; and those who give him a name are thereby naming only what is a living part of their clan, of their family. They are marking as theirs a part of their living capital, putting, as it were, their seal on the animal closest to their heart . . . or to their purse.

On the other hand, ancient history records that dogs gave their name to men and to cities. From "cynos" was to come Cynaras, who was king of Cyprus, Cynire the son of Perseus, and Cynortas the king of Sparta. From "canis" came the illustrious Roman names Caninus, Canuleius, Caninius . . .

not to mention, with Elzéar Blaze, the French families Canac, Canille and Canone; the Italian name Canino; the Spanish Perrito; the German Hundfeld, etc.

The following places also carried the name of the dog: the towns of Cynira in Argolis, Cynopolis in Egypt, Cynossema on the Hellespont, the Cynoscephalae Mountains, and the Canary Islands. There are modern towns that still carry dogs on their armorial bearings, such as Montdidier, which has the head of a Briard (in memory of Aubry, perhaps) in its arms, and Palermo, which has the head of a guard dog.

Certainly, not all of these etymologies are necessarily flattering. One has only to consider that a Roman priest who stroked a dog had to have himself purified before he could take part in any more sacrifices; that in Greece dogs were forbidden on the island of Delos; that in old Russia a nobleman would not have dreamed of touching a dog with his bare hand; and that the Turks and the Arabs have always considered the dog to be an unclean animal.

But for many others, the dog represents fidelity, courage, affection, and altruism. Because of this a great many people have been proud to take the dog as their emblem, either in their arms, on their crest, or on their flag.

THE DOG IN HERALDRY

In heraldic devices the dog appears, according to the circumstances, either "ramping, running, barking, lying down, seated, facing (when opposite another dog) or collared (depending whether or not it is wearing a collar)."

Among the principal families of France, there is the Canillac family who bear arms "Argent (silver) a greyhound rampant Sable (black) collared Gold"; the Des Barres family, "Gold a barking guard dog Azure (blue)"; the Du Lys family, "Azure three dogs courant in pale Gold"; the Baylens

family, "Gold a greyhound rampant Gules (red) collared Argent"; the Brechet Péruse family, "Gules three hunting dogs couchant (lying down) Silver"; the Dukes of Montmorency, Havray and Crussol bore the head of a dog on their helms. The great military leaders of France also had dogs on their Blazons, by which they wished to symbolize their vigilance and courage. Marshal the Baron de la Châtre (1536-1614) in his Arms had "three dogs' heads looking towards the sinister (left)"; Marshal de Gramont had "A dog Gules couchant in front of a tree Vert (green)"; and Marshal Massena, Duke of Rivoli (1756-1817), had "a grey dog couchant."

The German Barons and princes who placed a dog or dogs in their arms were so numerous that it would be impossible to name them all. Let us however, just mention the rather rare arms borne by the Heilgberg family in the 17th century: "A mastiff's head (so named as being originally from Molossus in Epirus [Greece], a hunting mountain dog).

As for the English, they had, among other canine devices, the greyhound of the honor of Richmond (in Yorkshire) "Argent with a collar Gules studded and ringed Gold holding a shield of the Tudor Arms with a crowned rose." Introduced into the Royal bestiary of England by Henry VII, first king of the Tudor dynasty, the Greyhound was adopted in 1513 by Henry VIII for his personal standard. Ever since, it has been the animal of honor of the House of York.

The Greyhound has often figured in Coats of Arms as the symbol of alertness, devotion, and affection until death; whether it be Greyhound, Saluki, or the slight Italian Greyhound, the dog is found on blazons in all attitudes, standing, running at speed, leaping or passant, i.e., walking with a front paw raised. According to the various books of heraldry published in France in the 19th century, the Greyhound is to be found in the arms of more than 400 noble families, and especially in Languedoc and Provence where the Egyptian Greyhound, introduced into Spain, was to have as its descendants the "charnigue" of the southern lands. "A Greyhound rampant Sable collared Gold" appears on the shield of the Archbishop of Catalonia (Comtat Venais in the 16th century). "A Greyhound courant Argent on a base Gules and a demi (bitch) Greyhound issuing out of a helm" form the Armorial Bearings of the Baron Texier de Hautefeuille. "A Greyhound rampant Argent collared Gules and Gold" is in the Arms of the Marquis Le Febvre de Laubrières (16th, 18th centuries). "A Greyhound passant Argent collared Gules" is a charge in the Arms of Chamillart (17th, 18th centuries). The Greyhound is the dog of the nobility, just as it is the noblest of dogs.

THE ORDER OF THE DOG. Writers seem unable to agree on the origins of this decora-

*The Indian village
of Kitvanga (British Columbia),
is protected against evil spirits
by a dog, wow-wow, sculpted in wood.*

*The arms of the Marquis of Nicolai.
(Vivarais. 17th to 18th centuries.)*

*Silver coin
found at Segesta in Sicily.
(5th century B.C.)*

*The seal of Simon de Montfort (1195).
(National Archives of France,
Department of Seals)*

Duchesne has emphasized, appears to have been the first to take the dog as its crest, in place of the peacock which was formerly to be seen there.

THE DOG IN NUMISMATISM

The dog is not only to be found in arms, as a crest upon standards, but also on many famous seals, such as that of Simon de Montfort (a Greyhound tied to the left stirrup of a knight who is galloping along blowing his horn), or that of Raoul d'Isoudun (a dog sitting on the hindquarters of a galloping horse and held in position by the knight). Old medallions often represent a hunter accompanied by a dog. Sometimes there is an eloquent allegorical detail; if, for example, the dog is holding a shell, this represents the town of Tyre and the discovery of Tyrian purple; if it is shown beside a caduceus, it is the servant of Mercury, the messenger of the gods; if it has a turned-up tail, it represents victory; if it lies at the feet of a warrior, it is Argus at the return of Ulysses.

In this connection the National Archives of France has the richest sigillographic collection in the world. In it there are seals of every form and type, kings' seals, knights' seals, and even ladies' seals, whose inspiration was sometimes disturbing. In fact, women have always had a preference for seals showing horses or the hunt which were personified in their jewels. In 1260 Adelaide, Duchess of Lothier and Brabant, is shown with a bird in her hand, while a small dog of the bird dog type trots between the feet of her mount. At about the same time Jean I, Duke of Brabant, had almost the same seal, but flanked on the top right-hand side by a little Greyhound bounding along. Much later, in 1477, there was the seal of Mary of Burgundy, daughter of Charles the Bold; the duchess is shown in a close-fitting gown, mounted on her white

tion. According to some, *"L'ordre du chien"* was created in 495 by Lidoye de Montmorency, a companion of Clovis, at the time of his conversion to Christianity. Others believe that it was Bouchard IV of Montmorency (nicknamed Barbe-Torte) who on his own initiative, sometime around 1120, gathered together a band of knights who wore a "collar" fashioned in the shape of a stag's head with a medallion representing a dog and bearing the motto "Vigiles." Then there are others who think that it is to the Marshal of France, Charles de Montmorency (one of whose sons was Jean, lord of Nivelle, the Jean de Nivelle of the legend) to whom must go the credit for the beginnings, in 1345, of the mysterious *"Ordre du Chien"* about which so much has been written. Whatever may be the truth of the matter, the house of Montmorency, as the heraldist

Mandarin's ivory button (Netsuke).
(From the collection of D. Rouvière)

V. DELAISSE

The Musicians of Bremen,
in which the dog occupies an important
position. (Bremen, Germany.)

palfrey with a falcon at her wrist, while a dog bounds along at her side in a flower-strewn meadow. As Meurgey de Tupigny points out, this is a poignant image, for Mary of Burgundy was to die at the age of twenty-five, after falling from her horse while out hunting.

The Greeks, Sicilians, and Romans all struck coins which bore the image of a dog (usually of the Greyhound type) shown either with its nose to the ground, sitting on its hindquarters, or even running after invisible game. The dog is also to be seen beside Aesculapius on the coins of the Magnetes in Thessaly. In modern times, it is perhaps reasonable to see as symbolic the name that the Spaniards have given to their two smallest bronze coins, *"la perra chica"* and *"la perra gorda"* ("little dog" and "fat dog," respectively 0.05 and 0.10 peseta), as if to compare the small value of these coins to the small esteem in which the dog is held. . . .

Some lesser-known symbols are the fire dogs. These are more or less ornate supports, made of iron or cast iron, which hold up the logs in the hearth, and they correspond, in the sweetness of life, to the peace of the eternal sleep of the recumbant figures of the dead, with their dogs at their feet.

THE DOG IN STANDARDS, SIGNS ADVERTISING, JEWELRY AND TOYS

The symbolic dog, the crude totem of the first ages, rose to the dignity of a god, becoming Anubis the dog-god of the Egyptians, who not only guided the dead to the other world but also gave warning of the Nile's flooding by barking as soon as the first brilliant star rose over the horizon. Then with heraldry the dog became the symbol of virtue; what it lost in the way of adoration as a divine creature it gained by taking a place closer and closer to the hearts of women, children, and nations.

ATLAS PHOTO – PETIT

A new industry, dog food.

Humorous sign, by J.-L. Gérôme.

From the standard or sign of war, the dog passed to the commercial sign. From the blazon it passed to the postage stamp, and the corollary of the seal of nobility was to be one day the label of "quality." From a jewel it became a toy, and the rock paintings of the Tassili prefigured the poster.

The fashion for shop and inn signs has almost disappeared today. Out of snobbery some luxury country inns still cling to a few, but the last of them are to be found in England, where the dog is really king. In Huntingdon, for example, the "Fox Inn" has a sign portraying a dog in delicately wrought iron, made in Andalusia. In Paris there is the cake-shop "Chien qui fume" (The Dog that Smokes), the saddlery shop "A la levrette" (At the Sign of the Greyhound), record-players and records by "His Master's Voice," and the dogs' hairdresser the "Caniche élégant" (The Elegant Poodle). . . . Germany symbolizes her fast cars with a greyhound. Japan makes paper dogs of all shapes, sizes, and colors just because they are delightfully unusual. China, across all her glazed, baked expanse of land, is re-introducing the fashion for her own true Pekingese. Italy draws out the necks of her "hippy" porcelain Dalmatians, until they look like giraffes. Advertising!

In a thesis for his doctorate in veterinary science, Guy Bénézeth takes as his subject the position of advertising in daily economic life from the 19th century on, and he explains the psychological reasons for the involvement of animals in this activity which was new to the world. There need be no connection between the animal and the firm or the product. What ought to be striking is the unexpected, or the obvious relationship between the name of the business man, for instance, and his product, or else the sheer likeableness of the animal whose job it is to promote a certain product.

The Suchard chocolate dog is good-natured, in the same way as every Saint Bernard is a rescue dog. The dog may also become an amusing personality. A Dachshund that ties its body into a knot is used to impress upon us the flexibility of a Bic pencil. An unhappy looking Basset Hound, by Peynet, tells how sorry he is because he did not buy a ticket for the national lottery (he would have bought himself a step-ladder!). Dubout does extraordinary advertising for an all-purpose glue, by mending the tail of a dog. A Fox Terrier by Sévignac gravely shares with Tintin the sweet taste of an orange juice. Siné, with ill-tempered humor, welcomes back his dog who brings him a packet of cigarettes, "But I told you, with filter!" Sometimes it is important to use a certain breed of dog because of its symbolic significance. In England, Patrick Tilley could choose only a snobbish Afghan Hound to bring the *Times* to its master. A Bulldog with a hang-dog look, perched on a sparkling table top, bears the caption "With Johnson's Polish, your furniture will be well guarded." In the United States, Tomi Ungerer's Setter must be a pedigree dog for "the shoe with a pedigree." Finally, in Italy, the tramp dog, drenched by the rain, but quite unruffled by the weather (what we call "raining cats and dogs") is the best possible graphic advertisement for a medicine for influenza! It is useless to advertise jewelry, expensive toys for those unsatisfied grown-up children, women. Every jeweler is at the mercy of the fairy "fashion" who must be served first, even before the desire is conceived or formulated within one. Brooches and clips in gold (or gold-plate), of diamonds (real or imitation) are modelled on many varied canine breeds. There are Poodles clipped in the old-fashioned manner, silver Greyhounds with gold collars, Pekingese or Pomeranians made of the sparkling fragments called "rose-diamonds," and the last word in fashion for a beautiful woman is to wear around her neck a real dog-collar set with gems!

Every age has its games and its toys. Four thousand years ago, during the Middle Empire of Egypt, the ancestor of backgammon was "the game of the dog." We know

HOLMÈS-LEBEL

J.L. GÉRÔME BARBOUILLAVIT ANNO DOMINI 1902

O PTI CIEN

HACHETTE

little of the rules. It was played with little ivory sticks and knuckle-bones, and gave the ladies especial pleasure. Today, the toy dog is the king of the menagerie in any proper nursery. For babies still on the bottle, there are rubber dogs for sensitive gums, or dog rattles to distract the attention of infants, reassuring Poodles to compete with good children's Teddy, and finally for adults, plush dogs, wooden dogs, papier-mâché dogs, with movable heads, grimacing or wagging their heads at the back of the car; and in the hallway, the latest thing is to have white plastic life-size Greyhounds, sitting quietly, to welcome visitors.

PROVERBS AND SAYINGS

"To bear the dog in your arms," says a manuscript treatise on the blazon of the 14th century, means that one is "A loyal warrior who does not wish to leave his lord, either in life or in death, but who is ready to suffer death in defending him."

What starts as a device easily becomes a saying and God knows how many thousands of proverbs there are which, directly or indirectly, concern the dog, which we see every day and which is our day-long companion.

From the 15th century on, they said, "You cannot recognize people by their clothes, nor dogs by their coats"—which has today become "the habit does not make the monk." We read in the Bible, "Whoever, passing by, gets angry over a quarrel that is not his own, is seizing a mad dog by the ears."

Direct observation was the foundation of the following sayings: "To have a dog's character," "To be received like a dog in a game of skittles," "To be as sick as a dog," "To be between the dog and the wolf" (because it is the hour when the wolf is going out and the dog coming home), "Bon chien chasse de race" (a good dog hunts with breeding), or even "He who sleeps with dogs gets up with fleas."

With the passing of time, people became more affectionately interested in the fate of animals, and sensitive people said, "It's a dog's life," "Weather one wouldn't even put a dog out in," "To be beaten like a dog," "Strike a dog and the women will come." These were all sayings which expressed the pity of the common people, and "To fight like a dog," their admiration.

Ecclesiastes in its wisdom declared "A live dog is better than a dead lion," and writers continued to enrich this folklore in their work. La Fontaine wrote "A snarling dog has always a torn ear," and in one of his plays Molière wrote "He who wishes to drown his dog accuses it of having rabies," a reflection which centuries earlier Eustache Deschamps had phrased thus *"Qui son chien het, on lui met sus la raige."* (Old French.)

Other proverbs are more specific, such as "The dogs of Orleans do not bark" (referring to a cannon which was called "the dog" and which remained silent during an attack); or again, "For wolf flesh, dog sauce—for dog flesh, wolf sauce" (meaning that in life, one has to adapt circumstances to suit oneself).

Every country has its own sayings.

Spain: *"Quien quiere a Bertran, quiere bien a su can"* (Love me, love my dog); *"Quieres que te diga, el can? Da le pan!"* (You want a dog to love you? Feed it!); *"Perro ladrador, nunca bien mordedor"* (A thieving dog rarely bites); *"El perro viejo: si ladra, da consejo"* (Listen to the old dog; when he barks, he is warning you).

Germany: an old proverb of the 16th century, "No dog would accept his bread" (said of the culpable hypocrite); and today, there is this prudent advice, "Place no faith in the lameness of the dog, the smile of the courtesan, or the word of a merchant."

THE DOG IN LEGEND

Legends are born of the uneasiness felt by men of all ages in the face of the mysterious forces whose secret escapes them. Most important is man's anguished anxiety about his fate after death, but he is also afraid of the forces of nature which he cannot dominate. Among these natural phenomena are fire, wind, light, darkness . . . and also all that is beyond his understanding in the animal world.

This is the origin of two very closely linked beliefs: totemism and metempsychosis. Totemism is man's identification of himself as a member of the great family of animals; he would like to attain the strength, cunning, or courage of the particular animal that he has idealized and taken as his totem. By metempsychosis (belief in the transmigration of souls) man seeks to find continuity after death; he would like to see himself reincarnated in the animal, who will become his new self.

This form of hope in survival after death was very widespread among primitive humanity; several Greek philosophers also clung to it and it survives today in the hearts of many Hindus and in certain primitive tribes of the island of Celebes and of Australia.

There is a painting by Bernard Picard which illustrates this myth very well: An oriental chieftain (Parsis or Ghever) is about to die. A woman holds to the lips of the dying man the dog that has served him, so that with his last breath he may transmit to the animal, together with his soul, all his qualities as a hunter.

Every people gave its preference to the animal it most admired. The dog rarely had such an honor bestowed on it, except by the Iranians, in whose mythology it occupied the first rank, together with the cock. In classical mythology, the dog appears even as the symbol of deceived vigilance, of exploited weakness, of strength overcome by cunning. Was Cerberus not sent to sleep by Orpheus' lute, gorged with honey by Aeneas, and finally chained by Hercules?

On the other hand, the legend told us by Gaston Phébus reflects only glory on the

dog. King Apollo of Léonnois in Brittany had come to Tours, to the court of King Clovis, with his wife and beloved Greyhound. He conversed with Clovis' own son, who, admiring the Breton queen, could not rest until he possessed her. So he followed the couple, killed the husband, threw the body into the river, and carried off the woman. But she threw herself into the water and was carried away by the current. The dog had followed the body of his master. He dragged it to the river bank, and by scratching the ground with his nails, buried him as well as he could, then lay down beside the tomb he had made. He remained there for days, then for weeks. Some time later Clovis passed the spot, recognized the faithful Greyhound and had the ditch opened. The body of Apollo was found, as intact as the day he died. King Clovis wanted to find the culprit. A lady had witnessed the crime; she told her story, and there and then Clovis ordered a fire to be lit and had his own son thrown into it. "That is why," concluded Messire Gaston Phébus in telling this story to Philip VI of France, "we value the dog as an instrument of vengeance, a pure soul, and the arm of the law!"

History tells us how sometimes some rather unexpected judgements were pronounced. For instance, a courtier had spoken ill of Queen Hedwig, in the presence of King Ladislas of Poland. Brought before the Diet of Cracow, the courtier was sentenced to stay under the table and bark like a dog at all future meals.

In 1313 François Dandolo was sent as ambassador to the court of Pope Clement Vth at Avignon, with the mission of obtaining the annulment of the excommunication laid on the Republic of Venice. Dandolo could think of nothing better to do than put a chain around his neck, throw himself at the feet of the Holy Father, and, crawling on four legs, assure the Sovereign Pontiff that he would continue to live like a dog until his native land was returned to a state

of grace. Clement V, amused, gave his pardon, and Venice, reconciled with the Church, was grateful to her ambassador for his success. It named Dandolo "Doge," but the nickname "Dog" remained with him.

THE DOG IN PHILATELY

In philately, the dog had to wait for nearly a century before it was thought suitable for him to appear on postage stamps. St. Pierre & Miquelon and Newfoundland set the example in 1931 with a superb Newfoundland dog (on a 5 franc stamp and a 50 franc stamp), and canine issues have continued with thirteen stamps dedicated to sled dogs.

There are also sled dogs on two Greenland stamps, and to celebrate polar expeditions, there is one on a Belgian stamp, a Russian stamp and a French stamp. As far as we know this is the only French stamp to bear the image of a dog, though France is the native land of the majority of hunting dogs and sheep dogs, and it would be in France's interest to maintain in this way the prestige of her sheep-herding dogs—Briards and Beauçerons; her hunting dogs—Breton Spaniels, Braques d'Auvergne, and Braques du Bourbonnais, to mention only the most important national breeds.

Switzerland has produced two stamps showing police dogs; the Netherlands, one of a dog for the blind; Russia, a stamp showing army and police dogs; and this initiative was followed by Rumania (two stamps) and Surinam (one stamp).

Naturally Afghanistan has paid homage to her "great greyhound," with its long silky coat and gazelle-like eyes; China has not neglicted the Chow Chow, the "Hong-Kong dog" as it was scornfully called less than half a century ago, and which has now become one of the most popular watch dogs and pet dogs.

Panama, strangely enough, has issued stamps bearing the image of a dog that once belonged to empresses and mandarins,

the Pekingese.

In 1957, Rumania, to whom we owe nine stamps with pictures of hunting and dogs, issued two very beautiful stamps to the memory of "Laika," the first dog to travel into space on board Sputnik II. Laika is the name of a type of pure-bred hunting and sled dog. This dog is like the Eskimo dog, with small erect ears, of medium size, white or grey in coloring, with more or less black or sometimes fawn markings on the back, the breast, the flanks, etc. It weighs anything from 55 to 65 pounds. Unfortunately the dog shown in the illustration with this legitimate claim," *"Laika primul calcator in cosmos,"* is only a nice little mongrel, probably a cross between a Spaniel and an English Fox Terrier.

Russia, Mongolia, Poland, Albania, Bulgaria, and Hungary have also paid their respects to the space dogs, whether these were called "Shelka, Tchernouchka, Zvedetchka or Belka."

Besides this, Hungary (Magyar Posta) has dedicated nine other stamps to dogs of various breeds (Setters, Pointers, Dogues, Greyhounds, Sheepdogs, Terriers, Great Danes, Braques, Poodles, etc.), and has been imitated in this by Czechoslovakia (six stamps), Russia (ten stamps), Yugoslavia (five stamps), Poland (nine stamps), Togoland (seven stamps), and the Emirat Um al Quiwain (eight stamps).

But it is the Republic of San Marino which has succeeded in issuing the most homogeneous collection of pure-bred dogs with its ten stamps, each of which shows one of the best types of dog, i.e., the Pointer, Borzoi, Maremma Sheepdog, etc.

In order that the record may be complete, let us mention the only two official stamps (as opposed to stamps issued on private initiative) that two countries have used to plead the cause of unfortunate animals; the United States issued such a stamp in 1966, and the Grand Duchy of Luxemburg has also issued a stamp on the subject of animal protection.

3
THE DOG
AND SCIENCE

10 MORPHOLOGY, ANATOMY, PHYSIOLOGY

Shave one cat, ten cats, a hundred cats—it does not matter whether they are Siamese cats, Persian cats, Istanbul cats or Monmartre cats, drawing-room cats, alley cats or wild cats—and you will always be left with a cat, morphologically identical with all the others.

With dogs, it is quite a different matter. What diversity of shape! There is no exterior resemblance whatsoever between the short, round Pug and the Borzoi with its long head, its spearhead jaws, and its overall lengthiness which make it look as if it has been spun out in every direction. Yet both really are dogs.

There are such great differences between the numerous breeds that there is not an "exterior" characteristic of all, nor can one talk of a "character" that is psychologically common to them all.

THE HEAD

The head of the Pekingese and the Bulldog is quite spherical; the head of most sporting dogs is wider and more oblong; but the head of the Fox Terrier and the Collie is narrow and compact. In the Pointer and the Spaniel, the "stop" (or the bridge of the nose) is very marked, while in the Borzoi it is nonexistent. The nose of the Japanese dog is squashed; in the Boxer it is almost straight. The lips of the Bloodhound are flaccid, the Sheepdog's lips are firm and neat. Finally, the ears of the Chow Chow are small and carried well forward, while in a dog like the Skye Terrier (prick-eared variety) they are held high and very erect, though in another dog they may be long and heavy, lying flat against the cheeks as in the Cocker Spaniel, or semi-erect as in the Collie, the Fox Terrier, and in almost all members of the Greyhound family.

THE BODY

As regards the body, the size of the chest is especially striking. Deep but narrow in the large, long dogs, it tends to be rounder and even wider in most of the shorter dogs. In dogs the line of the back and hindquarters is always pleasing and straight (level) as opposed to the obvious depression in the line of the backs of hyenas and wolves.

The tail of some Spaniels, the Pointer, and the Braque is quite long when undocked. In Cairn Terriers and Scottish Terriers it is short and held vertical; in the Alsatian (German Shepherd) and the Collie it is furry (full-coated) and held low; in the Pug, the Chow Chow, and the Papillon it is more or less curled, and curved up over the back. In the Bulldog the tail is almost non-existent or reduced to a stump; and in the "tailless" dogs, of which the massive, shaggy Old English Sheepdog (the Bobtail Sheepdog is a typical example) it is completely absent.

THE LIMBS

The limbs, depending on whether the bones are long and straight as in the Airedale Terrier, or short and bandy as in the Basset Hound, give the dog its correct stance or make it stand with its feet exaggeratedly wide apart. Sometimes there are digital irregularities, according to the breed or even the individual animal. Theoretically, the dog has five toes on its fore-feet and four on its hind-feet, but the presence of a simple or double dew-claw, in for instance the Beauceron, can mean that the dog has one or two of these supplementary toes.

The foot is in no way affected by these embryonic toes which do not come into contact with the ground. In French, a short, rounded dog's foot is called *"pied-de-chat"* (cat's foot), a long-toed foot is called *"pied-de-lievre"* (hare's foot).

THE COAT

What we call the "coat" is made up of the length and the texture of the hair. To be

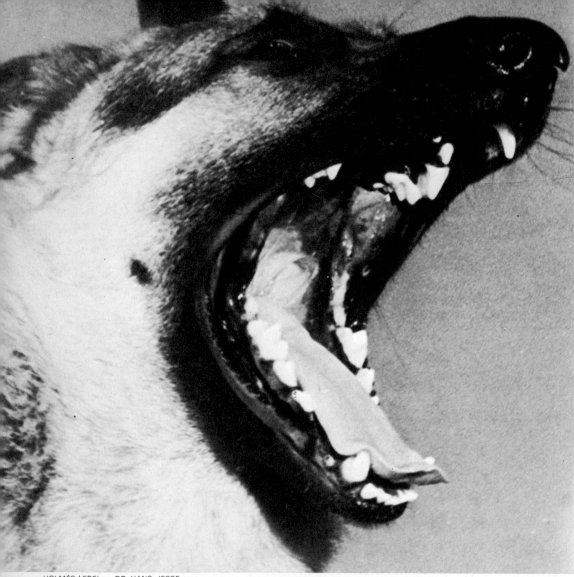

HOLMES-LEBEL — DR HANS JESSE

INTERNATIONAL NEWSPHOTO — ARTHUR SASSE

*The main weapon of all canines
is the teeth.*

absolutely comprehensive, we should also consider the skin, which is more or less pigmented, for some of the dogs of South America and China are almost completely bald. Inventive Nature has offered the canine race such a diversity of garments that all tastes and fashions are catered to!

The hair? In the different varieties of one breed, the Dachshund, the hair varies from short and tight as velvet to harsh hair, and then to silky, wavy hair. The Smooth-haired Fox Terrier's coat is like satin, the Wire-haired's is like bristles. The hair of the Korthals Griffon only looks rough. The Chow Chow and the Water Spaniels are protected by a woolly undercoat which easily becomes matted if it is not combed regularly, and the Greyhounds of the East (Salukis or Afghan Hounds), seen to be endowed with woman's hair which one's fingers caress fondly.

The coloring? Black, white, and red-brown are the dominant colors of the palette. But the homogeneous purity of coloring exemplified by the great black St. Hubert Hounds and the beautiful so-called "porcelain" dogs, is today seen less frequently in the Chow Chow and the Groenendael (Belgian Sheepdog). The red-brown colors range from sand, through a metallic orange, to chestnut. With a discreet infusion of white, the coloring may be cream all over. Black and white mingle to produce tones ranging from pearl grey to iron grey, from mouse grey to dark grey; sometimes (as in the Braques of Auvergne or the Dalmatian) there are more or less dark markings on a light ground. And finally the coat may be a complete mixture of very irregular markings, as in the so-called "harlequin" Great Danes, Anglo-French hounds, some Cocker Spaniels, and Bulldogs. The only dog whose coat never seems to change is a very old one, the typical Manchester Terrier (Black-and-Tan Terrier), in which there are mahogany-tan markings on the feet, the muzzle, inside the ears, and often below the eyes.

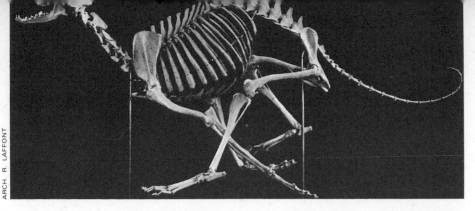

*The skelton of a large Borzoi,
running, by S.-H. Chubb.
(American Museum of Natural History)*

*In the Bloodhound,
the Pug, and the Bulldog,
the conjunctive tissue makes the skin
very wrinkled.*

This is also true of the Beauçeron, the Doberman, the English Toy Spaniel, and a few of the early German bassets, but is becoming progressively more rare.

Obviously, a whole book would be required to enumerate all the various guises of pure-bred dogs. And even then, how could one hope to describe all the other dogs, the innumerable mongrels, born of chance? Morphological variations in the dog defy any attempt at exhaustive classification; they are still one of the most mysterious phenomena in Nature.

ANATOMY

On the other hand, under the scalpel there is no mystery; the general anatomy is the same in all dogs, pure-bred or mongrel. It is astonishing that the skeleton, which accounts for at the most 8% of the weight of the body, is so strong: The explanation is that it is composed of tissues which are compact and very dense. There are in all 280 bones. We have already described the characteristics of the cranium (in talking of the dog's exterior); there is a wide frontal bone that it more or less convex, and the maxillae (longer or shorter according to the breed) are set with strong teeth.

The teeth can be grouped, according to their shape and function, as follows; incisors (I), carnassials (C), premolars (Pm), and molars (M), the last two of which are called "corner teeth."

Whatever the variety or the breed of the dog, its dentition always corresponds to the following formula:

in pups (before 6 months):

(I)	3/3
(C)	1/1
(M)	2/3

in adults:

(I)	3/3
(C)	1/1
(Pm)	3/3
(M)	2/3

The length of the spinal column depends, for instance, on whether the dog is a Greyhound or a Brabançon; but nevertheless it follows the same plan in both dogs. There are 7 cervical vertebrae, 13 dorsal vertebrae, 7 lumbar vertebrae, 3 sacral vertebrae (which joined together constitute the sacrum) and, according to the breed, anywhere from 1 to 22 vertebrae which constitute, or do not, the caudal appendage.

The rib-cage consists of 13 pairs of ribs, 9 of which lean against the sternum (which is itself made up of 8 sternebrae) while the 4 remaining pairs are directly attached to it.

The limbs, whose lines of bones vary only in their length, are anatomically very like those of our own skeleton, with this very important difference, that we must remember that every dog moves like a human being putting his weight on the ends of his toes. The dog literally tiptoes on all four feet.

The dog has at its disposal an extremely supple measure of articulation, which enables it to perform the extremes of movement imposed by its natural capabilities in running and jumping, according to norms or performance dictated by the morphology of the different breeds.

All dogs have a powerful musculature, tough tendons, and a very sensitive nervous system, which enable them to move rapidly and give them an unsuspected degree of pulling strength. In the head, this carnivore has platysma muscles, facial muscles, auricular muscles, masticatory muscles, etc., which give it a mobility of expression which the other higher animals (with the exception of the members of the monkey family) lack.

In general, the other muscles are surrounded by rather soft fat. This fat is far less developed in sporting dogs and the exceptional musculature of the Greyhound is therefore very apparent, as is that of the Whippet and of that other little athlete, the Dachshund.

TIERBILDER OKAPIA

DIM

A perfect example of the Chow Chow, with a wealth of coat.

The platysma muscles of the head give the dog a remarkable mobility of expression.

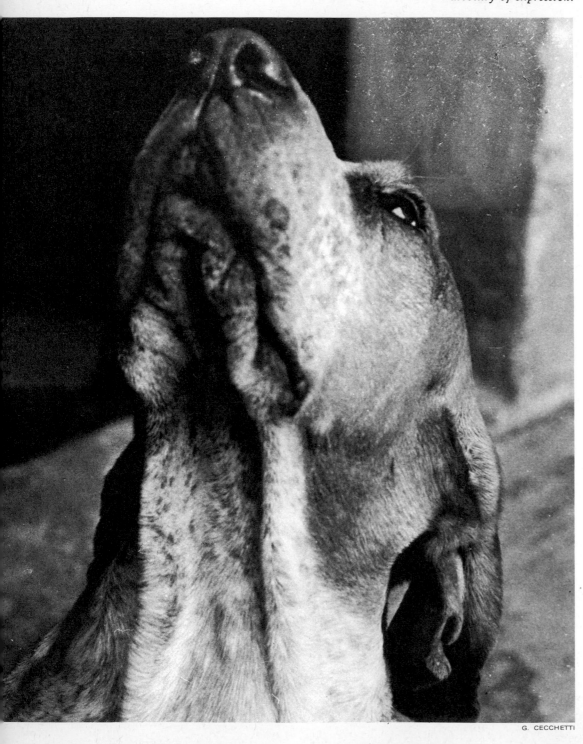

G. CECCHETTI

PHYSIOLOGY

The viscera, organs and larger internal systems of the dog present several peculiarities that it is as well to know about, because they give the animal its own physiology.

Digestion does not begin before the food reaches the stomach. The dog only tears and cuts food up, but does not bother to chew. It swallows the food quickly, thanks to a wide and extensible esophagus, which, however, is not invulnerable. One should be careful of giving a dog the hard sharp bones of duck, rabbit, lamb, etc. The gastric juices of the dog are incomparably richer and more acidic than those of most other mammals. The capacity of the stomach varies from individual to individual. In the Schnauzer, for instance, it varies between 1.22 pints and 12.32 pints, depending on whether one is talking of the miniature Schnauzer or the giant variety of Schnauzer. The meal always remains in the stomach for a long time; this is probably why almost all dogs usually lie down to rest as soon as they have eaten their food. The intestine is on the whole very short (as in most carnivores), with a spirated caecum; as for the anus, it has special marginal glands, whose function is still a matter of discussion.

There is nothing special about the lungs and the functioning of the respiratory system, except perhaps how at the least effort the dog (which, let us emphasize, does not sweat) quickly begins to breathe heavily in order to ensure a normal supply of oxygen by pulmonary ventilation.

On the other hand, the genital system of the male is represented on the exterior by a copulative organ in the form of a cavernulous member, extended to the front by the penial bone, with a very erectile pelvic urethra and a gland whose posterior turgescence is such that, in planting the penis in the vaginal passage of the female, it produces complete coarctation of the couple in copulation, which may last as long, and often longer, than 30 to 40 minutes.

*Large Greyhound
with short, smooth coat.*

Understand them, and you love them.

In the female, the relatively long vagina leads to the uterus which is made up of two cornua whose length varies from 3.9371 inches to 7.8742 inches. There are ten mammae, which are hardly noticeable in the young bitch; in females that have remained virgin, or that are not gestating, the mammae are often subject to congestion two months after the end of the oestrus.

The circulatory system merits particular attention in so far as the heart is concerned. The cardiac rhythm is more rapid than in man (normally 90 to 100 beats to the minute, and up to 120 in the pup) and though there may be frequent intermittences, these do not necessarily correspond to a true lesion.

For a complete study of canine psysiology we should have to add to these general elements which we have already discussed a study of the activity of the endocrine system and the urinary system, but we will have to discuss these when we come to speak of the psychology of the dog.

THE ORGANS RELATING TO THE VOICE: ALL DOGS TALK "DOG LANGUAGE"

The phonation of the dog, that is to say, everything that plays a part in producing the voice, varies considerably from breed to breed, because of differences in the length of the vocal chords; the volume and shape of the sound-box, which consists of the mouth, the nasal fossae, and the roof of the mouth; the speed and power with which air is expelled; and the pulmonary capacity. So it is easy to understand that though a wolf howls like any other wolf and a fox barks like any other fox, the little Pomeranian with its rapid, metallic yapping could not possibly produce the powerful barking of a pack dog, nor the dull grunting of a Saint Bernard.

Of all animals the dog has definitely the greatest potentiality and subtlety in the use

MAGNUM — ELLIOTT ERWITT

of its voice, almost to the point of possessing a "form of language." If, like all animals, it shows its feeling by its bearing, its mimicry, and its movements, it can also use its voice to express its desires, its joy, its fears, and its state of mind. No one needs an interpreter to understand the little groans of joy of a Fox Terrier, and even less to understand a frightening mastiff bounding towards one uttering terrible howls of anger.

Certainly, not all dogs have the same voice, but they all talk the same language, which man is still far from understanding, in spite of the claims of Rodolphe Darzens, the Parisian theatre director, to have suc-

ceeded in compiling a "dog dictionary."

On the other hand the dog is able to master a small "vocabulary of man language." From the age of eight to ten months, it is able to learn enough French, Russian, or Chinese to enable it to understand its master. But the master must not be frivolous and change from one language to another; if he were polyglot, his dog would no longer understand him.

SIGHT: MEDIOCRE AND SOMEWHAT DISORDERED

The sight of the dog seems to be weaker

All animals see . . .
the dog looks.

A perfect example of the English Setter.

than ours. It has long been known that a dog is hardly able to distinguish an immobile (and especially odorless) subject placed 300 yards in front of it.

My colleague Doctor Thieulin has put forward a scientific explanation of this fact.

The same object, seen from the same angle, produces an image on the retina of a dog which is three-quarters the size of that it will produce on the human eye. The total field of vision of the dog is 250 degrees (70 degrees more than man's) but, on the other hand, its binocular field of vision is much less. This is not surprising, if we compare the face of a Bulldog with that of a Collie. In brachycephalic dogs, descended from the mastiffs (the Pekingese, the Bull Terrier, the Pug) the field of vision is somewhere in the region of 85 degrees; for dolichocephalic dogs, of whom the Greyhound is typical, it is 75 degrees; while in man it is about 140 degrees.

But at night dogs see much better than we do, thanks to the extremely sensitive diaphragm of their optic system, and especially because their retina is richer is prisms than in cones. Now, prisms are much more sensitive than cones to the least stimulus from the slightest glimmer of light; cones are above all adapted to seeing colors in full daylight. So a small amount of light is enough to sensitize the eye of a dog. In man, almost the opposite occurs. We see better during the day. This detail was of little importance long ago, when man, a diurnal animal, ceased all activity at nightfall; today, with the artificial lengthening of daylight, man's sight is tending to fail, to become weaker, because it is used at all hours of day and night.

The dog's sight is also weakening. We see only too often the stricken eyes of our good old dogs, with their glassy, slightly greenish look that, from the age of eight to ten years, because of the opacity of the crystalline lens, often signifies the insidious onset of cataract.

So the optic system of the dog would cer-tainly not be good enough if the animal were not also capable of paying attention, if it did not show a certain kind of volition which sometimes gives its glance an intelligent keenness, unknown in most other creatures. When a dog does not see as clearly as it would like to, it "stares." It makes an effort to adapt. Perhaps it is one of the 52% of dogs with eyesight troubles that were the object of Doctor Joly's excellent study. According to this great specialist, 48% of dogs have normal vision; but myopia is very common. Bulldogs, and all dogs with pro-truding eyes, are more commonly afflicted than the others.

The best recently published studies seem to prove that the dog, even if its vision is nor-mal for its breed, sees shapes indistinctly, and does not perceive detail.

If a vague wooden shape, with the exact measurements of its master, is placed about 250 yards in front of the dog, and the master crouches immobile on the same plane as the wooden shape, the dog will rush towards the latter to begin with, and will continue to go towards it for the first 150 yards. After hesitating for a short time, and often stopping for a while, the dog will abandon the silhouette and finally rush in the direc-tion of its master; but from that instant, the sense of smell plays the determining role.

Can the dog see colors? Research so far carried out in color vision will only allow us to state that the dog is more sensitive to changes of tone (from pale to dark) than to colors themselves. But here too, one must take into account the differences in color of paints and dyes. Imperceptible to man, they are immediately registered even by a dog with the most mediocre sense of smell.

THE SENSE OF SMELL:
THE DOG'S SCENT IS ITS MIND

The dog's marvelous sense of smell will never cease to amaze us. Of course it has its limitations; it used to be thought that the

The mind of a dog is its sense of smell.

that it follows the "trail" (or "track") left by this individual. A dog following a man who first walked and then continued on his way by bicycle (or on stilts) finds its way easily; but should the man get into a little teleferic railway that glides along only a few inches above the ground, without touching the ground, then even the best dog stops dead in its tracks. This is also what usually happens when a track stops suddenly at the banks of a river.

So it is not only the scent of the man that guides the dog following him. One should also take into account the trampled earth, and crushed plants on which the man's residual magnetism persists, varying degrees of humidity, and, perhaps, some little-known transmitted waves. All these numerous and ephemeral perceptions are what constitute, during a maximum of from six to eight hours, what is usually called "a fresh track."

What is the explanation of the dog's wonderful sense of smell?

First of all, it is bound up with that part of the nervous system which forms the link between the brain and the nasal cavities, which has been given the name *"rhinencé-phale"*; this part of the anatomy is much more highly developed in dogs than in men. Réné Thévenin has given a perfect description of its various cavities: "A bulky inferior scroll-bone, with diverticula, and a pitted surface, occupies three-quarters of the cavity, which opens partly into the nose and partly into the throat. These scroll-bones are covered with mucous membranes that are very rich in nerve endings, which receive the least olfactory impression and transmit it to the brain. It is not only the internal architecture of the muzzle which plays a part in the functioning of this wonderful apparatus. The exterior has its own part to play. In fact the nose of a healthy dog is always humid. It is this wet surface that retains, and in some fashion absorbs, the emanations floating in the air and which probably communicate them to the taste papillae to reinforce their perception."

dog could not smell anything more than 16 inches deep, or 60 yards away on the surface—this is not the case, and the sensitivity of the dog's sense of smell is, in some circumstances, greatly superior to this estimate.

Apart from the fact that the dog can distinguish perfectly between two odors which to us seem identical, or even impossible to perceive (like the odor of magnesium sulphate and that of sodium sulphate), every normal dog is able to detect the presence of one drop of blood in five quarts of water, and to differentiate with the greatest of ease between the smells of

meats as similar as pork, beef, horsemeat, mutton etc.

Delegates of sixteen nations were brought together for the first time in 1936 in Frankfurt, for the World Canine Congress (Congress Mondial Canin). During this conference I was able, in my capacity as committee reporter to institute the analysis of all that had been discovered about the olfactory faculties of the dog. The very interesting work of the Austrian and German researchers (and particularly of Doctor Menzel) showed that the tracking dog does not seek out the odor, specifically, of a given individual, but

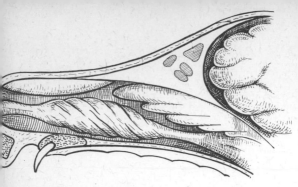

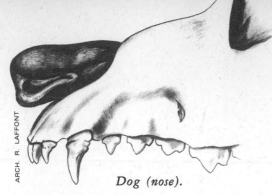

Dog (nose).

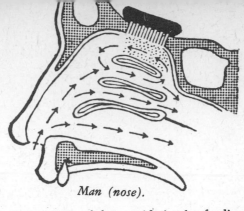

Man (nose).

If you compare the two drawings above and to the right, you will get an even clearer understanding of the dog's exceptional sense of smell.

Although man has a very large nose, four-fifths of it is taken up by scroll-bones whose mucous membranes are of little value to the sense of smell. But the part which contains the ethmoidal cells (which are essentially olfactory) is situated very far away, at the superior stage of the pituitary, i.e., at the top of the nose. Its volume is about 1½ cubic inches. What is its volume in the dog? In an Alsatian (German Shepherd), this same organ has a volume of 6 cubic inches.

The disproportion is even more clearly shown by the numbers of ethmoidal (olfactory) cells to be found in the dog and in man:

man has	5 million
a dachshund has	125 million
the average Fox Terrier has	147 to 150 million
an Alsatian has	200 million

It would however be a mistake to deduce

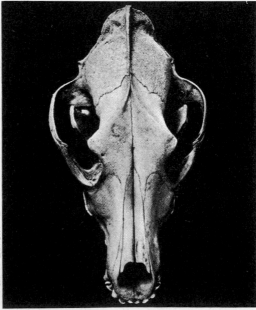

from these figures than at Alsatian must "smell" 44 times better than a man. The olfactometer, which is in use today, shows that the dog's sense of smell is in fact a million times superior to our own. The dog's sense of smell never ceases to astound us.

"The richness of the canine olfaction" writes Vitus B. Droscher, "is due not only to the enormous concentration of the sensory cells but also, and above all, to their manner of functioning."

This will make it clearer. One of the odors released by perspiration—either human or animal—is butyric acid, 1 gram of which contains 7 thousand milliard million molecules, an unimaginable number! Imagine that this acid is spread at a precise moment throughout all the rooms in a ten-story building. A man would only smell it if he were to take a breath of air at the window and then only at that precise moment. But if the same gram of odor were spread out over a city like Hamburg, a dog could perceive it from anywhere up to an altitude of 300 feet![1]

We ought also to bear in mind that there are more than 200 breeds of dog, and that each of these has its champions. In Holland and Denmark, Alsatians are used to discover the smallest leaks in gas piping. These specialized dogs are more reliable than the most modern instruments, and they are able to find the spot where a pipe is broken, several feet under the thickest tar macadamed road.

Professor Neuhaus has even succeeded in tripling the olfactory capacity of dogs. He made some dogs swallow one gram of fatty acid. Two hours later, their sense of smell was considerably diminished. On the other hand, after four or five days of fasting, these same dogs were able to follow the trace of anything that might contain these fatty acids, and they did this three times better than at the beginning of the experiment. This shows

[1] *"Le merveilleux dans le régne animal"* (The Marvelous in the Animal Kingdom). Coll. Jeune Science. Ed. Robert Laffont, 1968.

the importance of fatty acids in the feeding of carnivores. When a dog is deprived of these elements, its sense of smell is heightened and this helps it to follow the oldest and most worn tracks. One can understand why hunters instinctively starve their dogs for a whole day before the opening of the shooting season.

This on the whole is the structure and functioning of the olfactory system of our friend the dog.

There have been thousands of experimental tests carried out to define the thresholds of this rich sense of smell. The best known of these is that carried out by Professor Buytendijk (of Gröningen). In the presence of a dog, each of six persons unknown to the animal throws a pebble far away. One of them makes the dog sniff his fingers and then orders, "Go fetch!" The dog at once runs toward the pebbles, patiently sniffs them one after the other, then suddenly wags its tail. It picks up a stone, and brings it back to the person whose scent it has recognized on the pebble.

The test Romanes carried out with his Setter was more complicated. Romanes stood at the head of a line of a dozen men. They followed him one after the other, each man placing his feet in the exact footprints of the preceding man. After walking for several hundred yards, Romanes turned to the right at the same time as five of his companions. The rest of the little group turned to the left, with, at the very end of the line, a game-keeper whom the dog knew as well as his own master. Romanes' Setter was immediately afterwards let loose. It set off without hesitation, then when it arrived at the parting of the ways, it turned right in the direction Romanes had taken, paying no attention to the last track, which was that of its friend the game-keeper, and without being confused for even a moment by the footsteps or emanations of the other men. So it had found the scent of its master, Romanes, which was however the first and (to us) the least perceptible under those

*Section of the olfactory passages
of the dog.*

*Detail of the truffle (nose).
(Drawing by R. Dallet.)*

*Section of the nasal passages in man.
(Drawing by Vitus B. Droscher.)*

*Skull of a wild dog.
(Museum of Natural History, Senckenberg)*

*Absolutely no need
to signpost the way,
he will find
his own house.*

of twelve other men.

Another extraordinary demonstration of the keenness of the dog's sense of smell was carried out by H. Kalmus, using two young Alsatians belonging to the British police. Having first made sure that these dogs could easily recognize the various garments of the members of a family, Kalmus wondered if the dogs could distinguish between the scents of twins, mixed up with other twins, male and female. The results varied according to the procedures adopted. If the dog was first allowed to sniff the hand of one of the twins, who was alone present, and then taken into the presence of numerous handkerchiefs among which was the handkerchief of the other twin (the absent one), it was this handkerchief that it chose. Exactly the same result was obtained if the handkerchiefs of both twins were mixed with the others. One of the dogs, "Chloe," then brought back, at random, the first of the two handkerchiefs that fell under her nose.

Another experiment was carried out with the twins walking along together. After some time, one of them let his handkerchief fall, then they both went off in different directions. "Kim," the second dog, was brought to the place, and followed the track of the twin who had dropped his handkerchief. It was thus demonstrated that the dog is able to differentiate between the scents of twins, even if the two scents are mingled!

Other experiments enabled Kalmus to affirm that the dog is always able to find the handkerchief of the twin in question, whatever part of the body (face, hand, armpit) may have been used to permeate the object, and even if the handkerchief has then been sprinkled with the most violent chemical perfumes!

An Alsatian belonging to the Cairo police was put on the scent of a donkey which had taken a rocky path four days beforehand. In three hours, the dog found the animal a mile away; it stopped, sat down, and began to bark in front of an old tumbledown cottage where the donkey had been hidden.

SNARK INTERNATIONAL — MARKER

Is the dog a music lover?
Snoopy and Schroeder,
by Charles R. Schultz.
(United Features Syndicate)

Ten books would not be enough to recount all similar happenings.

However, in some cases it happens that the dog becomes confused. If a dog is set loose in a place which several men have trampled over in every direction before going to an agreed meeting place, even the best bloodhound is unable to find that spot, unless it has a man beside it who knows the spot they are aiming for and the way to it, and who will guide the dog either by word or gesture when it hesitates, and warn it of its mistakes. In this way the man becomes a "means" of success for the dog. This is what dog-handlers and whippers-in of the "laying-on of the pack" do when one or several dogs are for the time being completely confused.

Why? Because man "intellectually" recognizes signs and tracks and transmits his discoveries to the dog.

Should we conclude from this that the dog is deficient in intelligence? This would be to misunderstand its particular physio-psychology. The dog which finds or follows a track knows nothing of the path, less still of the itinerary, of which it cannot form an idea. It acts in obedience to a chain of sensory impressions, a chain which comes in more or less quick relays and is more or less fortunate. Man's assistance is part of this chain.

HEARING: DOGS CAN PERCEIVE ULTRA-SOUND

Among all these different kinds of relays, we must give a very important position to sensations and perceptions of the accoustic order.

In fact the dog's hearing is almost as highly developed as its keen sense of smell. We should not forget that it is sensitive to ultra-sound. Our ear can only just perceive 30,000 cycles per second, while that of the dog (according to the latest research carried out in Russia) is able to perceive waves of the frequency of 100,000 cycles per second. Pavlov had already demonstrated that the

dog registered 75,000 cycles. The use of the famous silent whistle (so-called because to man it is inaudible), is in itself sufficient proof that in this domain we cannot bear the least comparison with the dog.

This peculiarly keen sense of hearing has for a long time been demonstrated by the use of controlled tests. Engelmann was the first to note that a slight noise, imperceptible to the human ear at a distance of four yards, could be heard perfectly well by a dog at a distance of 25 yards. Later, Engelmann and Katz conducted other experiments to determine the ability of the dog to locate the sound. To do this, they trained a bitch to respond to an electric buzz which lasted for only a third of a second, emitted by an apparatus placed behind a small plank. When the dog was thoroughly conditioned, it was placed at the centre of a circle six yards in diameter. At regular intervals around this circle were positioned sixty identical planks from behind any of which the twenty-two could come. The dog immediately located the plank from behind which the sound was actually coming, whether this plank were put in front or behind her.

These results were confirmed at a later date. Keller and Bruckner placed a dog at the centre of a circle eight yards in diameter, around which were positioned 64 planks, each with the same apparatus attached to them. Without any hesitation the dog went towards the plank behind which the buzzing was sounded. Then another experiment was carried out; two planks were placed at a distance of eight inches from each other, and the buzzing could be made to come from behind either. The dog was supposed to go toward the plank from behind which the sound came. It did manage to distinguish between them, even when they were four or five yards away from him.

Katz, when he learned of these experiments, thought that the dog could locate the sound because it was able to note the difference in the time the sound took to reach one or the other of its ears. (Keller and Bruckner

were doubtful of this). The experiment was again performed, and this time is was noted that if one of the dog's ears were plugged, the dog was no longer able to locate the sound correctly. In fact, it was better able to do this if both its ears were plugged!

Katz then performed the same experiments in a modified form, by placing the sources of the sounds at different levels. Unless they were placed above its head, the dog could distinguish between them. Above this level, it could not differentiate between them.

Is then the normal limit of the sight, the sense of smell, and the hearing of the dog—of the whole world of its senses in fact—situated three feet above the ground? This is unlikely.

Katz was intrigued, and did not rest there. He wanted to find out next if his dog was able to distinguish between three sources of sound placed on the same level, but one behind the other. In this situation, it should be emphasized, the dog was not at all successful. It ran in the right direction, but stopped dead in front of the first plank, unable to work out whether the noise was coming from that plank or from one of the others.

If a man takes part in the same experiment, he finds the solution better and more quickly, because he brings to the task of solving the problem a measure of intellectual reflection which is lacking in even the most alert dog.

In conclusion, we can say that because its auricle is mobile and perfected by very sensitive hairs, and because its external ear, middle ear, and internal ear are very much superior to ours, the dog can determine the direction of a sound much better than we can, but does not judge distance as well as we do.

ARE DOGS MUSIC-LOVERS?

Because the hearing of the dog is extraordinarily sensitive, several people have believed it to be susceptible to the charm of music. In spite of the legend of Orpheus, it is wise not to pay too much attention to amusing stories like the following:

In *"L'Ami de la Nature"* (The Friend of Nature), Toscan recounts that in 1789, "Parade," a mongrel, was gamboling with joy alongside some of the musicians of the traveling show at the Tuileries. The musicians had become friendly with him and each evening one of them invited him to dine. The word "dinner" was enough to ensure that Parade would follow his host home. When the meal was finished, he would leave to go to the Comédie Italienne, the Feydeau Theatre, or to the Opera House, and there he would slip into a corner and enjoy the rapture of the harmony, says Toscan, like any true music-lover.

Easier to check, but no less suspect of anthropomorphism, was the reputation in our own day of "Bemol," a Dachshund which Reynaldo Hahn loved like a child. "I love him so much," he used to tell us, "because he loves music as much as I do." So Bemol too was said to have a musical ear. When the lady who created "Ciboulette" performed, accompanied on the piano by the author of the song, Bemol slept right up against the pedals, not moving a muscle. From time to time he would heave a deep sigh, but if the charming Edmée Favert happened to miss a note, then, but only then, Bemol would lift his head and comically begin to bark to show his disappointment.

"And that is why," Reynaldo Hahn confided one evening, "I had to make a change in the line *'Nous avons fait un beau voyage';* there was one note in it which the interpreter stumbled over, and dear little Bemol couldn't stand it!"

This of course was just a charming caprice, for Bemol was always at his master's side, and the latter only had to sigh with disappointment or give the least shake of impatience, and the dog associated itself with his emotion. So much so that, secretly flattered by this artistic communion, Reynaldo Hahn never failed to praise the little Dachshund for its good judgement and to reward it for it.

In fact dogs are much more susceptible than one would imagine to admiration, flattery, and compliments, or at least to our way of expressing them. A sudden gentleness in our voice, an indefinable change in our behavior, always surprises them agreeably, and reaffirms the mysterious communication between them and us without which no dog on this earth can be happy.

TASTE AND TOUCH:
THE LEAST KNOWN SENSES

We know less about the dog's sense of taste than about any other part of its physiology. In fact the dog does not "taste," it swallows quickly, without chewing. The preferences it shows are perhaps nothing more than the results of an instinctive tendency to consume vitamins, mineral salts, etc., all of which are often lacking in the pet dog.

Although we are all aware that the dog is sensitive to stroking and to beating, our scientific knowledge of the dog's sense of touch is still rudimentary. The dog's skin, lips, hair, vibrissae, and whiskers constitute a whole keyboard of sensitivity which still holds many mysteries for us.

We only know that the cutaneous vestiture is so sensitive that a gentle touch is enough to alert the muscles of horripilation and make the hair stand up on end. We know that a few drops of oil of turpentine on the back of the most wiry-haired dog are as painful to him as knettle-stings are to the skin of a child; but that, on the other hand, a Nordic dog can sleep all night long in a blizzard, and awaken in the morning in a shell of ice, without seeming to suffer at all. We know that the dog's feet can be badly hurt by asphalt, grit, and stubble. Finally we know that stroking and beating are forms of contact to which even the most lethargic dog is sensitive and able to understand; but we have no understanding of the exact role of the vibrissae nor of that of the acid modifications of the skin.

11 PSYCHO-PHYSIOLOGY

"Where are the dogs going?
you people who pay so little
attention ask. They are going
about their business.
And they are very punctilious, without wallets,
notes . . . and without brief-cases."

BAUDELAIRE

It is by no means my intention to try to establish a precise dividing line between psycho-physiology and pure psychology. Nothing in this sphere is more uncertain than what we know about man, unless it is what we know about the dog.

This is however the best means of arranging the problems, and even more, of extricating animal psychology from a sidetrack which though doubtless dear to the hearts of literary men and poets, nevertheless contains little elment of truth, for it is always falsified by a predisposition to suppose an analogy with the behavior of man. "It all happens as if . . ." they have unthinkingly said, for so long. But nothing ever happens "as if." Between human intelligence and animal intelligence there is a vast gulf, a gulf which results from the fact that it is impossible for an animal to attain to conceptual or logical thinking, just as it cannot attain to the kind of verbal language which enables man to express himself.

Indeed we should not speak of the "intelligence" of animals without bearing in mind the essential differences between them; the bee leads the life of an insect, the nightingale the life of a bird, and the dog leads the life of a dog. To place these three forms of life on the same plane would be to commit a grave error. There can be no value, for instance, in a comparison between the behavior of a hen and that of a dog. Here is proof: If a chick is placed behind a screen starts to cheep, its mother comes running. But if the chick is placed under a transparent cover (and so remains completely visible to the hen) the mother pays no more attention to it. One can well imagine that a dog in a similar situation would be terribly upset.

On the other hand, a vulture will fly three feet above a dead body, hidden under some leaves, and not notice it; but if the dead body is placed under a glass cover, a dozen vultures will swoop out of the sky to feed on it.

Why are the reactions of the hen and the vulture so different? This is because their organs of perception are not of the same keenness; in the hen, hearing is the most important sense; in the vulture, sight.

As it is not my intention to impose upon the reader an arid technical exposition of the subject, I will give only some of the essential elements of canine psycho-physiology, which I think are helpful to a better understanding of the relationships dogs have with each other and with men.

THEY LACK ONLY WORDS

We will not return here to the subject of phonation, the method of inter-communication about which we know so little. The dog has at its disposal other means of expression, other codes, made up of signs, stances, and odors which enable them, specifically, to understand each other.

When two dogs meet, their whole bodies, from the ears to the tail, do in fact act as a sort of code. If the ears are held more or less erect, the attention is concentrated; if they are pointing forward, the dog is on the alert. If the tail is held high and wags, this conveys joy and confidence on the part of the dog; if it is held almost still, the dog is unsure; if it is held low and does not move, the dog is feeling insecure; if it is brought right down between the legs, the dog is afraid. If the lips are drawn back and tremble, with deep growls, this betokens intimidation; if there is no growl, this is the ultimate sign of defiance before the dog attacks.

But is it necessary to define these familiar reactions? There are others, not seen so frequently, which are of more interest to the layman. The dog that offers you his paw is either worried or has been trained to do so. The dog that lies on its back is a passive creature; but if it takes up this sudden "dead" attitude at the beginning of a fight, it is a coward—or a wise dog, for in canine language (just as in the language of the

*When a dog lies on its back
it is a mark of confidence
or allegiance.*

wolves) this attitude is a sign of allegiance, it automatically results in complete indulgence in response to the surrender: "You're beaten? Good, you admit it? That's fine then! Let's say no more about it!"

A SOCIAL HIERARCHY AS OLD AS THE WORLD ITSELF

When the weak or the less brave submits, this entails the instinctive establishment of a social hierarchy that is important to know about, for it shows that in spite of their domestication, dogs have retained, in a dormant form, their primitive instincts.

Every dog, whether it is descended from the jackal or the wolf, belongs to a species which has always led a communal life. Now, in every community of superior animals—whether it is a herd of elephants or of dairy cows—there must be a leader. The role of the leader is to precede, watch over, command, guide, punish, or protect its fellows. The leader ought to be the finest (the most alert, bravest, and the strongest) of the animals. The law of nature will not allow the community to be endangered because of the deficiency or incapacity of the leader in performing his task. Hence the law of the "dominant animal," which is no more than strict obedience to the instinct of the preservation of the species, by means of the voluntary submission of the individual animals.

The dog, even though it has long been protected, fed, and cared for by man, is not exempt from this law. Its life may no longer have anything at all in common with that of the wolf or the coyote, but its instinct has remained the same. It is as strong in the domestic dog as in the wild dog, and if the dog we love is so closely bound to us, it is precisely because, separated from its fellows for thousands of years, it now finds itself alone in the heart of the human family. It has become part of this family-pack; it humbly takes its place there just because the person who feeds and protects it is still, in

its eyes, not only a friend, but the leader.

It should however be noted that the hierarchy establishes itself differently, according to whether the dog belongs morphologically, and above all psychically, to the wolf type or the jackal type.

The Chow Chow, which belongs to the wolf type, respects the well-established hierarchy of the wolves, in which the No. 1 animal takes precedence over the No. 2, No. 2 over No. 3, and so on. The sheep dog and the pointing dog, on the other hand, belonging to the jackal type, will defer before the leader, but will not establish any distinction of superiority or obedience among the rest of the pack.

As we will see later, the supremacy of the leader is never a life-long privilege for the animal that enjoys it. Constantly challenged, the deficient leader is soon ousted by a more valiant rival.

Because we so often see the gentleness and faithfulness of the domestic dog, we tend to forget too easily this original law of the pack. So it is wrong to interpret the dog's hostility and naughtiness as ingratitude, for their true cause may be the failing of the master.

It would be equally wrong to believe that the instincts of the dainty lap-dogs can be any different from those which actuate the tough dogs of a sled team, or the pack hounds. The inner life is the same, only the intensity of the reactions differs. Too many dog owners do not know about, or do not wish to know about, this essential element in the psyche of the dog, and this sometimes leads to tragic, or comic, consequences.

In one of the historic chateaux of the Loire Valley, where for a long time there had been the tradition of maintaining a pack of large hounds, one summer's day the huntsman in charge of the kennels went off in the afternoon to a family party about three miles away. He came back during the night, doubtless rather tight, and went to bed. But he had neglected to feed the dogs before he went out, and they welcomed him home with a deafening concert of barks

which, if it left off for a moment, only started the next second louder than ever. After two hours, the exasperated huntsman jumped out of bed, put on his slippers and went down to the kennel in his nightshirt, whip in hand, meaning to reestablish order and silence. It was a mild, but dark night. He had no sooner opened the door than the dogs, stupified for a second, jumped on him. The man had hardly time to raise his arms. Maddened by the unexpected appearance of this white ghost which stank of alcohol and in whom they could no longer discern the strong and familiar odor of their "master," thirty "devouring dogs" threw themselves on him. The staff, hearing the savage cries, ran to the scene. Too late. Nothing was left of the careless fellow but "a horrible mixture of bone and ravaged flesh."

Here is a parallel, though totally different, story, in which the comic vies with the ridiculous.

A few years ago an old maiden lady was so lonely that she got a very gentle, affectionate little Teneriffe poodle-like bitch. Having raised it from a very young puppy, she retained such happy memories of this tender experience that it was not long before an excessive transference of maternal solicitude took root in her heart. The little dog is now seven years old. But ever since it was weaned, the poor little creature has been subjected, every day, at mid-day and in the evening, to forcible feeding from a spoon. The dog and her mistress are now conditioned to such an extent that the animal, whose appetite is long since satiated, is no longer able to eat like other dogs; that is to say, it cannot feed itself. The result? Understandably resenting being stuffed like a goose, the dog reacts each time; it tries to impose its own will, which, as one can imagine, causes a certain amount of trouble. The mistress, who does not want to punish her pet, has found a strange weapon against the dog's bites, that are caused more by annoyance than by badness. To catch hold of the dog without endangering herself, she throws a napkin over

*The joy of playing
diminishes with age.*

*Among sled dogs,
the social hierarchy is always
being challenged.*

its head . . . and to the satisfaction (secretly selfish) of the spinster, the fragile Teneriffe submits. Not that it has renounced its intention to be victorious one day; quite the contrary, since it need fear no reprisal! So every day for seven years, twice a day, the pantomine is repeated; the revolt of the victim and the ephemeral and very relative victory of its unconscious tormentor.

These two stories, both true, underline how wrong it would be to endow the dog with our own psychology, to treat them as little men or children. There will always be something in the canine psyche which is a mystery to us, and which easily disconcerts us.

In Bar Harbor, Maine, U.S.A., an attempt is being made to reach a clearer understanding of this. Domestic dogs are being studied, over a period of a few years, completely at liberty, i.e., removed as far as possible from the influence of communal life with man. At Bar Harbor the Rockefeller Foundation has set up a Center of Canine Psychology, where dogs of all ages and breeds are kept. In the course of the research being carried out the conditions of their habitat and food are modified, and their play is monitored. Tiny radio transmitters are attached to each animal which enable the respiratory and cardiac activity of each to be registered from afar, for future study. The dog can also be watched, without its being aware of this, by means of eyepieces placed in disguised posts.

The information obtained from this research is interesting; it has been found that the hierarchy which we have just been speaking about exists already in a litter of pups, in the first hours after birth. It exists between the greedy glutton who pushes all the others aside to get the best teat, and the timid little runt. It has also been noted that the old dog who used to be the leader is quickly replaced by a younger, stronger, more aggressive dog and that it then descends, gradually or brutally, depending on the breed, to the bottom rank in the community.

Finally, the researchers have been able to

ATLAS PHOTO — MERLET

HOLMÈS-LEBEL/CAMERA PRESS — R. HARRINGTON

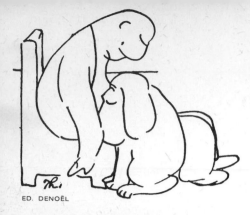

ED. DENOËL

His master's apartment
is the dog's territory.

White huskies (Samoyeds)
in the Great North.
(RAPHO-MARRY.)

confirm a theory which has always been dear to me—that each breed manifests its own constant characteristics. Films are shown in front of the dogs; poodles and hounds rush forward or bark excitedly at the sight of the game as it leaps onto the screen, while Scottish Terriers remain impassive.

Qualitative modifications in the daily diet have brought to light the role played by certain vitamins in the formation of the character of the individual dog. The value of Vitamin C as an agent of resistance was already known. The group of *liposolubles* vitamins (Vit. B/1, B/2, B/3, B/12, etc.) has shown itself able to transform a timid, unaggressive dog into a quarreller who seeks to impose its own will. Deprived of this precious contribution to its diet, within a few months the same dog is again afflicted by its former fears and feelings of inferiority.

The Center at Bar Harbor has already contributed more to our knowledge of the psychology of the dog than a lot of other experimental work on this subject, more so than many books written by dog-lovers whose dangerous tendencies are only too well known.

THE SENSE OF TERRITORY: TO FEEL AT HOME

It is well known that many animals like to feel they are masters of a territory, which they feel to be their own exclusive domain.

Like the other mammals, and perhaps even more strongly, the dog has the same instinct of "his own place," which wild animals mark for themselves either by rubbing themselves against the trees or by scratching the bark, or by leaving their droppings here and there on the land.

It would seem logical to suppose that the behavior of a domestic dog is only very slightly related to that of a wild dog. This is by no means the case. Just like the wolf, the most domesticated of dogs will "mark"

J. RIBIÈRE

CAVE CANEM

The dog defends its "home" . . .

and always returns to it.

the frontiers of its piece of land either with a spurt or a few drops of urine, or with an odorous liquid secreted by the anal glands, or even sometimes in a less discreet manner. This causes many misunderstandings, starting with our human incomprehension of the dog's act of relieving itself. The dog we take out for its little "walk" does not always obey the need to relieve itself. If he nearly always leaves his smelly visiting cards in the same places, he is marking, for the benefit of any ill-bred dog who may come along, that this is his place, and this is his manner of affirming it.

I know a pair of very beautiful Greyhounds, which, although very clean, intelligent and perfectly well aware of the reprisals to which they expose themselves, nevertheless, since a parrot has come to share their home, cannot help "forgetting themselves" in their master's flat just as often as the traces of their ownership are effaced.

Tibergen has shown when, and under what conditions, the sense of territory is born in the consciousness of the dog. The young male dogs of the packs of the Far North leave the protection of the family and wander about aimlessly for some months. During this time they violate the boundaries of other dogs' territories, in spite of the severe punishment these incursions entail. It is only when they become sexually adult that within a few days they learn to differentiate between the forbidden zones and those which are still available. Then, but only then, do they take possession of their own territory.

Fortunately the dogs have other weapons for use in defending their territory than the simple marking of its boundaries by their droppings. The first of these weapons is their aggressiveness; this is the natural aggressiveness of the dog against which the Romans warned their visitors at the threshold of their households. Today the classic *"cave canem"* is made even clearer with the warning, often untrue, "savage dog."

Although it cannot live alone, even the most peaceful of contented dogs holds great store by his own place. He has made the territory of his master his own and will show a slight inclination to defend it whenever a stranger appears. If it is quite free its manifestations of hostility will range, according to its size, from desultory yappings to deep meaningful barks. If, however, it is held on a short or long chain, and so limited in its movements, it will immediately feel anger and fear. Fear above all, for dogs are rarely brave, and strength and weight count for nothing in this context. There are some minute little Pomeranians who would die rather than retreat a yard; there are some fine Boxers who are beside themselves with terror when confronted by one of them in such a mood.

Ulrich Klever amused himself by giving the layman some valuable advice on this subject. Never go within the circle of ground which can be covered by a tied-up guard dog (especially if the dog is attached to a sliding system, which enables it to move along a rope). When the dog is simply tied to its kennel, let it go on with its outburst. Give it a wide berth as you pass, and smile! In the presence of a threatening Chow Chow or any other dog which runs at you from the bottom of the garden, never beat a retreat. You would let loose a "tropism," exciting the instinct to pursue; there is no surer way of being caught up with, and bitten. But if you really are frightened, move backwards slowly, without crying out and without gesturing. This is the language of wisdom; the aggressor knows he is master, and he knows that you know it!

Just as long as, you do not throw yourself on the ground (and your back), remembering all you have learned of the generosity of dogs towards a floored adversary, in the hope that all the dogs in the world know their duty . . . and your rights!

This is certainly precise factual advice, but it would be prudent not to rely on it too much.

HOW THE DOG FINDS HIS WAY

Another problem is the dog's ability, of which we still know so little, to find its way home from a great distance. All students of the subject admit to the fact that if a dog is carried in the dark ten miles away from its usual home, it is perfectly well able to travel in a straight line right to its home, across country that is completely unknown to it, and to do this without any difficulty.

It seems to have been proved that this need to go home is the result of insecurity and emotional upset. The dog tries to assuage its distress; it feels all alone, it is afraid of falling into the hands of strangers, it wants to be back in its own home.

*The male usually
remains untouched by the maternal instinct.*

"And the dog walked, walked. . . ."
J Prevert.

SALLY ANNE THOMPSON

But how does it find its way? Because of its excellent associative memory, there is no problem when it is a case of country already known to the dog; but it is more difficult to say how it find its way to an old home which it left a very long time before, and when it does not seem possible that it could have registered in its memory the path to follow to get back there.

This is the story of a dog who for twenty years was my beloved companion. "Miche" was an old Wire-haired Pointing Griffon bitch who was at that time more than sixteen years old. She was deaf and almost blind; one day she disappeared. I thought that she must have been upset by my absence, jumped into the back of some car and been driven a few miles away, then discovered and set at liberty again. For a fortnight I searched for her all over Paris, first in the district we lived in, the familiar territory she had wandered over for the last fifteen years. Then one morning, when we had abandoned all hope, a friend who lived in a distant part of

town, where we had lived fifteen years previously (when Miche was at the most six months old), telephoned us on the off chance to say that there was a terrified, trembling dog, whom he thought he recognized as my bitch, taking refuge in his garage.

I dashed over there; it was Miche! And this is the curious part of the story—during the last fifteen years, neither the dog nor any other member of the family had had one single occasion to go back there. But she had ended up in the very place where she had spent her young puppyhood.

There are many examples of similar happenings, but they baffle us humans. Dogs, no doubt admirably served by their senses, and by a reliable topographical sense, do not proceed in the same way men do. Motivated by hunger, anxiety, and loneliness, the dog probably sets off in a general direction, according to a process that we do not understand, then chance intervenes and also various stimuli (favorable or otherwise). Then the dog is guided by every familiar noise, every

odor it has at some previous time perceived, every inch of ground it has previously been over. It sets off, makes a mistake, hesitates, begins again, testing its progress by the well-known method of trial and error. All these various stimuli re-echo; this auditory perception leads to another, either olfactory or kinetic, for instance, which may or may not be helpful. It makes corrections, changes direction, and progresses more and more quickly until it is finally successful.

It is difficult to understand the wanderings of Miche. Although it appears natural to us that she should have wanted to get home (I learned, by making enquiries, that she had been seen, and sheltered for a while here and there), why on earth had she gone to a place so far away, braving the thousand and one dangers of the center of Paris as she crossed the city?

I only understood this much later, when Conrad Lorenz showed that every creature starts its education and registers its experiences most deeply in the first days, even in the first hours, of life, because it is during this very fleeting period that the wax is still virgin, and that what is called the "myelinization of the cephalic neurons" takes place.

But where logic—our logic—fails, is in the case of a dog which has never made the journey between its old and its new home (if for instance it was taken in a train or a boat, and is sometimes separated from its old home by a very great distance), and in spite of all these difficulties it succeeds in finding its way back!

Let us give one example out of thousands. Monsieur Lechat, an auctioneer in Brest, relates that an old huntsman from Audierne died, leaving two setters neither of which had ever been out of the town and its immediate surroundings. The family decided to give one of these dogs to a friend who was in Brest, and it was sent in a boat from Audierne, arriving at Brest by sea. A few days later the dog escaped and, it was later learned, returned across country to Audierne,

The bitch is full of tenderness.　　　　　　　　　　　　　　　*The first steps.*

which is about 100 kilometers from Brest.

How does a dog manage to get back to its territory (or its master) in spite of so many obstacles, difficulties, such great distances? The fact that they do is proved by the amazing performances reported by reliable witnesses who are blinded neither by imagination nor by anthropomorphism.

This is still the dog's secret.

Jean Nourry has told of a strange observation which is of interest in this context. There was an old dog that used habitually to go to the next village which was very near to its own, taking a route that struck everyone as very strange. By chance the secretary at the town hall discovered that the dog was following exactly an old cross-country path, which in the course of time had become almost obliterated. It had been gradually eaten up by the riverside landowners, and only a few sections of it remained here and there, passing along the side of, or leading to, isolated fields; but the path the dog took corresponded with the path shown in the old cadastral survey dating from before the modern road, which itself dated from the time of Louis-Philippe (1830-1848). So it would seem that the dog was able to pick up the subtle emanations which still rose out of the ground, trampled for centuries, by thousands of animals and people.

This extraordinarily ability is even more astounding in view of the fact that the dog is not one of the animals which perform best when this ability is tested in the laboratory. It is only with difficulty that it comes sixth after the monkey, the dolphin, the rat, the cat, and even the pig. But, if we except the dolphin (for it lives in a different medium), there is hardly a cat, a monkey or a rat which is able to find its way home under similar circumstances!

Well then? We are forced to recognize that there is here some unknown factor. The difference between the psyche of the dog and our own is not one of degree (either more or less) but rather a difference of nature.

SEXUAL BEHAVIOR

Like all living creatures, the dog is influenced by the wonderful instinct of reproduction, through which endocrine activity makes the bitch available to the male, makes this female a mother who gives birth to pups, who in turn will obey the same instinct, without there being the least need for the agency of the intelligence.

Biologically, the physiology of the individual and the preservation of the species are sufficiently dominating instincts.

In the bitch, the sexual urge provoked by internal hormonal stimuli incites every normal adult female to seek the male and, at the same time, to flee from him. The congestive phenomena appear from the age of six to eight months. They last for about three weeks, with a period which is "favorable" to gestation between the eighth and the fifteenth day, according to the breed. At this time the bitch is rather nervous and her appetite is not good. The oedamatic vulva secretes a hemorrhagic fluid which decreases as the region returns to its normal volume and appearance.

In the male dog there is almost no sexual display, little or no simulated combat nor serious conflict between the stud dogs. As soon as the female "emits," this odor attracts the male. For bitches who are at large, there follows a frantic flight from an excited pack of suitors of all ages and sizes. They will follow her for hours on end, without thought of food or rest; the boldest are quick to try their luck as soon as the bitch stops running to get her breath back. Finally, the lady makes her choice, or simply submits to the law of the least tired, the most ardent, or the nearest, and as in many animals, the mating takes place as the bitch is mounted. There is however one detail which should be noted; because of a special anatomical peculiarity of the male organ, when copulation is completed the mating sometimes goes on for up to thirty or forty minutes, when the male is the prisoner of the female and can only

Cleaning the new-born pup.   *One month later.*

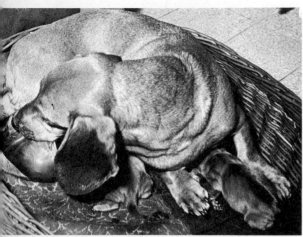

ATLAS PHOTO – KURT KLEIN

ATLAS PHOTO – KURT KLEIN

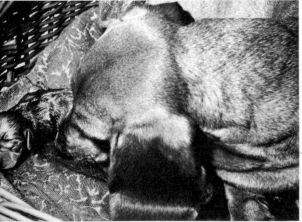

ATLAS PHOTO – KURT KLEIN

escape from her by tearing himself away painfully.

What is the reason for this mysterious "trapping," by which the mates, their ardor appeased, wait with comic resignation for their sweet embrace to come to an end?

Hardly any scientific observations have been carried out on the subject of this strange mating which is peculiar to the canine race; and it would be very risky to put forward any explanation as final. Besides, in the face of the life process which ends in a position that one must at least admit is strange, one can only wonder, with Conard Lorenz, "What use does this fulfil?"

THE MATERNAL INSTINCT

There is nothing out of the ordinary about the gestation, which lasts a little longer than two months (63 days, on average). At the end of this time appear the signs of approaching birth. Then the bitch—without trying to hide away any more than she hid when she abandoned herself to the embrace of the male—scratches the ground, and accomplishes quite well, and wherever she can, the very elementary birth during which her young come into the world. Some delicate and cosseted bitches accept the basket full of rags or straw provided for them, and settle down gratefully in it. From then on this place will become the center of the "territory" where for two months she will clean, lick, suckle, and defend her pups, and finally wean them.

The male usually remains aloof from all this. Used for thousands of years to count on humans for their livelihood, male dogs have gradually become estranged from the obligations of family life. So the females look after their offspring alone.

But it does sometimes happen that the male, under the influence of the paternal instinct, shows some interest in his young, and an unexpected liking for them, especially when they are very young.

A superb Irish Setter was walking along the banks of the river Paillon in Nice one day with his mistress. He suddenly jumped into the river and came back carrying in his mouth a puppy that was at the most a few hours old, deaf and blind, as they are during the first twelve days of their lives. He dropped his fragile burden at his mistress's feet, went off again, threw himself once more into the water and returned with two more new-born pups in very bad shape, who only lived for a few minutes. The lady, upset, went home; her dog followed her carrying the first, living, puppy carefully in its mouth. When he got home, the Setter climbed the three flights of stairs, laid the puppy on the floor, picked it up again as soon as the door was opened, and having settled it in his basket, lay down around it and began to lick it to remove all the mud. The most surprising thing about the whole story is that for two whole months the surprising savior of the puppy showed himself a nurse jealous of everyone, except his mistress, who dared come near the puppy. The lady was touched, and accepted this new Moses, fed it with a bottle, and brought it up to be a large, fine, and good dog.

But let us return to the behavior of the bitch who is suckling her young.

Under normal conditions, weaning takes place after approximately seven or eight weeks, when the intensity of the endocrine stimuli diminishes, causing a rapid lessening in the production of milk. Everything that would tempt the little pup to prolong its baby life (brutal sucking, impatient kicks from the little feet) becomes painful for the mother and she becomes more and more detached from her offspring. She gradually abandons her puppies, whom before she would have defended furiously and whom she used to lick over and over again with a sort of frenzy. In fact even the weakest of bitches is capable of courage and sacrifice in the protection of her puppies, as witness the Fox Terrier bitch who in the course of one night brought back her three new-born pups, one at a time, from Paris to Versailles, to return them to the "territory" from which they had been removed. In all a journey of more than 120 kilometers!

Many authors have thought it proper to call such behavior virtuous. Actually, one should see in it only what Jean Rostand calls an "integral of reflexes." This phenomenon is easily set in motion in any female mammal by the action of a series of hormonal injections alone, or by a graft. Only woman is able to purify this instinct and to be animated by the true sentiment of maternal love. Of course, if one removes two of the pups from a bitch's litter, she will be anxious, become agitated, and show all the signs of confusion; but one has only to place at least the same number of foster-children in her box, and even if they are strangers, and of a different breed, she will immediately accept them as her own.

When the suckling is over, if the human family does not intervene to provide the pups with a new form of food, the most domesticated of bitches will behave in exactly the same way as all other carnivorous females do; she will eat far more food than she needs and will bring it up during the next half hour. Thus the pups eat partly digested food, and less than a week later they are able to feed themselves like adults. From then on, the indifference the mother shows them only bcomes more marked from day to day. The pups grow and develop. In six to eight months they attain sexual maturity which shows itself in the females by the first manifestations of the oestrus, and in the males by the stance they acquire at this time when they "lift their legs" to urinate. Let us note that a castrated dog of any age immediately loses this characteristic stance, but that it is possible to make it reappear by injections of testosterone, though naturally this does not entail a reawakening of the sexual instinct.

The cycle is now complete. Maternal behavior disappears entirely, and the mother, who retains not the slightest memory of it, regains her peace of mind.

REUTERPHOTO

12 PSYCHOLOGY

*"The love of a dog for its
master will one day
no doubt be a 'scientific fact,'
amenable to the same
objective tests as is study
of the laying of eggs in the insect."
(J. Lecomte.)*

Domestication has brought about no changes in either the reindeer, the horse, or the ass. Has it had any effect on the instincts of the primitive dog, to the point of modifying its psyche?

At this point difficulties and scruples arise, if one wishes both to respect the scientific basis of modern animal psychology, and to interest the most "reasonable" of animal-lovers in this discipline.

DOMESTICATION AND PSYCHOLOGY

Of all animals, the dog is indisputably the one that has most easily adapted itself to life in a human environment. The results of this have been of fundamental importance. The dog has not only become used to the presence of man, but it has also bowed before this dominating creature who has liberated its life from all disagreeable or dangerous surprise, and indirectly ensured its supply of food.

From the time when man finally became sedentary, the consequences of this adaptation became even more striking—the dog ceased to be a wanderer. Its protected life was prolonged much longer than that of so many other animals whom the biological law obliges to become isolated from their community, or to die, as soon as they are no longer able to be useful or to do battle successfully.

What words could one use to convey that slow, very slow, process whereby, over the ages, dogs ceased living only "among dogs"?

Of course, the primitive instincts have not entirely disappeared; but from that time on the *canis familiaris* led a life quite different from that of its paleolithic ancestors. Exterior conditions had changed, so the relative importance of instinct had also to evolve.

The direction taken by this evolution was towards a reciprocal affection between man and dog; man loving the dog in his human way, dog becoming fond of man in its own dog-like manner. This development of the

affections is explained by the fact that the dog was domesticated not only by means of coercion, rewards, and punishment, as was the case with the other animals that man has "conquered." This communion of affection was brought about largely by the sharing of food and shelter. This resulted, as H. Pieron says, "in an affectionate and intelligent cooperation through which the dog has become truly integrated into human society."

Nowadays scholars try to discover, by means of laboratory experiments carried out on dogs that are given their liberty, the instinctive activities and potential intelligence of the dog beneath the layers of knowledge it has acquired from domestication and training.

THE UNDERSTANDING OF RELATIONSHIPS AS REVEALED BY EXPERIMENTS

The classical experiments are based on the "mechanical box." They have shown how the dog reacts when confronted by a problem depending for its solution on an understanding of causal relationships, and some "maze" experiments have shown its aptitude for spatial relationships.

If it is simply a question of opening a door, the subject, after a few groping attempts, suddenly discovers the solution (it is true that many dogs instinctively push the handle to open a door!), but more complete series of experiments have shown that the dog is capable of "comprehending" the situation to some extent.

"If a dog which is used to moving around inside houses is shut into a case," says J. C. Filloux, "and the case taken up to the first floor of an unknown house, and if the dog is then set free, at the call of his master, whom the dog can see below (through a window), the dog will leave the room, go down the stair and out of the door."

You can also train a dog to go back to its

The French Bulldog is becoming very rare.

Waiting for happier days.

basket in a room when it is told to do so. Then one day when you are both several hundred yards away from home, order it in a commanding tone. "To your basket." Your dog will certainly obey you. It will cover the distance very quickly and without stopping, even if it has to climb several flights of stairs.

In both these cases there intervenes what is called the comprehension of spatial relationships and the combination of isolated experiences.

HAS THE DOG ANY SENSE OF TIME?

In an attempt to answer this question, Hunter, with the aid of a piece of apparatus called a "temporal labyrinth," reproduced in the laboratory situations in which the apprehension of a rhythm was necessary to the finding of the solution.

In fact it is amazing with what precision a dog, used to receiving scraps of food at a given time (for instance at the door of a restaurant), will arrive at that place punctually, almost to the minute. Experimental studies have shown that this has nothing to do with a notion of time, but is the result of a simple "biological rhythm" bound up with the association of ideas.

In this context there springs to mind a spaniel we once knew, which was left during the week by its master in a boarding kennel. The master used to come and fetch it every Saturday at mid-day to take it hunting. The dog behaved perfectly normally all through the week; but come Saturday, from 11:30 on, it would not keep still; it jumped around, barked and refused to touch the food left out at 11 o'clock. It was obvious that it could think of nothing except the arrival of its master. Was it conscious that seven days had elapsed, and could it deduce from that fact that it was nearly time for it to go off hunting? Certainly not. It would be more realistic to believe that a few unaccustomed details (the telephone ringing, some show of

HOLMÈS-LEBEL/CAMERA PRESS — BILL BRIDGES

zeal on the part of the kennel-hand, a meaningful accoustic or olfactory stimulus) were responsible for this happy expectation. The rest was a chain of associated ideas. This was nothing more than a conditioned reflex.

THE DOG'S MEMORY

One must make a distinction between the associative memory and the so-called true memory of the dog. According to the work of Hunter and Maier, the true memory, i.e. the capacity of the dog to "remember," is of short duration (a few hours at the most), without one being able to speak of a "representative" memory.

In the absence of any exterior stimulus, or sense signal, no dog is able to evoke a memory; no dog in fact is able to think, "Where is my master right now?" But if at any time of the day or night, it hears its master's voice or step, perceives and recognizes his smell, or spies in the distance his silhouette, there will be an immediate passionate outburst, the sign of a real emotional state linked to its associative memory, whose existence is indisputable.

There are cases in which this associative memory never ceases to confound us.

Some time ago, while I was staying abroad, I struck up a friendship with the little Pekingese of a family I knew. When I left, I gave him a little rubber toy (which I afterwards learned he never set great store by). Time passed. Then chance took me once more to that country and that town, and I thought I would go and give my friends a surprise. A few minutes later, I learned all the details of the following little scene. Hardly had my taxi turned the corner of the road than the dog (who was snoozing quietly in its basket), jumped up, wide awake. It immediately rushed into the kitchen, hastily grabbed hold of the toy I had once given it, and joyfully ran towards the door, the door at which, as I was not expected, I was only to ring a quarter of an hour later. The fuss

*Man is the dog's
"perfect leader."*

this lap dog made on seeing me was as nothing compared to the surprise of the people who were watching this scene.

Let us try to unravel the mystery a little. What was the trigger, the secret warning that had been able to cause such excitement in a dog I hardly knew? A whiff of odor? Through the walls, doors, corridors of an apartment situated on the fifth floor of a large building? This is hardly probable. Something which affected the sense of sight, of touch, or of taste? In a case like this, three senses seem to be eliminated. There only remains the sense of hearing. Fair enough. But the auditory perception *of what?* Of the anonymous taxi which was bringing me? Such a possibility is not worth examining. Is this then a case of some other kind of stimulus? An unusual gesture of the lady of the house which might indirectly have been enough to set in motion the association of ideas? A book which I had at some time touched? A word, a name associated with my memory? I really do not know!

"We were certainly not thinking about you!" the dog's masters assured me. "We were astonished to see Tang wake up suddenly and go and fetch, out of that corner, that old toy which he has almost never played with. . . ."

Well then? We must admit humbly that we are still looking for the rational explanation of this mystery.

THE DOG, MAN'S FRIEND

In trying to discover what constitutes the fondness a dog bears its master, we must be especially careful, and avoid any transference from our conscious life to that of the dog—that is, we must not bestow human feelings on dogs.

Among all the superior social animals the hierarchy, once established, is as a rule accepted. None of the "dominated" animals would feel any desire (or more precisely,

Does the dog experience real suffering?

The "string" test.

the instinctive propulsion) to set himself against the "dominant" animal unless the latter had manifestly given proof of his weakness.

The dog observes this law of the pack, of the flock, out of instinctive necessity. In its relationship with man, the latter is the perfect dominant. This state of obedience has lasted for thousands of years, so it is natural that the human family, the human clan, has become the dog's ideal pack, the privileged place where it knows security and tranquility. It is on this that the mental poise of the happy dog depends. When, for any reason at all, this euphoric environment is upset (by the unaccustomed, the absence of the master, by quarrelling between the loved ones, and, *a fortiori,* by scolding and corporal punishment), the dog immediately loses this poise.

"He's so unhappy," we sometimes think to ourselves.

But can the dog really feel unhappy? Also, is it able to take a part in our sorrows, to "suffer" affectively, in the "sentimental" meaning of the word?

It is very difficult to find a reply to this delicate question.

Here for example are two facts of everyday observation: All dogs are greatly upset by a quarrel in the household, sometimes even by a fit of the sulks between their master and mistress; all dogs are shocked and disconcerted by punishment. At times like these we are touched by their obvious efforts to escape from this painful tension. They hold out their paw to us with an anguished look; and we draw the conclusion from this that they want, in the first case, "to console us," and in the second, "to beg pardon."

No doubt the reality is simpler. A dog is absolutely incapable of understanding the real reasons for our moods. It only knows of our problem because when we are angry, for instance, our cutaneous acidity is modified, and consequently so is our odor. At other times our shouts and insults reach such an unusual pitch that they intrude upon its

peace of mind. And it is precisely because it does not understand that the dog is much more perturbed than we ourselves are, and that it instinctively tries to regain its lost tranquility.

The same thing applies to the dog's joy.

Still in the psychic sense of the word, animal joy and human joy are not on the same level. The (apparent) gaiety of the dog is an unleashing, a more or less brutal liberation, a kind of psychic unraveling; but, as Jean C. Filloux thinks, it cannot be "the intoxication, the euphoria, which allows us to transcend the human condition itself."

As these two sorts of state, one emotional and the other affective, are well differentiated, it would not be anthropomorphic to think that the emotiveness of the dog is always the result of being far removed from its home and the absence of the people to whom it is attached. In this way we could explain the very characteristic state of anguish of the lost dog.

Is the dog that is put into a boarding kennel not also a (relatively) lost dog? Veterinary surgeons are well aware of this, and they ask the owner of the hospitalized dog (whether it be wounded or ill) to take it home again as soon as its health no longer requires constant care, as soon as its convalescence has begun.

The canine practitioner and his staff know that while the sick dog is in the clinic, it must become familiarized with its surroundings before it will accept any form of treatment (taking of temperature, dressings, administration of medicines, etc.), and also to give it a good chance of being cured. In the medical treatment of farm and stable animals, of course, such details are of secondary importance, but in the case of pet animals it is of the utmost importance that the shock of separation and being taken away from its "territory" is reduced to the minimum.

Under the circumstances, moreover, there is nothing to be gained by haste. The process of familiarization will never be accom-

"In front of some netting which separates it from an appetizing dish."

plished within the first few hours, however great may be the "human contact" (soothing words, titbits, and even caresses). The absence of the dog's master, the unaccustomed surroundings, the presence of strangers—all this in fact creates at first in the dog that is hospitalized or boarded out a more or less hostile, guarded attitude. On the other hand, the situation is reversed eight or ten hours later. The emotional tension is relaxed. From then on the dog needs to cease feeling alone and abandoned, and wants to be helped. So it is ready to integrate socially (or, as we would say were we talking of men, ready to make friends).

This explains how it is that dogs can accept a new master with equal devotion. Among the higher animals the dog is undoubtedly the best able to inhibit its innate reactions. It is overcome with fright if it no longer has a "leader of the pack," no longer has any friends. If it loses its master, it needs a new one. In the example of the clinic which we have just given, the remedy which ought to be applied to this "neurotic" beginning is that only someone whom the dog has neither seen, heard nor smelled, should come into contact with the dog for about ten hours after its arrival. In fact the presence of any other person who was present at its arrival can only serve, by association of ideas, to renew the emotional state of the first hours.

THE INTELLIGENCE OF THE DOG, AS COMPARED TO THAT OF THE CAT, THE RAT AND THE PARROT

Can one talk of intelligence, when it is only a case of adapting to a situation, to an environment? This is a process of learning by experience, of conditioning, with no recourse to intellectual activity. An intelligent act only occurs when the subject proposes an act which is not directly governed by its natural impulses and instincts, but whose consequences it foresees in advance.

The methods used in the study of the in-telligent actions of the dog are the same as those used with all other animals in experiments.

The most elementary problem is that of the "maze," to arrive at whose solution the subject must get around such and such an obstacle to arrive at the desired or hoped-for reward. A dog placed in front of a grill separating it from an appetizing and visible meal does not hesitate; it goes around it, while other animals only succeed in finding this solution after some time, and then always by chance.

In a further test, the problem is more complicated. This time the subject must make use of an intermediary object in order to attain the same end. The subject is shut into a cage, a string is attached to an inaccessible titbit and left within reach of the animal (if necessary the string may have a ring at its end to facilitate grasping).

A cat, a parrot, and a rat pull the string to get the titbit.

According to P. Guillaume and his assistants, the dog is altogether incapable of working out this link. On the other hand, the cat understands perfectly the function of this "intermediary-string"; if the string is placed diagonally in relation to the titbit, the cat positions itself opposite the handle or at the end of the string, and not opposite the food!

Is the dog then the intellectual inferior of so many other animals? No. And here we will quote *in extenso* the very words of the great Russian physiologist to whom we owe the discovery of the conditioned reflex.

Pavlov, whom no one could suspect of anthropomorphic tendencies, noted particularly the intelligence of the dog used in experiments. In this case the dog was a cross-bred Fox Terrier, that had a gastric fistula, as a result of which there was a constant irritation of the skin caused by the digestive juices which, as they flowed, soiled the exterior skin.

"It began," said Pavlov, "to feel the ulcerating effect of the gastric juices two weeks after the operation. One morning, to our great annoyance, we found beside the animal, which was tied to its leash and in general very well behaved, a whole pile of plaster which it had scratched off the wall. We tied the dog up in another place; the next morning we found the same thing. For the second time, one of the projections in the wall of our laboratory had been demolished. At the same time, we noticed that the animal's belly was dry and the marks of irritation on the skin were less marked. In the end we guessed what it was all about; the dog had discovered a means of stopping the irritation and in fact, of curing itself! Its intelligence had helped not only itself, but had shown us the way to a new method of treatment. In fact, we made the dog a bed of sand, that is, a porous bed (one can

163

*There is no safer
companion for a child
than a dog.*

also use lime), and from then on it stopped demolishing the wall, and at the same time the gastric juices, absorbed by the porous substance, stopped irritating the wound."

In contrast to this undeniably "intelligent" action, whereby the dog showed indisputably that it was able on its own to make use of substances for a desired end, here is the astonishing result of an experiment in comparative psychology which is called the Adams Test.

Adams trained some cats to pull lightweight but rigid boxes by means of a string attached to one end. Then he put a piece of liver quite high up on a shelf so that the cats could only get to it by jumping. To make the jump easier he put, not far away, a box which could be pulled along by the usual string.

"After a minute," wrote Adams, "the cat (this was the most cunning of the selected cats) stopped and stayed still for four or five seconds, in the attitude of a cat that is stalking something. Holding one of its back

legs out horizontally, it was ready to spring, and all this while, it gazed fixedly at the liver. At the end of this immobile phase, the cat suddenly stood up on its four legs, ran to the box and made obvious efforts to get at the coveted morsel. After several vain attempts, the cat sat down and began to look alternatively from the liver to the box on which it was sitting. Then suddenly it climbed down from the box, seized the string, pulled the box right under the liver, over a distance of more than 12 inches . . . and climbing quickly onto the box, seized the liver."

No one would deny that this cat had shown proof of intelligence in finding the solution, not by trial and error, or by groping attempts, but by reasoning.

The same experiment has been carried out with several dogs. We all know that dogs are much more skillful than cats at pulling a string to drag along a box. None of the dogs, however, found the means of success, or even tried; they all just barked.

They barked, because the dog has an instinctive impulse to bark in the face of the unaccustomed. For example, in front of a closed door which they do not know how to open, dogs will bark. People who do not know any better say that they are barking "so that someone will open the door for them." "This is a mistake, says Revesz, "the dog that scratches at a door and asks someone present in the room to help by turning towards him, is instancing what is called an attitude "of the utilization of means." In short, it does not bark in the hope that someone will open the door for it, but because it is shut in.

DOGS AND CHILDREN

In any case, is this not what happens with a very small child, just as incapable as a dog of abstract thought? An infant starts to cry as soon as his mother wants to put him back in his cradle, but these cries do not mean "I don't want you to go away!" They can be translated as meaning, quite simply, that it is less agreeable to be left all alone than to be nestling in mother's soft lap.

The dog acts like this all its life. One can never repeat too often that in spite of its strength, its teeth, and the wealth of its sensual perceptions, the dog is an eternal child.

Perhaps it is in this resemblance that there lies the secret of the tacit accord which springs up between dogs and small children, and of the disarming confidence that the latter place in the most fearful-looking and largest dogs.

A strange American theory has been put forward that this sympathy (and especially that of the dog towards very young children) has something to do with chemistry. The organic make-up of very young children—in French they are said to "smell like chickens"—is richer in potassium and magnesium than that of adults. It would seem that the same is true of young animals. Hence this attitude of parental indulgence, of common games, which we always interpret from our own ethical point of view. "The dog is better than the man," "There are no ill-treated children among animals," etc.)

There are numerous examples of surprising behavior in dogs of uncertain temper who will accept anything at the hands of any little scallywag who cares to pull their ears, shove little fingers into their mouths or eyes, etc. Is this also the explanation of the strange mysterious instinct which causes so many dogs to save careless children and those in danger?

At L'Horne (Loire) a Bouvier de Flandre was walking along the side of the highway with its little mistress. Suddenly, the little girl walked forward onto the road just at the moment when the Saint-Etienne-Lyons bus arrived at great speed. In a tenth of a second, the dog had leaped, risen on its hind legs, and pushed the child with all its strength out of the way of the vehicle.

If there is an element of affection in the bond between a dog and its master, this is even more true of the bond which exists between a dog and a child.

One morning, in the Landes, a dog belonging to a Monsieur André Saubourguet disappeared. Three days later, it made an astonishing entry into a school at Bayonne (50 miles away). It wanted to rejoin a child of the Saubourguet family who had been a boarder at the school for a week.

One could mention hundreds of similar cases. To what should they be attributed? To an innate instinct to protect the young? Certainly. But also perhaps to some possible means of communication which defies our understanding . . . to the fact that the child and the animal can communicate with each other because they live in a different world, a world into which we adults, in spite and perhaps because of our intelligence, cannot enter.

In any case, there is no more safe and appropriate companion for a child than a dog. There is no domestic animal (trained or not) which has more hereditary aptitude for being a child's playmate and defender.

As far back as one can go in the history of man, it is true that children and dogs have always had this common link—they play. They play together. The horse, the cat, and the bird and all the other animals are more or less tolerant, and more or less submissive, but they all remain passive. They are only "toys." But the dog enters into the game. It gets excited, pretends, participates. It is not a toy, it is a partner. It is "the player and the game."

However, as soon as the child gets bigger, begins to be harsh and hypocritical, as soon as he tries to establish his supremacy over the animal, the behavior of the dog changes. Why? How? We do not know, but it will no longer tolerate from the child what it put up with from the infant. Just as nursing bitches of the heavier breeds (Briards, Great Danes, etc.), when their pups scratch them, pull too violently on their teats, or are strong enough to show signs of aggressive-

SALLY ANNE THOMPSON

They are free?
The invitation to play.

ness, say to the growing children, "Careful! You are going too far," by means of the warning growl or the harmless snap.

Of course, there is no moral significance in these growls, these changes of mood. It is only our interpretation of them by analogy with our own behavior that gives them this qualification. But children are never misled.

Without a doubt, this communication that they have with the dog, on a strictly instinctive plane, gives them a better understanding of the mystery of the dog than we can ever achieve.

How is it that there are no accidents between dogs and children? They happen very rarely indeed. Yet does it not sometimes happen that underfed or sick bitches wound or kill their own young?

THE BEHAVIOR OF DOGS
WITH OTHER DOGS

Although laboratory tests are scientifically indispensable, the observation of dogs in everyday life is no less necessary. Certainly, it leads to some controversial interpretations, but because of the original insights it brings, it can only serve to broaden our knowledge of canine psychology.

Caught up in human life, two dogs come across one another. At once their curiosity and anxiety are awakened. If they are on leashes, and so tied to a "territory," they utter the furious barks of combat, and the more restrained and tied they feel at the end of their leashes, the more aggressive will be their reactions.

But if they are free, their behavior will be quite different. There will be a rapid interrogation, impartial observation, olfactory contact, the tails will wag and almost always there will follow an invitation to play, a form of pretended combat.

Animal psychologists refuse to see, in such emotional states, anything more than instinctive, spontaneous acts which follow one another (confirming or annulling them-

selves) and which can be replaced by others, according to the reaction of the adversary. If however, one seeks a clear understanding of the matter, it is helpful to follow the example of the school of Lorenz, and while not being content just to "note" what happens, not to draw any conclusions either.

In particular, it is impossible to explain the differences of behavior occurring in dogs of different breeds without recognizing that these instincts bear the psychic imprint of distant forebears.

Greyhounds alone seem to be imperturbable. They are all very highly strung. But their hypersensitivity is not expressed in barking or unseemly aggression. Their hearts begin to beat a little faster, their breathing is accelerated. In Greyhounds there is often a noticeable perspiration of the toes and a sudden rhinitis which are of neuro-sympathetic origin. One of our dogs, a racing Greyhound, displayed a strange symptom. Every time it got into the car to go to the racetrack (and only on those days) its nose ran continuously, drop after drop, while there was not the least muscular tremble, the least change in its behavior, to otherwise betray its emotion.

Dogs of the mastiff type, and especially the large mountain dogs, are usually good, placid, patient, affectionate creatures. Great Danes, because they have Greyhound blood, are much more timid than one would imagine. Mastiffs and Bulldogs are very rarely bad-tempered, and the proverbial good nature of the Old English Sheepdog, the Newfoundland, and the Briard are well known. With a few exceptions, hunting dogs are also placid. In fact it is among the hounds and their descendants, Braques and Griffons, that one most often finds dogs completely dependent on man, because atavistically they feel the need of the pack from which they feel isolated.

The Wolf-type dogs (sled dogs, Chow Chows, Finnish Spitz, etc.) have more personality. I hesitate to speak here of loyalty, pride, and courage, but if these are qualities

that do not belong exclusively to man, no one could deny that these dogs possess them.

To get nearer to the heart of the problem, we must go back to the two great ancestors, the jackal and the wolf, whose racial characteristics are so different. The more or less latent psyche of one or the other is to be found in all dogs according to their breed. To return to the case of the two dogs that chance brings face to face with one another, that are drawn together by a common social instinct. Are they friends or enemies? There is an immediate opposition or attraction between them. "Wolves do not eat each other," says the French proverb. Dogs that have a fair proportion of wolf blood in their veins will rarely fight each other; but they are always ready to fight the others, and preferably those that have remained fairly jackal-like.

Examples? They crop up every day. You have only to see a Chow Chow in the street, indifferent to everything except its master, from whom it rarely strays far. It will not even look at the Poodle that crosses its path, nor at the Alsatian that is coming towards it. But as soon as another Chow Chow appears on the scene, its ears point forward, it leans squarely on its fore-legs, with its feet well apart and its eyes shining —the Chow Chow (which is descended from the wolf) has eyes only for its fellow Chow, as if it were finding a long lost friend!

This frequently happens with a few old breeds, Dachshunds, Greyhounds, and all the varieties of Spitz. I am emphasizing this phenomenon to underline the extent to which some of our dogs' reactions, which to us seem incoherent, can be bound up with their confused origins; hence the unconscious conflicts which move them and which are so difficult to explain.

The Chow Chow, more than any other breed, is a good illustration of this peculiarity of the species. The Chow Chow comes from northern China where the monks and

*Behavior that we would be tempted
to call "brotherly."*

the merchants of Manchuria have used it to pull their sleds to the towns of central China. But "chow-chow" means food. The Chow is still, to this day, looked upon in the Far East as "butcher meat." In the course of long journeys through the wind and snow they have in fact very often provided the dinner. If they arrived at their destination without trouble their masters would take off their harnesses and give them their liberty without another thought for what would become of them! And during the following days, these half wild dogs, to feed themselves, would have to fight with the packs of mongrels of the great towns, over the garbage and refuse. Centuries spent in this way, fighting (sometimes ten to one) with dogs of all sorts of mixed blood, have made the Chow Chow (the "Hong Kong dog" as it is sometimes called) a ferocious wolf.

We have tried throughout this study to concentrate as much as possible on the real behavior of the dog, foregoing any idealization. This is certainly the best way to get to know and love the dog, as it really is, and not in so far as it conforms to some fantasy born of our imagination.

In the same spirit, let us now consider what there is in the behavior of the dog that we might be tempted to call "fraternity," or "charity."

For example, two dogs sometimes get together to hunt. It is not a case of the dog having any conception of solidarity, but that its partner is to him a means, a help in the accomplishment of the desired end of finding food.

"The characteristic manifestation of partnership does not extend to the comprehension of the fact that it is possible to create collective forms of action," says Filloux, who adds, "Perhaps this is one reason for the stagnation of animal societies and of animal life in general."

Yet is there not some other factor at work in a situation like this: A dog that had been run over by a car dragged itself to the side of the road to get out of the way of other vehicles. A second dog came to join it, and stayed beside it all night.

This is what led Hediger to speak of a "tendency to assimilate with the other," for apart from the fact that one cannot see how the wounded dog could have solicited "the instrumental value" of its partner, no more can one see what "self-interest" the dog that was not wounded might have been obeying.

Certainly we would agree that a dog is incapable of grasping the "idea" of altruism, but is it not just as disturbing as mysterious that a dog can throw itself into the water to save a child, and can equally well save, or help to save, another dog?

13 PSYCHIATRY

The type of behavior we have been discussing up to now, difficult though it may be to confine within scientific terminology, nevertheless conforms to the normal. It is not "anomalous." It does not reveal any of the peculiarities of character, aberrations of instinct, neuroses, or psychoses which have only been studied in the animal during the last half century at the most.

Yet it was inevitable that the dog, more than any other domestic animal, should have been exposed to psychic disorders, just because of the close tie that has for centuries bound it to man. We have not only assumed the right to control the feeding, the liberty, and the reproduction of the dog, but we have also made it the slave of our requirements, our needs, and our whims, by adapting its instincts and, if need be, modifying them in order to make use of the dog in all sorts of different ways. Even worse, through selfishness or because we are blinded by the affection we bear it, we protect the dog (sometimes unreasonably) from illness and death, even to the extent of preserving sires that are neuropsychologically unsound. The hereditary consequences of this are that their descendants are really unstable.

So it is easy to understand that the dog has a great, but painful, contribution to make to animal psychology. This is a very young science, and in this book we can only hope to make a very incomplete survey of it, but it seems important to us to set down the essentials so that this attempt at unravelling the mystery of our reciprocal affection may serve to make the dog as well understood as it is loved.

ANOMALOUS BEHAVIOR

Instinctual disorders are as frequent as they are varied. In some cases they affect the behavior to such an extent that it becomes extremely difficult to clarify the puzzling phenomena.

These disorders can show themselves by sense aberrations, of the hearing, touch, taste, etc. In the case of the pica (scavenger), for example, the best fed of dogs will throw itself on refuse and garbage, without there being any discernable dietary deficiency.

Sometimes there are recorded cases of disorders provoked by emotional factors. This happens in the case of a racing Greyhound which trembles like a woman. One has only to raise one's voice to scold it, and this is enough to activate a sudden bulimia, by the action of substitution.

Other disorders occur in dogs one would describe as independent and fond of their liberty, when they are in fact the victims of the fugue state, an equivalent of epilepsy. This disorder can take on different forms. For ten years we had a Wire-haired Fox Terrier; it was the calmest of dogs, and as long as it was held on its leash, it seemed to be perfectly well balanced. But as soon as the snap-fastener was released it would rush straight ahead, no matter where it was, absolutely deaf to our cries, and only stopped several miles away, out of breath, sobered and calmed. It would then become once more the gentle obedient dog we loved.

One of our famous friends, the great writer André Billy, also has a little chestnut Spaniel that is loving and faithful to him, but whose behavior is a problem too. To go out in the car for a walk in the forest induces in this dog something like drunkenness. Whatever the time and whatever the place, the same strange performance repeats itself each time. No sooner is the car door opened than the little Spaniel jumps onto the ground, yaps a few times and literally dashes backwards like a streak of lightning, in exactly the opposite direction to that the car has just taken, only to stop 300 yards away. It will only come back if one pretends to start the motor, to shut the doors, and go off without it. This stereotyped performance is repeated every time the dog gets out of the car and is set at liberty. Does

"There are no wicked dogs . . .

*. . . only disturbed dogs
whose natural aggression is
exacerbated."*

it want to assure itself of its retreat? Whatever the truth may be, it seems that such an
irresistable psychomotor impulse should be
put down to hysterical epilepsy.

DOGS ARE NEVER "WICKED"

We are no less in the dark when it comes
to interpreting the psychic disorders in
which are found—with no anatomical substratum—a disturbance of the defensive instinct.

Canine aggression is not an anomaly. It
is a natural phenomenon. Characteristic of
carnivores in general, it should however
have its limits, otherwise it endangers the
status of the dog as a domestic animal.
Education, apprenticeship, and training have
helped to fix these limits. If this natural
aggression is too marked, it irritates us and
we are quick to pronounce, wrongly, that
these dogs are wicked, stupid, or cruel.

There are no wicked dogs. There are
disturbed dogs, dogs which, for different
reasons, are constantly in a state of insecurity. These dogs have an obvious propensity
to bite, so much so that they become in
our eyes anti-social. Such dogs are half mad,
for it seems that their behavior can only be
explained by an internal disturbance of their
"consciousness" (as dogs). In this context,
it is important to know that it is around the
age of one and a half to two months that
the pup begins to adjust itself to its life as a
domestic dog. If it is not well adjusted, it
may become abnormally aggressive, but a
well-directed course of treatment ought to
cure this.

On the other hand there are the dogs,
equally stricken pathologically, that are too
submissive, depressed, and fearful. We ought
to try to improve their lot, without feeling
authorized to judge their responsibility or
penalize their cowardice.

This quite frequent type of anomaly is
sometimes linked to what science calls a
"long-standing disorganization of the spon-

The best way to get bitten is to take flight!

Some dogs break off the fight when they are attacked.

taneous reactions." This is true in the case of dogs that bite because they have been too spoiled and too well loved, as they have never experienced anxiety. More than any other dogs, they are led to risk challenging once again man's domination over them. This is also true of lethargic dogs, which are scolded all day long, corrected for every little misdemeanor and consequently remain stupid, relegated forever to the bottom rank in the pack.

The way to train a dog to be well adjusted and well behaved is to use neither cruelty nor ragging. The way to do it is to make it a happy dog.

This is not always easy. Psychic disorders of the aggressive instinct can in fact appear at any age, without there having been any ill-adjustment, as the following observation shows. Was this an affective conflict, or a real psychosis caused by amnesia? Who can tell?

This is a true story of what happened to a dog and a child who loved one another and lived in the same family.

Pierrot, the child, was seven years old. "Eva," the bitch, was eight. She was a mastiff, and unusually powerful. They were inseparable. The protective fury of the animal was instantly unleashed by the slightest unfriendly gesture or the approach of any strange person. Holiday time arrived. Madame E——, the grandmother, took Pierrot into the country in the neighboring province. Eva, of course, went along too; but the day after they arrived at the villa an unfortunate thing happened. Chasing a cat which had ventured into the garden, Eva bounded forward and out of the open gate just as a car was passing. She was bowled over, but got up without being hurt, howling with fear. But instead of coming into the house to her little master who was calling her, she ran as fast as she could along the road and disappeared. No one was able to find her for a whole week. Such a large dog cannot go unseen for very long. Two days later, the dog was seen wandering in the

mountains about 15 miles way. Madame E—— immediately went there with the child, who was full of hope. But for three days a countryman and the impatient child scoured the district in vain, calling the dog. Two weeks passed thus, then suddenly there was a new alert; Eva had returned to the villa's surroundings. She was in the neighboring field. Everyone ran out there. Gently, the child walked towards her and spoke to her, his heart beating furiously. The dog stared at him for a long time, but retreated a few steps at the least tentative approach. Then, as Madame E——intervened, the enormous mastiff, jumped backwards frightened, and fled. She was never seen again.

Was this amnesia? Or a trauma of a punitive nature caused by the car (the dog chased the cat and gone through the gate, betraying its role as the child's guardian)? Was the "punitive" nature of the accident enough to make it impossible for the dog to

accept another (in her eyes possible) punishment of the same sort, and to make her want to escape from this by any means— even though she was influenced by what had been, until then, her whole life, and by her parental instinct for the child, and at the same time held back, inhibited by the searing memory of the car looming up just when she was at fault? It would at any rate seem logical to eliminate a profound traumatic lesion. Eva was still in perfect health after the accident and, from all the evidence, she tried to return and roam around the house. The psychiatric aspect of a case like this appears to be indisputable. Its true nature remains nevertheless inexplicable.

FEAR: THE ROUTING OF INSTINCT

Fear, which, as Bancels has emphasized, is

*Some bitches,
if they are deprived of their young,
will blindly adopt
any step-children.*

more than any other dynamic response or motor inhibition "a routing of instinct," is frequently observed in dogs. The speed of modern life is too great. Dogs have not all become sufficiently "civilized" to be able to remain indifferent to the many forms of the unaccustomed or the unexpected, especially if they have been ill-prepared for social adaptation towards their fellows or towards humans.

Fear is expressed differently by different individuals and different breeds. The Wirehaired Fox Terrier takes flight wildly; the Pug displays cataleptic inhibition; in the Schnauzer, there is a whole syndrome—the hair rises, the lips are drawn back, the whole body is shaken with trembling; in the minute Mexican Chihuahua there is paradoxical aggression; and finally the Boxer lies flat on the ground, its breathing becomes irregular, and it submits completely.

There is even a real "illness of fear" with psychomotor crises. Recognized for the last thirty years, it has several times been observed in whole kennels, following ptomaine poisoning by flours treated with *trichloride* of nitrogen. First one dog panics, and very quickly the others do the same, running hither and thither if they are enclosed, or straight ahead if they are free, with the same obvious panic as is seen in the audience of a theatre when fire breaks out. This same contagious fear can also be seen in all the dogs in a kennel before a storm, or in a whole pack of hounds when they return from an exhausting hunt.

ABERRATIONS OF THE SEXUAL INSTINCT

Sexuality is one of the essential poles of animal life. Disorders of this instinct are all the more numerous in so far as they are linked to the most varied social relationships from the time when the wild dog of long ago, separated from its own kind, became the domesticated dog.

First studied in the monkey, the most unforeseen sexual aberrations, ranging from onanism to sadism, have been observed in the dog. Among other examples of disorders in sexual behavior, Villemin has described that of a little mongrel, whose conduct was only discovered by chance. His master, an innkeeper at P——, had noticed that several of his hens were lame or had been found dead, as if they had been throttled by a fox. The hen house was watched and the real culprit discovered—the little dog! He committed sodomy with the poultry, holding their heads in his mouth, without making a sound. He was castrated, but the operation did not cure him of his vice, or at least of his desires. All the hens died off except one who had resigned herself to her fate and put up with the passion of the obstinate creature!

Dracoulides has noted and recorded an instance of a Poodle that was a passive homosexual. Dehner has recorded the deviation of a Doberman who had also tried his luck in the hen house and had returned to the family and their friends; it took advantage of every occasion which offered to straddle any woman's leg held out to him in play. Vaivre has cited a similar passion in a Cocker Spaniel who never took any notice of the most solicitous of bitches.

Anomalies such as these constitute real sexual perversions, due perhaps to some accidental conditioning.

DISORDERS OF THE MATERNAL INSTINCT

We have seen that the maternal instinct can be aroused in the male, yet behavioral disorders and aberrations of this instinct are more noticeable in the female. Some bitches, deprived of their young, blindly adopt any kind of infants, even though these may be animals of a different species and though these adoptive children may be anatomically incapable of suckling. Thus an English Setter bitch adopted as her own several chicks which she feverishly kept snuggled against

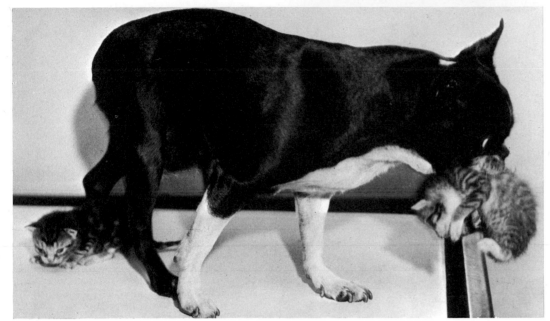

her belly. As soon as anyone tried to take them away from her, she became fiercely protective. Besides, any bitch whose own young are removed and replaced, for example, by kittens, shows them exactly the same care as she would her own offspring. When these kittens are weaned, she will if need be defend them from her own pups, whom, though she brought them into the world, she did not suckle and does not know.

Sometimes the activity of the endocrine system acts blindly. This is the basic reason for the classic instances of milk coming in, and false pregnancies, which everyone who owns a bitch, even if she is a virgin, has had the occasion to observe. They express themselves in exactly the same kind of behavior (the making of a "nest," an attitude of protection and defense, etc.) toward the most extraordinary objects—gloves, slippers, toys, etc., as toward puppies. Disorders of this nature are no doubt due to a hyperfunctioning of the ovaries, but one cannot exclude factors of a psychological nature. Thus

it has been noted that 90% of cases of false pregnancy occur in bitches belonging to delicate breeds, who receive an exaggerated amount of fond attention as soon as they start whimpering. Chertok and Fontaine have revealed the existence of these psychological factors by administering a tranquilizer to the bitch or by sending her away from the surroundings in which she lived. Everything goes back to normal and the flow of milk stops. We can definitely say that false pregnancies are as much of psychosomatic origin as they are due to the hormonal release of the procreative instinct.

There are other familiar anomalies which are clinically quite common, such as puerperal cannibalism or total indifference. After giving birth to their young, some females abandon their little ones, and even go so far as devouring them. Factors of all sorts play a part in cases like this: insufficient calcium in the blood, almost nonexistant lactation, chronic constipation, an irresistable onslaught of *placentophagia* (this is an innate craving which leads the females to eat

placentas that are rich in galactozymes). It is not however unreasonable to suppose that affective or emotional disorders may play a part in this sort of infanticide. Here again, insecurity certainly comes into it, especially with female sled dogs or baggage dogs who have not managed to isolate themselves for the birth of their young.

In pet dogs, jealousy is often responsible. Finally, more profound disorders have been noted during the last few years, the results of supersonic booms. In a kennel at Ottignies, the sonic boom has caused the death of 212 dogs in two years. The more nervous breeds have suffered most. Out of 30 whelpings, only four litters have survived. Bitches which are suckling their young are terrified by the noise which is as violent as it is unexpected, and it is impossible for them to project their defense reflex onto any precise object. They throw themselves on their pups and, obeying the protective instinct, bury them quickly (they die of asphyxiation); or else, under the influence of a substitution reflex, they are seized by bulimia, and decapitate and swallow their pups. This phenomenon is all the more violent because, in this highly populated environment, the sonic boom sets all the dogs barking and causes a true collective panic.

REGRETTABLE ERRORS

Among the disturbed instincts, one should also mention the frequent and regrettable error made by guard dogs at the sight of a human being lying immobile on the ground. They go up to him, looking at the same time curious and anxious, and begin by licking him, tugging at his clothes a little, nibbling at random, without understanding why, and sometimes throwing themselves on him with catastrophic results.

What has happened? The natural aggression of the dog was moulded by its training, with a view to making it defend the in-

The "spleen" of the Bulldog.

The cruelest of Boxers can be disarmed by a tortoise.

GALLIPHOT — AUREL SALA

paroxysms similar to those the real disaster had caused in them.

Also natural was the psychosis of a dog that survived a railway accident and that was thought to be unharmed. After this ordeal, wherever it was, and however spoilt by its four successive masters, it would howl despairingly as soon as it heard a train whistle, would forget itself at once and refuse food for days on end.

Fontaine, Leroy, and Gaudino have observed a curious form of neurosis, caused by a combination of conditioned reflexes (and this, they say, puts in question the whole problem of determinism by conditioning of neurotic states). A Setter bitch regularly displayed all the symptoms of an emotive fit (anxiety, fear, barking, trembling, urinating, etc.) when she saw a child and a child's car. Contact with young dogs, kittens, and kids set off identical outbursts. The same thing happened in the presence of objects used in baby care (diapers, baby bottles, rattles, etc.). Anamnesic research revealed that the bitch had been reared alone on a large estate, with her master as her one and only human contact, and that the character changes she suffered from had been caused by the aggressive behavior of another bitch, whose young had excited her curiosity.

INDUCED NEUROSES

Unfortunately the various neuroses induced in dogs used for experiments are very numerous. We would like to pass over them in silence. We shall mention three at random, the first two to show how quickly laboratory experimentation can lead to neurosis, the third because of the moral one can draw from it.

The two first cases are related by Y. Ruckebusch. Chenger-Krestovnikova had conditioned a dog to have a "positive" feeding reflex at the sight of a circle, and a "negative" one at the sight of an ellipse. When the larger axis of the ellipse was

dividual and the species, but in this case, which the dog has never before come across, the animal is incapable of controlling its reactions, and its original aggression is aroused. This is by way of being a misunderstanding, for which the dog cannot be held responsible. Man is able to use his reason to regain his poise, but not even the most intelligent and devoted of dogs is endowed with reason and so has no ability to regain its mental balance. So it is prey to true neuroses, which one should recognize as "natural," as they conform to its nature as an animal. This is so whether these neuroses be provoked by circumstances or

(artificially) in the experimental laboratory.

The neurosis which struck all the dogs in Pavlov's laboratory during the great flood in Leningrad was a natural one. The cages were full of water and a violent storm broke out when efforts were being made to save the dogs. These efforts had to be postponed for 24 hours, but in the end all the dogs were saved. The youngest and the weakest were in the grip of a neurosis. This lasted for several months, so much so that it was enough to let some water flow noisily along the floor and to create gusts of wind artificially with a drier, and the subjects, upset by this, at once suffered

174

reduced to nine-eighths of the smaller axis, differentiation became impossible, and the subject immediately had an hysterical fit. Rikman, in his turn, induced an experimental neurosis in a dog whose secretion of saliva was conditioned to the sound of a metronome, by submitting it to simultaneous assaults. The platform on which it was placed was made to oscillate, a continuous noise was produced with a handrattle; there were sudden noises, or a grimacing mask was suddenly made to appear! For 16 days the dog showed signs of motor excitement, with the disappearance of all the feeding responses, both conditioned and absolute. After that, the slightest experimental sound stimulus was enough to cause an epileptic type of fit, and the sight of the oscillating platform was alone enough to inhibit all the conditioned reflexes.

And here is the most moving story of all. Some adult dogs were trained to cross and take their meals at fixed times at the ringing of a small bell. Then, these same meals were refused them at the ringing of another little bell, whose sound became progressively identical to that of the first. Thus, very quickly, the poor creatures became neurotic. In fact, as soon as the signal was heard, they rushed forward, then stopped, set off again, came back, stopped again to listen, until in the end they really broke down. The experiment continued. Alcohol was added to every second meal, and the anxiety of the animals was seen to lessen rapidly. Their behavior improved. From then on, between the two meals, one of which contained alcohol and the other which did not, they showed an undeniable preference for the ones with alcohol in them. Was that all? No, for these were the unexpected results of the experiment: As soon as their nerves were calmed and they had become used to the bell nightmare, the dogs of their own accord abandoned the alcoholic meals and passed onto a "dry" diet.

Humorists would say that proves "that alcohol is not for dogs!" This is a happy fact, but is it not disturbing to note that the animal, by means of its instinct alone, knows when to stop, while man, with all his intelligence, only persists, sinks ever lower and poisons himself to death?

IS IT POSSIBLE TO TREAT AND CURE DOGS THAT SUFFER FROM PSYCHIATRIC ILLNESSES?

This is the question that the reader will naturally ask himself after this brief incursion into canine psychiatry.

Can one cure dogs that are neurotic, ill adjusted, psychically abnormal? Why not? Animal psychology is not an imaginary utopia. Though still young, this science will make progress, and it is not impossible that from this new field of medical research, the psychology and psychiatry of man will gain some benefit. Certainly, animals are intelligent, but in their own way. Although their psyche is not of the same nature as ours, their physiological substratum is very close to our own. Like us, the dog can be disturbed by very precise circumstances in which one can attach no blame to any injury or pathogenic agent, but only to an emotional trauma. No one can deny that dogs do suffer from neuroses and psychoses. Their collective panics, and their hysterical epilepsy with all its corresponding forms, are recognized. There has been a beginning to the discovery in dogs of true psychosomatic disorders; for instance, hormonal activity is not alone enough to cause a false pregnancy. If dogs were only machines, would they suffer from emotional alopecia? This, it is true, is a rare condition, but Guilhon has recorded several cases in the hospitals at Alfort, and private clinics often observe it. Of course it is impossible to question a dog as one would a sick person, and therefore many psychic disorders will always remain mysterious, but there can be no doubt that we are sometimes faced with obvious cases of canine neurosis. Are they

K.P. MEIER

*A hundred years ago,
Charles Darwin
and M. Wood were already beginning
to study the nervous cerebral disorders
of the canine species.*

*In this dog's death howl,
should one see the cry of the wolf?*

*Reynolds: ►
Miss Bowles.*
(ARCH. R. LAFFONT.)

HOLMES-LEBEL — LISA

curable? It all depends on the circumstances.

Environmental therapy (comfort, diversion, affection) can be of use in veterinary psychiatry. This has been shown experimentally with rats, even though they do not live on terms of intimacy with man. Forty rats were fed in the same way, surrounded with the same hygiene. But half of them were housed in dreary, dark, individual cages, while the other twenty lived together in an enormous enclosure which was well ventilated, very well lit during the day, copiously provided with swings, little stepladders, tunnels, and various toys which they could play with as much as they wanted. Three months later, at the autopsy, it was noted that the rats who had played together in the light environment had better irrigated cortexes, their brains were 5% heavier than those of the rats that had been isolated, their cerebral cells were better developed and their enzymes more active. It follows that one can never repeat too often that, to have any chance of modifying the psychotic reactions of a dog, the first requirement is that its master keeps an even temper with it, talks to it gently and reassures it.

It must be added that modern chemical therapy is also very valuable, and that in this field calming, stabilizing, tranquilizing, and, if necessary, energizing drugs are of as great benefit as they are in human medicine.

To have one's dog killed just because it has bitten someone ("He who wants to drown a dog says it has rabies") is a facile solution. Because of the place the dog has taken in our homes and hearts we will not put up with the unjust or the absurd. In the future more and more care will be showered on the Pomeranians that never stop barking when they feel lonely; on the Boxers that stupidly run after cars; on the Setters that forget themselves during a storm; on the Alsatians that kill cats and sheep. . . .

The method has today become classical. In a canine psychiatric clinic at Watford, near London, England, this service is performed by young women who are calm, affectionate young nurses with gentle movements and measured voices. In cases where the whip, shouts, and a man's violent actions would only madden the sick dog, these girls intervene without haste, stroking the animals, offering them titbits, and in the end winning their confidence. This however is only a beginning, the preparation for treatment. Animal psychiatrists believe that a successful cure can only be accomplished with the dog's master present. This is the principle which everyone has tried to follow since the director of an American hospital, Dare Miller, declared, *"One can only be sure of curing a dog if one has first psychoanalyzed its owner."*

In fact, the dogs' masters have often had something to do with the psychic disturbance. This is what happens in the case of a dog that is half deaf and whom the master (who does not know of this infirmity) wants to make obey a whistle at any price, and so punctuates his orders with blows from a hunting crop. It is also true in the case of a nervous lady who jumps, cries out, and runs forward as soon as the telephone rings, and who complains that her Poodle immediately leaps up behind her, sometimes going so far as to bite her (because it is itself terrified by her behavior). It is true of the boy with the weak constitution, born shy but arrogant, who suffers from an inferiority complex and who cannot understand why his dog, after being tied up all day long, muzzled, and held severely on a leash to go out, bewildered by incessant and contradictory orders, does not welcome him with joy, submission, and affection!

Dr. Dare Miller, in his clinic at Los Angeles, has as his clients the dogs belonging to the celebrities of Hollywood—of Zsa-Zsa Gabor and Bob Hope, of Don Adams, Frank Sinatra, and many others. All these people are too taken up with their professional obligations to do more for their four-legged companions than stuff them with goodies.

*Can he "think"
that he "is" a dog?*

*In the dog, the fugue state
is a symptom of a type of
epilepsy.*

All dogs, whether they are famous or unknown, need to love and to serve someone. No dog can be happy unless it is reassured by and through its master. Yet this master is always surprised when it can be proved to him that his dog is disturbed, often because of himself. And this is equally true of the lady who quickly picks up her delicate little dog and hugs him close to her (because the others "want to eat him up"), and of the master who holds his large dog with a heavy hand "because he would eat all the others up." In both cases, it is indeed the master who needs to be calmed and made to see reason.

SHEEP KILLERS

Can one psychoanalyze a sick dog? There can be no question of this, for it is hard to imagine the practitioner saying to one of his patients, "Lie down and bark away!" So he has to use methods more like those of the investigator, of the detective. This is what happened in the case of an old Schnauzer that belongs to some friends of ours. Its master tried in vain to prevent it from attacking every white dog it came across, from the harmless Tenerife to the powerful Pyrenean Dog (which, happily, is seldom seen). One day in the course of conversation it was discovered by chance that when it was just a young pup, hardly weaned, the Schnauzer was assaulted and "bowled over" by a mad Poodle that was on a leash, and under whose nose it had come to preen itself. The Schnauzer, when it grew up, retained an incurable hostility towards all white dogs. Unfortunately it was too late to cure it.

This is not always true of dogs that bite sadistically, or kill sheep or poultry. There are various forms of treatment. A Chow Chow that was a terrible poultry killer was only cured of this destructive mania when its mistress one day hung the latest of its victims round its neck as a cruel joke. For a whole day the terrible killer was forced to wander around bearing the weight and the stench of its own crime. It never killed again.

There is another cure that is worthy of mention, for it is the very justified pride and joy of its inventor, Frank Pettit. Since it was discovered there have been no killer dogs in England. They are cured by "Sidney" alone. Let us explain. "Sidney" is a sheep, a sheep "that does not know he is a sheep," because as soon as he was born, he was reared by a bitch in the midst of her pups. The dogs and Sidney, being weaned, fed, and raised together, very naturally came to terms with each other, and lived happily together as a group. If any of the dogs threatened his daily quota of milky gruel or his own personal corner of the territory, Sidney, a shaggy sheep, simply sent his canine brother spinning with one great push of the head.

The dog that kills sheep is first left alone for two days in a dark cage, to isolate it psychologically. On the third day it is let into a small enclosure containing Sidney, just at the moment when the latter is about to tuck into the milky gruel he likes so much. What happens? The dog catches sight of the sheep and is ready to attack him just as he has all sheep until then; but Sidney knows what he is about. He lets the dog come forward and when it comes right up to him, with one pompous blow of the head he sends it rolling in the dust. The "sheepshock" has done its work. The dog gets up again, astonished, humiliated, already beaten. The rest is just a question of useless relapses on the part of the dog, and the passage of time, but in the majority of cases the dog understands! From then on the dog mixes every day with other dogs, the step-brothers of Sidney, who are fond of him and if necessary only too ready to bare their fangs. There only remains the process of consolidating the treatment by kindness and rewards, to convince the killer dog that it must accept the inevitable. After the dog leaves the clinic, sheep can graze in peace.

It is obvious that we have come a long way from the "dog's life" of primitive hordes. Dogs living today are exposed to the complications of our lives, of us mad people.

The amazing thing is that they are still, on the whole, able to adjust themselves to it!

F. MERLET

14 PARAPSYCHOLOGY

It has seemed more logical to us to group together under this heading several psychological phenomena which are as yet insufficiently studied and which are difficult to place within the well-defined bounds of psychophysiology, animal psychology, or animal psychiatry, phenomena which are metaphysical and consist of behavior which is anarchical. Each age has been more and more tempted to tackle them, so that imagination and fantasy could easily reveal their hidden secrets: dogs and hypnosis and catalepsy; dogs and death and suicide; dogs and sleep and dreams, hallucinations and premonitions, etc.

All these are states which, in the final analysis, one can relate back to sensor-motor physiology and to the concept (as yet very imprecise) of the state of consciousness (or of unconsciousness) of the animal.

HYPNOSIS AND CATALEPSY

Three hundred years ago, to the stupefaction of the religious circles in which he moved in Rome, Father Kirchner succeeded in hypnotizing a hen. All he did was to tie together the bird's feet and to draw along the ground a chalk line from the exact point where the beak of the bird rested. At first the hen was agitated, then she became calm. When she was set free, her eye was fixed on the white line and she stayed quite still.

And after three hundred years we still have not succeeded in discovering what hypnosis is.

Chertok gave the following definition for animal hypnosis: "Animal hypnosis is regressive behavior characterized by inhibition and torpor, obtained by various procedures which put the animal into an unaccustomed position or situation and alter the normal pattern of its relationships with the outside world."

Using this definition it would not seem that the dog is particularly susceptible to hypnosis. Hypnosis implies both a mechanical and a psychological inhibition; but, though the mechanical inhibition is relatively easy, the same cannot be said for the psychological inhibition. Although there are exceptions, which result from a sudden and up to now inexplicable sympathy, a dog is always on the defensive with strangers. Only the person whom the dog has chosen as its master is likely to have any success with hypnosis. However, veterinary surgeons who specialize in canine medicine are used to treating dogs of every breed and age, and they have every day to handle them without fear so that they can examine them thoroughly. In these cases, the dog undergoes an inhibition which is part somatic and part psychological, in which the personality of the practitioner, his authority, and his instinctive skill are the means whereby he succeeds.

A general observation: All vets are able, without the smallest difficulty, to immobilize a big dog without muzzling it or tying it up. To do this, they simply take hold of the front and back leg furthest from them, make the animal lose its balance and turn it over quickly but gently on to the examination table. However, a vet will never display the same unconscious skill if he is subsequently told that the dog he has just handled with such ease is snappy and a biter.

That would suffice to underline the part psychology plays in hypnosis. The vet who, to examine his patient, suddenly shines the beam of his oculoscope in its face, holding it at his mercy for several minutes, also puts the dog in a relative state of inhibition.

But is this really hypnosis? As soon as the intervention is finished, the dog jumps down. The period of immobilization has been very short and the "inhibited" behavior has ceased spontaneously. It is this that is the attribute of the catéleptic state. Where hypnosis has taken place, however, the animal would only awake after an appreciable period of drowsiness or torpor or sleep. Now this is never evident in cases such as the professional one we have just discussed.

The instinctive attitude of a young pointer.

Pointing, a primitive American painting.
(Grand Palais Exhibition)

the head stretched out as a continuation of the neck, to the point where the lower jaw is sometimes pressed against the ground. Here again it is clearly a case of catalepsy, if one is willing to accept the phenomenon as a result of motor changes with an ecological (or more or less biological) significance, because they are of use to the dog.

One must seek the origins of "down" in the Middle Ages at a time when the "bird dogs" had the job of nosing about in the thickets and furrows to seek out and put to flight the hidden birds and the crouching rabbits. As the game would begin to move, the dog would pause, and the servants of the noble huntsman would take the pause as a signal to throw the great net, called a "drag net." However, the net, which was weighted with lead along its edges, would hit the dogs as it settled on the ground, trapping all the animals. Very soon the dogs learned by experience that by flattening themselves on the ground they could dodge the shock, and they would remain in this position until the servants had collected the trapped game.

It is to this hunting practice, which is many centuries old (and which must have been passed on as a hereditary factor to the descendants of the "bird dogs"), that one must equally attach the classic word "spaniel." The derivation of this word is not necessarily from the Spanish origin of the dogs but more likely from the old French word *"s'espagnir"*—to crouch down on one's stomach.

Having made these observations on catalepsy and hypnosis, let me say that in more than half a century of veterinary work with dogs, I have never once seen a dog in a state of induced hypnosis.

SLEEP AND DREAMS

Light sleep, paradoxical sleep—the essence of this subject was discovered in 1957 when encephalography was first applied to animals, to study the rhythm of their cerebral activity.

Catalepsy, on the other hand, is much more common than one would think among dogs. It is a phenomenon that a hunter could observe daily.

Two cases are classic: the behavior of the "pointers" and the "down" dogs.

In the case of the first, hounds or setters, among other breeds used for this purpose, literally fall into catalepsy, by motor inhibition, as soon as they have exposed the hare or the pheasant, if the creature stays motionless on the ground. The dog acts like a sleepwalker, unresponsive to any other attraction of his surroundings. After slowly moving a few steps forwards, the dog suddenly takes up a characteristic stance: the neck stretched forward, the head held horizontal; it is frozen on three rigid legs, the fourth bent at the knee joint, its tail stiff and parallel to the ground. He will stay in this strange position for several seconds or for minutes on end, as long as the fascinated game itself remains still. It is remarkable to see the concentration and tension sustained by the pointer.

In the second case the position which the dog takes up is quite different. It is the attitude adopted by the crouching dogs and which the English call "down" dogs. As soon as the little spaniels (Breton [Brittany] Spaniels, Cocker Spaniels, Springers, etc.), seek out an animal which stays quite still, they take up and spontaneously maintain this position: lying flat on their stomachs,

RAPHO — CHATILLON

We know, however, that sleep is not a period of uniform rest but that it is broken by cycles and intervals. Today, one is even led to think that sleep is linked to chemical rather than nervous phenomena. There has been brought to light a series of cells, found in the furrow which separates the two cerebral hemispheres, and these cells secrete a dormative horemone. There is no difference from a neurological point of view between dogs and cats. The states of vigilance are the same: 1) the state of wakefulness, with rapid cortical and sub-cortical activity; 2) deep sleep, when breathing is regular, and the heart beats more calmly than in the state of wakefulness; and 3) the mysterious oneiric sleep (during which one dreams) which consists of waves of various lengths, with cortical and sub-cortical activity. One can also observe movements of the eyeballs, trembling of the lips, spasmodic twitchings of the extremities, groans and little cries, and above all the total relaxation of tension in the neck muscles. It is in this period that the dog dreams.

German researchers, currently working in this field, have carried out numerous experiments. Dr. Menzel states that dogs begin to dream at the age of eight days. With the help of biological stimulants, Dr. Saris has provoked artificial dreams. He has placed a piece of strong smelling meat (smoked sausage, for example) three inches in front of the nose of a deeply sleeping dog. Three seconds afterwards, the dog, while remaining asleep, begins to spasmodically contract its upper lip and to make chewing movements, which continue for two or three minutes; then it becomes still. After awakening (with the sausage still close to its nose) the dog will take up to five minutes before it begins to repeat the movements which were induced in the dream. Where there is a scent of dead leaves or of game, a sleeping hunting dog will display movements which we can equate with the chase. This is, however, only an analogical interpretation. To really know if an animal is dreaming, one has to see it make a movement in its sleep which is not natural, a movement which might have been taught and which could be provoked

Of what do sleeping dogs dream?

A rude awakening by an hallucination.

by association with a certain sensation (in the sleeping state as in the state of wakefulness). Unfortunately, it has never been possible to perform this experiment.

Of course, it is very risky to put forward precise interpretations of these dreams. However, the behavior of our hunting dogs, in particular, so conforms to a stereotype that one is led to think that in their dreams they continue to hunt the game they did not take or the hare they could not catch. In fact, for the dog, all hunting is a fraud, as the dogs themselves are never allowed to finish the struggle; except in hunting and coursing, it is only the huntsman and his gun who reach a satisfying conclusion.

The experiments conducted at the Ames Research Center in California have shown how dogs and cats, during the period of "paradoxical sleep" (so named because there is a paradox between the sleep and the varying degrees of agitation which accompany it) can pass into a light sleep. As soon as the oxygen is reduced in the air that the animals are breathing, they fall into a very deep somnolence and dreams no longer occur. If oxygen is put back into the air, the sleep becomes lighter and the periods of dreaming increase in proportion. There is not only in this experiment, therefore, proof that deep sleep is linked to the metabolism of oxygen in the brain, but there is something else. Does not such a "rebound" pose another unsuspected question? Is perhaps this rapid return to the dreaming period a response to a real need, to a psycho-physiological necessity for dreams?

In ending, let us note that no studies have been made in the dog of that period of consciousness, halfway between the oneiric state and the state of wakefulness, when we ourselves know that we are dreaming.

HALLUCINATIONS

So many phenomena still escape us in the canine psyche. Can dogs be subject to those

*In its sleep
it keeps chasing after . . .*

*An insurmountable terror
at some imaginary danger.*

"dreams" we experience when we are awake, which we call hallucinations? It has been said of hallucinations that they are emotions without object, a kind of "delirium of the emotions." Dogs, which are so susceptible to epilepsy and vegetative disorders, suffer (perhaps more than do cats) that psycho-motor epilepsy which throws them (apparently without reason) into frightening states.

However desirous one may be of not falling into anthropomorphism, how can one not see in some of their actions what they are expressing. In one case, one sees sudden rage with staring eyes, an aggressive attitude, unusual barking, etc.; in another case, there is insurmountable terror at some imaginary danger from which the animal wishes to flee at any price; he takes refuge under any piece of furniture, tries to hide himself in any corner, even though he remains perfectly visible. The state of mental confusion is evident.

Most often it is a question of less spectacular manifestations, to which an observer attaches no importance, as when dogs snap at non-existent flies as soon as they are exposed to a bright light. It would be reasonable here to take into account the possibilities of ocular disturbances well known to human oculists as "floating specks." Arterial hypertension too is not reserved for our species; a number of hallucinatory states can be due to this circulatory trouble, which is still insufficiently studied in dogs.

Another familiar manifestation is that of the drowsy dog which suddenly jumps up, gulps in the air for several seconds, then, with its nose to the ground, begins to explore the room, sniffing the legs of each piece of furniture, the cushions in each chair, as if it were looking for game or for some object whose smell had suddenly caused this sensor-motor activity. Is the animal continuing an interrupted dream? Or has it really perceived a smell or a noise which we could not. On one single occasion we had the chance to lift the veil of this apparent mystery. Often

What is going on?
The significance of so much sudden and unusual
behavior escapes us still.

*She has no need
of a sixth sense
to guide her.*

ERWIN LOWE

our Wire-haired Pointing Griffon was given to this type of behavior. Once, by chance, we noticed a mouse run not a yard from the nose of our sleeping dog, which explained her immediate awakening and her strange behavior.

This simple personal observation shows quite clearly the difficulties into which animal psychiatric research will always run, and how much of the realm of sensory investigation will long remain closed to us and of which we can scarcely begin to suspect the possibilities.

PREMONITIONS AND EXTRA-SENSORY PERCEPTION

When discussing premonitions, we are yet again treading on ground which we well know to be dangerous. However, how can we not class in the realm of parapsychology these phenomena which are still the subject of much argument but which are talked about so often.

There comes to mind a very moving letter from Paul Bourget which we received a few weeks before his death, in which he told us of what he described as a "telepathic message" that he witnessed. A dog was fast asleep on the terrace of a villa at Antibes, when Bourget saw it suddenly leap up and run howling to the railings. It was called back and quietened, but then it began to behave even more strangely. It crouched under the bed of its master and wailed incessantly. It so happened that at the same moment when the dog was wrenched from sleep on the terrace, its owner was killed in a car accident several miles from Nice.

We are wary of drawing conclusions. Yet here is another example. About eighteen years ago, at Montana-Vermala in Switzerland, we were playing with an Alsatian which was chewing a woolen glove, when suddenly it let go of the glove, backed away, and flattened itself on the ground, trembling all over. We had begun to calm the dog by

saying "What's the matter?" when suddenly a dramatic and deep rumbling shook the ground and cracks opened in the walls of the room and the ceiling rocked. The dog had been on the alert for several minutes before our poor human senses were made aware of what was happening by the seismic shock.

One can only cite from memory the hundreds of identical cases of this premonitory type, witnessed in birds and dogs in Turkey, Greece, Algeria, Yugoslavia, or wherever earthquakes are frequent. One has to be very cautious about some of the tales but others ought to be remembered, such as the description given by a school-master in Saint-Pierre of the behavior of his dog two days before the unforgettable drama of Martinique in 1902. Because of the symptoms he observed, his description has become classic. More recently, a German zoologist, Dr. E. Kilian, during several earthquakes in Chile in 1960 noticed that the slightest tremors (to which he personally had long been used) were felt so strongly in advance by the dogs, that each time the little town of Valdivia echoed for several minutes with their baleful barking.

It seems that one must consider such phenomena as these as indisputable cases of premonition in the most precise sense of the term: "A sensation which comes before, and announces an event," according to the dictionary. Whatever is the source of this sensory knowledge is inaudible to our ears: imperceptible shivers in the ground; tiny changes in the smell of the ground caused by gases; storms in the magnetic field. The emotional response that they provoke in the dog is just as much premonition as the function of a seismograph is registration.

These are many other cases of extra-sensory activity which are disturbing, but from which modern psychophysiology is slowly stripping the mystery. A long time ago, when I was a passionate devotee of shooting, I was intrigued by something which hunters have often witnessed and which they accept as being quite natural. My best dog used to

behave strangely when I fired at a bird. She was used to going shooting with me, and would stay at my heels except when she ran a short distance to retrieve. She knew (or at least seemed to have some presentiment) if my shot would hit its target or not. Each time I used to feel a secret humiliation.

Feuder's recent work has taught us that the eye is a veritable mini-computer which acts rather like a computer controlled gun which fires "in front of its target." Can dogs, in the full heat of the chase, enjoy these unknown sensory possibilities which allow them to judge in advance with inconceivable speed the outcome of a rifle shot?

It is in the realms of the extra-sensory that this mental tracking belongs, but which literature insists on attributing to a "sixth sense," a category which is as imaginary as it is convenient. According to modern knowledge there is no sixth sense, or we must be prepared to revise all our system of knowledge and consider as "senses" all the possible physio-chemical reactions which are not clear to us. This would really result in a state of confusion and disorder, of which a scientific mind must, at all costs, beware.

CAN DOGS COMMIT SUICIDE?

No myth is more deeply rooted in the minds of men than the idea of suicide in the higher animals. The dog, who displays so tenderly emotions of despair when separated from its master, cannot escape this naive belief.

Dogs do not commit suicide. To will your own death and to seek in it means of escaping grief or physical pain, it is first necessary to have a concept of death—an abstract concept—and the most intelligent of dogs always run up against the insurmountable barrier of abstraction. It is, therefore, with the greatest scepticism that one must receive the innumerable stories of this kind. Many writers at the beginning of the century were deceived. There cannot be suicide where there is no conscious action; even when men com-

From incomprehension to uneasiness.

No dog ever died of grief.

DIM

mit suicide in a state of mental confusion, deep psychosis or madness, they are performing a conscious act.

On this point devoted dog-lovers are sometimes difficult to convince. "There are, however, dogs who allow themselves to die of grief," they say as a final argument." Is this not an indisputable form of suicide?"

Here again, we must remember that no dog has ever died of grief. When the person disappears whom the dog loves and upon whom it depends for its existence, the animal often refuses its food and falls into a state of inhibition which ends in death. This is not suicide.

To explain such behavior one msut speak scientifically of "conditioning," particularly if the animal is accustomed to being fed exclusively by its master, exercised only by him, etc. It is in fact a case of anxiety which is sometimes deep, of depression which can sometimes end in death; but a dog in such a situation does not "know" that his master has disappeared for ever. Could one say that it is waiting for his return? That would be to admit that it could call his master to mind; and that too is impossible. Snatch a dog from its surroundings, separate it completely from its master and from everything which, by association, could awake memories in it, and in a few days it will slip into a new life.

It is naturally the same for dogs that "die of despair on the grave of their lost master." They too are only reacting to an association of emotions where faithfulness to memory is nothing but a sentimental interpretation. We have known a little dog who followed the funeral procession of its master to the cemetery. After it had spent a day and a night lying on the freshly filled-in grave, it was kept indoors for almost a week while the funeral masons erected a tomb. It is true that it returned to the cemetery as soon as it was released and that it did so each day at the same time as the burial had taken place. It would stay there for an hour or two until, motivated by a more basic instinct, it would go home. It was returning to its "territory" where its daily disappointment did not deprive it of his daily need for food. Three months later it went away on holiday with the family and when it came back it never repeated its touching behavior.

How many of us act much differently in similar situations! But here we touch on another and much more complex side of the problem where ethics and conscious memory come into play.

In conclusion, let us simply recall the point of view of Guillaume: "Man is more emancipated than any other animal that exists around us at present; he can see further into the past and into the future. The stagnation of animals results from the lesser flexibility of their perceptive organization and to the poverty of their imagination."

AFFECTION AND HEREDITY

This title might be surprising. It is well known that scientists are not agreed on the questions of heredity. So far as we are concerned, as long as there is no agreement on some scientific certainty, we will stick to the facts of experience that show us there is apparently a transmission of certain psychological as well as anatomical characteristics.

Certainly there are numerous specialists who are entrenched in their beliefs that only physical features can be transmitted by heredity. Professor Pieron has written that "on the question of hereditary transmission of acquired characteristics, the negative attitude of theoreticians is out of place, faced with certain facts which one could wish them to examine. It is useless to deny any possibility of the transmission of modifications in behavior, as it is to deny the role of mutations in evolution, the sudden changes affecting the instincts just as much as the forms."

One can admit without difficulty that a Tibetan Mastiff, over thousands and thousands of years, might have ended up as a Chihuahua, but it is virtually denied that a savage wolf could have evolved into a loving lap-dog.

It is not, however, our opinion to maintain that Briards are necessarily born sheep dogs, that Pekingese are born affectionate dogs, Braques d'Auvergne hunting dogs, when we know how many crosses and what mixtures (natural or produced) have gone into the making of the domestic dog. However, the explanation we have already given for the particular crouching attitude of some special

Heir
not only to its anatomy
but also its mysterious attachment
to man.

hunting dogs—fear of the net—seems to constitute an argument which is worth pursuing. Cocker Spaniels put themselves in this "down" position spontaneously from the age of three months, and pointers or spaniels do not decide to "declare' 'themselves—that is, show some interest in game—before the age of twelve or fifteen months, and, without any training, take up the marking position. Depending on the dogs and on the successive generations, the folded position of the foreleg will develop from uncertain mimicry to the pre-cataleptic state.

Hunters, trainers of circus dogs, and breeders in general are fully aware of this. They prefer dogs that are descended from those which seem susceptible to the transmission of predispositions and sensory qualities which have made their ancestors famous. (This does not mean, however, that a dog will walk on its hind legs because it comes from a line trained to do these tricks, unless it in turn is trained to place itself in this unnatural position.)

However, can one really hold the view today that cavemen's dogs are in every way psychologically the same as civilized dogs? In wolves as in jackals or wild dogs, the pack has always remained a community where each individual is dominated by the instinct to defend the species. But the domestic dog, descended from this same species, has been transformed. Not only has the dog itself integrated, as a minority, into a different pack where it is subject to superiors, and into a different psyche, but on the emotional plane it has adapted itself to this group. This took place at the same time and under the same circumstances as Neanderthal Man mysteriously became Homo sapiens.

And since then, the dog, whose intelligence is animal and thus of a different nature from ours, has never ceased to adapt more and more his perceptiveness to the emotional states of our species.

His innate characteristics have, like ours, remained the same; but the climate, the means of existence, the environment, and

the people have changed over the millennia. Are we so certain that, under so many varying influences, imperceptible, slow and complex modifications in the psycho-physiological order have not brought with them new predispositions? And why would these not be hereditarily transmitted, not so much as definite acquired characteristics but as a certain malleability, such as a predisposition to reactions adapted to special circumstances and special uses. We have always, on this question, shared the opinion of our colleague and friend, Edmond Déchambre, and we regret that we have set out badly the whole problem of the inheritance of acquired characteristics, in assimilating them with a reaction which is only the outward manifestation. It would be very desirable for the classical animal psychologists to consider in more depth such a problem, because it is worthy of far more interest than it has received.

SNARK INTERNATIONAL — CHAVANNES

SNARK INTERNATIONAL — CHAVANNES

*The immediate sympathy
of the dog which chooses some individual
and recognizes him as
its master.*

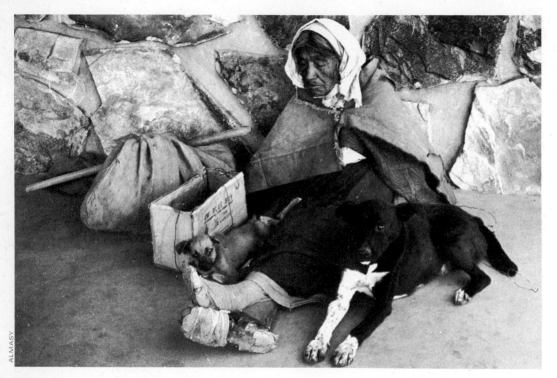

ALMASY

Affection—and we mean by this the true nature of tenderness, fidelity, and natural attachment of the dog for man—will perhaps also come to light one day.

Psychologically, affection is not only dependence. Cattle, horses, and all the other animals in man's service are not attached to him to the same degree as the dog—at least with such spontaneity and total selflessness. The cat, one tends to forget, came last of all to the mind and hearts of men. It has not yet shown what it is capable of, but anyone who has known and observed a cat knows very well that it will never be the servant or the slave of man.

Without going into depth, we would like to recall Flourens' famous neurological experiments. His results are classic. He found that the suppression of the encephalon (the anterior part of the brain) brings about an end to all intellectual and emotional life in the dog, while the reflexes of the vegetative life are preserved, so long as the subject is fed and watered.

This was a disturbing discovery in its time. Since then, research has progressed far in this realm. The electric activity of the brain has been discovered and the thousands of millions of cells of which it is composed are beginning to divulge their secrets. Through examination of lesions (whether accidental or produced), we have discovered the sensory or motor zones, the areas of integrative associations. We know the exact spots that one can stimulate, and (even at a distance) transform in a moment a wild guard dog into the most gentle and obedient of beasts. We can provoke or satisfy at will an unquenchable thirst in one dog, an insatiable appetite in another, violent itching in another. We know that the functioning of memory does not depend only on the nerve centers and junctures but also on cellular chemistry. We know (almost) why people are born alcoholics, geniuses, or murderers. But what do we know about love, affection, and tenderness? Very little, to be truthful. What enigmatic phenomena of

*What do we know
of tenderness?*

mental organization are at the birth or death of affection?

With even more reason we know nothing of the exceptional evolution which has transformed the dog—an animal like all the others—to such a level that it is on the emotional plane of man.

Without this evolution, how can we explain the immediate sympathies which make a dog choose some stranger as its master, and without any self-interest or apprentice-

ship, show him blind devotion, fidelity, and obedience. This strikingly resembles what we call love.

No scientist has succeeded, up to now, in explaining this total and mysterious understanding which exists between man and his companion the dog.

And that is why, in the final analysis, it seems to us that we lose nothing of our dignity or of our honor, by allowing ourselves to indulge in this sentimental analogy.

*It has integrated
into a different pack
and on the emotional plane
has adapted to it.*

SNARK INTERNATIONAL — MARKER

4
THE DOG
IN THE SERVICE
OF MAN

15 DOGS TRAINED IN SPECIALIZED WORK

"When the dog was created, it licked the hand of God and God stroked its head, saying 'What do you want, dog?' It replied, 'My Lord, I want to stay with you, in heaven, on a mat in front of the gate . . .'" MARIE NOEL

Throughout the different ages of literature, art, and symbolism of man, we have been able to follow the evolution of the dog and its adaptation to the needs and caprices of successive civilizations. The dog's different uses have imperceptibly produced morphological modifications which it is interesting to discuss further.

The respiratory effort and strength of Greyhounds and other hounds have developed greatly and have led to a hereditary change in the narrow, deep rib cage, to lengthened bones and a leaner and more obvious musculature. Even the shape of the ears has been modified; for at the same time their innate fear began to disappear (a fear which is always near the surface in wild dogs), their sense of smell took the place of their hearing, and the external ear gradually subsided in dogs used to chase or raise game, to the point where today there exist no hunting dogs with erect ears. The ears of the Ancient Egyptian Greyhound, which hunts only by sight and which through domestication has lost all fear, have also collapsed. With other, essentially brachycephalic breeds, which led more sedentary and less active lives, the ears also subsided and became bulkier. Also their craniums became more rounded, their noses more flattened, and their jaws shorter. Their descendants gradually took on genetic modifications resulting from endocrine disorders and imbalance, and have become giants or dwarfs, whose bodies are covered with short, close furry or hairy coats.

Meanwhile, the development of cavalry and the invention of firearms put an end to dogs of war. The democratization of hunting brought the art of venery to a standstill —as it had also put falconry in the shade— and only a few historic Anglo-French packs of hounds still exist. Other dog varieties of recent formation used for daily hunting, which were often delicate and difficult to handle, also soon disappeared. As a result there are practically no Saintonge, Ceris, Billy, or even porcelain dogs in France, almost no Wolfhounds in England, and practically no Borzois in Russia. But on the other hand, various other breeds were born and developed for practical or affectionate reasons, or even purely on aesthetic grounds whenever fashion dictated.

A new use for dogs has now become apparent, and that is for scientific purposes. In the absence of a modern Mastiff, the dog renders services to man which are far from being negligible.

DOGS TRAINED IN SPECIALIZED WORK

In general, the 20th century has continued to value highly any physical or psycho-physiological peculiarity which is natural to the various canine breeds and which was already well known in ancient times, for their development and exploitation.

RACING GREYHOUNDS

Tremendous power of acceleration and great running speed (40-45 m.p.h.) are the Greyhound's gifts. Quite apart from all cynegetic interest in coursing (the chasing of a living hare by sight by two Greyhounds set loose at the same time), the speed of these "arrows" is a spectacle in itself. At the beginning of the 20th century Owen Smith, an American engineer from Illinois, had the idea of transforming the ancient art of coursing into a sport, which led to the birth of Greyhound-racing in a Greyhound stadium. This kind of test had many advantages. First, such races do not end in the brutal cruelty of the attack, during which the hare is torn to death; second, the race can be followed from start to finish by thousands of spectators, a privilege which until then had been reserved for the privileged few; and, finally, betting on the uncertain results doubles the attraction. The principle is simple: a mechanical hare, propelled round the course by electricity, which enables the speed to be regu-

BAVARIA — LEIDMANN

The compression of the Greyhound is impressive.

A coursing Greyhound in full flight.

The leaping Borzois adapt badly to professional racing.

RAPHO — LANE

BAVARIA — PLÖSSER

lated, moves round an elliptical course on a rail. The Greyhounds throw themselves into its pursuit; the winner is the one which is closest to the decoy when it vanishes into a trap at a set point before the dogs' eyes.

In the first years, all types of hounds were run on the track, but experience quickly showed that only Greyhounds and Whippets continued to follow the course with enough enthusiasm to demonstrate the qualities that the spectators have the right to expect from them.

It is not that other hounds were less easy to deceive. It has been thought in fact that some racing Greyhounds might end up by guessing that the hare, made of wood and hair (or zinc), was unattainable. But that would overlook a fundamental principle of all training: dogs are capable of certain reasoning, but the messages to their brains only make them glimpse certain realities in a rapid and incomplete fashion. They immediately lapse into the domain of primary instincts and their rational judgement is of little weight next to the formidable impulses of instinct, to which the trainer's art binds all their education. And this is in addition to the ordinary training methods among which "giving them an appetite" and "reward" are soon made to condition the competitors.

We should not however forget that the Greyhound, which evolved in the African deserts and the steppes of Central Asia, had to hunt to eat, almost always in open country, and that its only weapon of attack (and defense) was and remains its speed. Therefore there was no need for it to use trickery or to scent the presence of game; this is probably the reason for its lack of olfactory senses and (as popular opinion quite unjustly would have it) its lack of intellect.

Today, England, America, Italy, and Algeria are among the countries where this sport continues to enjoy the greatest success. Greyhound racing in France, organized on the totalisator system of betting in 1933, has been suspended since World War II, and the *Société d'Encouragement* officially ceased all

A dog fight in Japan.

activities in 1951. It would be nice however to encourage the renewal and development of these exciting shows. They constitute, in fact—like horse racing—a true sport, which imples knowledge and experience as much from the point of view of breeding as from that of selection and training, and also a means of preserving a breed which has remained one of the most ancient, purest, and most interesting to preserve.

FIGHTING DOGS

When the organizers of dog fights, for economy's sake, stopped obtaining such ferocious beasts, we would have liked to think that contests between mastiffs and lions or bears or even between themselves were a thing of the remote past, leaving only painful memories of such circus spectacles. In reality, it was only in 1834 in France, and 1835 in England, that these revolting spectacles ceased. It is painful to read the descriptions by Alfred de Musset, Lamartine, Chateaubriand, and other sensitive Romantics whose eyes were wide open and dancing with cruel joy at such spectacles. Théophile Gautier, who himself was also one of the greatest aficionados of these spectacles, has left horrifying descriptions.

However, even in our time, despite legal prohibition, America has not succeeded in completely suppressing clandestine societies which organize these merciless fights. In Louisiana, Missouri, Texas, and Maryland, lovers of the sport are notified of a match by personal letter or by discreetly distributed programs. The meetings generally take place on Sunday in large farms a long way from towns, and the dogs are set loose into a circular arena six yards in diameter, surrounded by bars, behind which the public watches.

We will refrain from describing the savagery and ferocity of these odious duels, in which good husbands and honest fathers of families take so great an interest, men who

The showman of Augsburg and his dog. (German engraving, 1860.) (Bibliothèque nationale, Paris)

How many fractures are sustained before arriving at the polished performance.

cease to reason sanely when it comes to this passion. The combatants are selected from two-year-old dogs, which show a certain aggressiveness, and which are generally large and of a weight between 60 and 70 lbs.

A pleasure for unthinking outcasts of fortune? Amusement for poor blighters? Not a bit of it. A fighting dog eats more than four pounds of meat a day, it is trained for two years at least, and it has already cost its owner 200 to 250 dollars before it takes part in a fight. Before its ordeal, registration and general expenses will have amounted to 100 dollars, to which must be added on the following days all the expenses of a veterinary surgeon. All that to win prizes for the owner which amount to 400 to 500 dollars, but also for the amazing pride in being the victor, thanks to HIS dog. And yet the best fighting dog survives no more than three encounters. We could muse a long time on the murky parts of the human soul, especially when we hear, for instance, Leon C———, an American building contractor from Tucson, of French origin, make this dumbfounding statement: "If we have a passion for such a sport, it is because we are proud of our dogs and because we love them!"

RATTERS

Again it is the aggressiveness in a dog and also a particular predisposition for hunting down and killing rodents (without eating them) that has been exploited for a long time in ratting competitions.

The best breeds are the different varieties of Terriers, particularly the medium-sized dogs (from the Welsh Terirer to the Border Terrier) or the large ones (from the Bedlington to the Airedale). Yet the German Schnauzer; the little Belgian barge dog, the Schipperke; and Germany's Dachshund have also been used successfully.

Until 1939 most countries used the keen little Fox Terrier for ratting and it effectively did great service in destroying these undesir-

ZALEWSKI

able rodents, which were both fearful pillagers and spreaders of disease. The average best performance registered for competitions was from eight to ten rats killed in thirty seconds. Since then, the rat has been discovered to be the principal carrier of jaundice, for which dogs in cities pay so heavily. The numerous canine clubs and groups which devoted themselves to this kind of useful sport have wisely renounced the competitions which they used to organize.

DOGS OF THE CIRCUS AND MUSIC-HALL

We come here to a somewhat peculiar aspect of the dog's service to man. Acrobat dogs, tight-rope-walking dogs, comic dogs, dogs walking on their hind legs—are all these little *artistes,* which are often dressed up in our clothes and hairstyles, ever happy dogs? Who can say? Before World War I there existed a Jack London Club, whose protective aims extended to cover all circus and music-hall animals. The club's most useful documents denounced these exercises as dangerous and the training procedures inadmissible. Dogs were forced to execute dangerous jumps backwards or were thrown into the air to make a pirouette and land on one front leg. How many fractures and deaths must have occurred before the tricks were mastered! But how can one hope to turn away from their pleasure a public that has always been fond of such performances but is no less affectionately moved by the joyful complicity, at least from appearances, which seem to unite the showmen and their animals.

The problem, however, is not that simple. When all is said and done, these Fox Terriers and Pomeranians, mostly stray, are at least assured some care and affection on the part of those who keep them alive.

That leaves "performing dogs," dogs that work out square roots, read your thoughts, and show no lack of humor or philosophy in their responses.

*Football-playing dogs
have known great success
in the circus.*

It is certainly not a question of education or of the slightest divinatory gift, but simply a matter of training. At the beginning of this century, the Eberfeld horses astounded thousands of spectators and even confused some scientists. Since then we have had dogs that can count and even dogs that seem quite intelligent. They are all brought up by the same methods: They are taught to solve precise problems by yelping a certain number of times to solve an arithmetical problem or even to reply to various questions by choosing letters and assembling them into words. I have known a number of these astounding dogs. All had an engaging manner, but I was dumbfounded when one of them had this embarrassing question put to it (by its master): "What is man?" And the little Poodle replied in code with tiny, rapid taps of its foot: "Man is an irrational animal!" That was too good to be true!

We must recognize that at times dogs of a gentleness and exceptional psychic are found. But they are not prodigies as some children are. They are simply capable of perceiving the smallest scratching of the nail (inaudible to our ears), or of hearing the tiniest signal from their trainer.

And then there are the sincere dog-lovers who are absolutely convinced that their dog is a phenomenon. I have met some of them and I am afraid that I disappointed them and even irritated them. They made their little companion work wonders, but away from their presence even the most gifted performing dog was unable to give the slightest intelligent response. The truth is that these beings of good faith are quite simply either very calculating or very talented mimics. Unwittingly, the owners, by a quick glimmer in their eye, by an imperceptible twitch in a muscle, or by quickened breath (all phenomena which are independent of their own wills), transmit the elements of their responses to the observant animal, which is content to translate it without knowing it, in the same way that a parrot talks.

The misunderstanding arises from the way

197

FRED BRUEMMER

*In Holland,
dogs are still used
to pull loads.*

the dog itself sincerely plays the game; or from the belief that it is in collusion with the clever showman and obeys his commands; or even the possibility that it knows its master better than its master knows himself. We should therefore consider these stories as fantasies of the mind and charming diversions.

DRAUGHT DOGS AND SNOW DOGS

Is the dog really a draught animal? Well, why not? It is very tempting to think that it must have been in days gone by, and that prehistoric man used it for years as a partner in his efforts to pull his heavy loads along the ground, especially when we know how easily all kinds of dogs have adapted themselves in our times to such training. And more easily than the horse, we might add, since the horse is a member of the genus Equidae—as in the zebra—which in practice is not easily harnessed. If canine traction has not been exploited more, it is because the horse has always been king, and the sight of a dog, straining, panting, with its tongue hanging out, has always had something unfamiliar and pathetic about it.

In France, the first serious attempts at bringing the dog into general use as a draught animal date from the beginning of the 19th century. It caused such an outcry that the Prefect of Police forbade it in 1824, and was soon followed by all his provincial colleagues. In Belgium, Switzerland, Holland, and some German provinces dogs are allowed as draught animals, but the practice is strictly regulated. We can be sure that the powerful, docile dogs of the Belgium milkman or of the Dutch florist are to be no more pitied than the solid Newfoundland which, in St Pierre & Miquelon, daily renders valuable services to man in the almost total absence of any other draught animal.

Paradoxically, dogs pulling sleds shock our sensibilities less, even though such haulage demands an effort from the dog both harder and more sustained and in conditions of climate that we can only imagine.

With origins very close to the wolf, sled dogs have scarcely ever moved from these regions of cold, snow, and icy winds. Because they are mostly used in teams, they have more contact with each other than they have with humans, and thus they are guided by the pack instinct. Psychically, it is an imperious instinct, which must be given serious consideration because it differs distantly from the "adapted instinct" of the majority of dogs.

Whether it is a native of the great Canadian north, of Greenland, or of the furthermost regions of Asia, the sled dog is the same: it is a wolf, a wolf very probably mixed with the *canis palustris,* its official ancestor. Although it is stockier, stouter and with a wider chest than the wolf, it is no less a wolf in its ardor, its resistance, and its pack instinct. This instinct makes it obey the strictest law, particularly if it is the strongest dog—to "maintain" its rank and its prerogatives.

The head of the team is harnessed by itself. It is the spearhead of the team. Its job is to guide, encourage, and direct all the others which follow it in pairs. At the beginning of a trip, the head dog very wisely reserves its energy. Above all it busies itself with overseeing the others. If one of them seems to be a slacker, not playing its full part in the communal task, the head dog makes it clear by its barks, by sign language, and with its teeth that it is no fool and will allow no such behavior. But towards the end of the journey, when everyone's energy begins to run out, it is the head dog which sets the example to the very end. It must also be said that it is the head dog which will be fed first and unharnessed first, for it is necessary to demonstrate its privilege and value in the eyes of the rest of the pack.

Much has been written about these dogs, which are capable even when old of covering distances of up to 300 miles across the polar regions, where men are cut off from the world. Can you imagine the terrible cold of temperatures of 40 degrees below zero and winds of 100 m.p.h., which last for weeks on end? Sometimes, when it is almost impossible to find shelter and difficult to feed them in blinding flurries, their masters have to crawl to them to give them their indispensable fish or dried meat, and leave them outside, still harnessed, only to find them in the morning buried in ice.

In the course of the 1950 polar expedition of P.E. Victor in the Adélie Coast in the Antarctic, the handler in charge of the dogs sent this dramatic SOS to Paris: "Dogs' fur completely covered in thick ice. Attempts to free them tears the skin. Urgent, cable advice." We cannot comprehend such ordeals. Moreover, dogs in the polar regions are no use after the age of seven. And this especially goes for the lead dog which gives more of itself than any other.

"Boss," the most famous of them all, was the king of dogs of this character. A Husky, it had shown itself to have so much courage that it became a type of "chief." Such supremacy can hardly last forever. Four or five years at the maximum and then comes the day when a younger, stronger dog attacks it, overcomes it, and takes its place. Boss did remain the great, invincible conqueror for ten years. He had held his own against all, in spite of his age, until the day when one of his own descendants, "Fram the Bold," suddenly provoked him and laid him low without wounding him too much, and Boss, exhausted, abdicated.

However, luck did not abandon him. He was brought back to France and was adopted the moment he arrived by a kind-hearted lady. This hero of the polar nights, having settled down nicely to a middle-class existence in a villa in Chennevières, died two years later after unwisely going out one day when it was raining.

Another death no less famous was that of "Barry," a St. Bernard, who in twelve years

SNARK INTERNATIONAL

Renoir: ▶
Madame Charpentier and her children.
(Metropolitan Museum of Art)

Mountain dogs: the Pyrenean
and the St. Bernard.

of service had saved 40 travelers lost in blizzards and who was killed stupidly by a blow from an ice-axe belonging to the 41st, who was terrified at the sight of what looked like a bear running towards him.

AVALANCHE AND MOUNTAIN DOGS

By a strange irony of words the name "Barry" comes from "bari," which in a German patois means precisely "little bear." Barry, whose marvelous sense of smell was equalled only by his high intelligence, knew such fame that for more than a century this breed was called "barryhüng" (or Barry dogs), and even today the most beautiful puppy born in each year traditionally still bears his name.

Where and how did these mountain dogs, which are very close to the Pyrenean Mountain Dogs, acquire their protective instinct? It is difficult to say. However, their great olfactory powers are generally accompanied by another natural aptitude— that of returning with its prey. The St. Bernards probably acquired it from their ancestors, who, in their turn, were descended from the Assyrian mastiffs and their brothers the Bloodhounds. The have been changed over the years by training towards peaceable ends, and their qualities have resulted in our time in that cynegetic perfection seen the Bloodhound, which itself inherits them from the great mastiffs.

Whatever it may be, the St. Bernards have not changed since 1750, a date when they were utilized for the first time in a much more prosaic purpose. Until then one of the monks, called the "marronnier," every morning had the duty of testing the fresh snow which had fallen the previous night with his long staff, to establish whether a track, called the "pion" (foot-soldier or pawn), between the two sides of the neck of the mountain were open, but often this track had disappeared beneath snow of several feet before it could be marked. Thus

*Fiction often goes
beyond the truth: These rescue dogs have never
carried little casks round their necks.*

*On the Adélie Coast,
the dogs were often covered
with frozen ice and snow
in the morning.*

was the start of the St. Bernard's main role of being used as radar-guides for the hospice monks who followed them. It was only in the course of the following years that their sense of smell came to be fully appreciated and henceforth to be utilized.

(Unfortunately, it is necessary for us to destroy a legend: no dog from the famous St. Bernard hospice has ever carried round its neck any kind of little keg!)

Are such dogs born in the high mountains, and which seem ecologically created for them, capable of foreseeing avalanches? At one time this was believed, but from all the signs these purely mechanical phenomena do not seem any more discernible to dogs than to men. Therefore it is wrong to sometimes use the expression "avalanche dogs" to indicate dogs which are purely rescue dogs.

In France, such rescue dogs are virtually non-existent. In Switzerland, the army and private organizations have worked closely together to found, encourage, and train dogs for defense and search work. The Swiss Société Cynologique and Dr. Abrezol's teams, in particular, have turned their efforts to finding a type of dog, which is capable of responding to these two disciplines. Today, they are chosen, in the great majority of cases, from German Shepherds. The teaching and training courses are mixed, in the sense that their aims are to educate the master (or guide) and his dog at the same time. All the guides have to be, above all, dog-lovers, and good skiers, trained in night as well as day climbing, and unaffected by claustrophobia. One of the regular exercises demanded of these dogs is to find a man buried in a deep hole, which is tiny yet ventilated. The guide must play the role of the first victim for the dog to discover in this way. Very quickly the dog learns that its duty does not consist only of searching for its master but for any person thus buried. Regular annual competitions contribute in maintaining the standard among voluntary guides, who take a justified pride in having saved from suffocation many people who

have been surprised by an avalanche and swept incredible distances away.

Avalanche and mountain accidents are obviously not the only occasion when rescue dogs prove themselves invaluable in the service of man. In earthquakes and landslides and all kinds of disasters in which it is necessary to detect and free a human being, whether dead or alive, from a pile of debris, rescue dogs enable us to save a great deal of time and effort. According to experts, their work is hardly ever handicapped by darkness or blinding searchlights, and even less by smells which are intolerable to man. They indicate by eloquent sign language the results of their search or their discoveries by showing very different reactions as to whether the victims are still alive or dead. For over

ten years England, Holland, and West Germany have shown as much interest in the formation of such auxiliary forces as in police dogs or customs dogs.

POLICE AND CUSTOMS DOGS

Except mountain dogs such as the St. Bernard, rescue dogs are generally of the same type as those which are used as a kind of "radar" and as an extra arm of the law. Experience has shown that the Alsatian has the qualities for this work far more than any other breed. These qualities are: a highly developed sense of smell, enormous

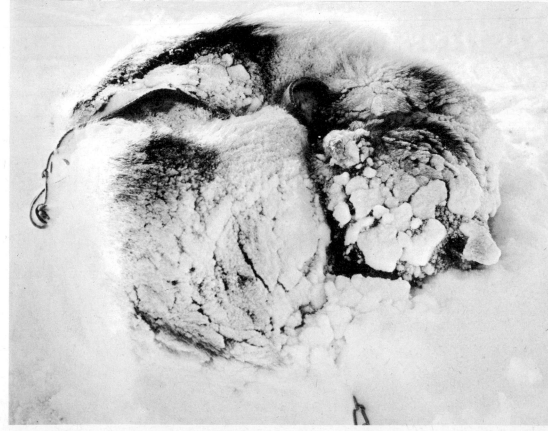

ZALEWSKI

Disregard for
fire and flame is the most difficult thing
to train in a dog.

courage, intrepidness, agility, and, despite its
aggressiveness, great obedience. Whether its
tasks are uncovering the traces of a wrong-
doer, holding someone in check, or exposing
the presence of opium, tobacco, hashish etc.,
the well-trained dog infallibly succeeds when
all other machines of detection fail.

We cannot refrain from wondering at such
performances as these: "Ajax III" found an
inn-keeper's assailant in a few hours after
the crime, hidden in a tumbledown cottage
only a few miles from the crime. "Xales,"
at Alfortville, went along the banks of the
Seine, its nose to the ground, then dived
into the river and brought out the body of
an eleven-year-old child who had disappeared
some days before. "Sultan," belonging to the
St. Denis police, after three days of tracking
and a night's watch discovered the burglars
who had broken into a house three months
before. "Dux," with a revolver bullet in its
shoulder, continued to follow a bandit's
trail for two hours . . . and stopped him.
And lastly, a police dog that found a
three-year-old child still alive sleeping under
a coat about five miles from the place where
she had wandered away from her parents.
The honor-list of these brave animals could
fill pages and pages.

Paradoxical as it may seem, the police dog
has a soft heart. It cannot help becoming
attached to the person who feeds it and gives
it orders, strokes it and rewards it, to the
person who is its master and god. It is incapable of being a mechanism. And the same
is true for the man who uses this dog, for he
cannot be indifferent to their common
activity, to the personal satisfaction which a
successful performance gives or should give
to him.

Now, every dog gives only in proportion
to the confidence and friendship it receives.
And that is the tragedy. Let us take the case
of a policeman to whom a dog is assigned.
For five, six, or seven years this man will
have the professional duty of becoming attached to this animal, of establishing closer
and closer links between himself and the dog.

Whatever the services rendered, "Brutus" (let us thus call the chosen dog) is then scrapped and put up for auction. What does it matter to the administration that the policeman may experience pain, and that Brutus, because of its age, has a 90% chance of not finding a buyer . . . and will be put to death without more ado.

Certainly, the policeman has the right to buy back his companion. But that is when the difficulties start. According to Article 90 of the French regulations, policemen can own rabbits, chickens, ducks, cats . . . but there is no provision for dogs. It therefore depends on the superintendent of the section to expel the brave animal or allow his master to maintain him with his own money, which the ungrateful State refuses to do.

ARMY DOGS

On the 21st of January, 1799, Napoleon Bonaparte wrote to Marmont: "There must be at Alexandria many dogs, which would be of much service to you in the outposts." It was certainly not in the mind of the future emperor to bring back the fighting dogs of the past, the killers of horses and men, but simply a suggestion that one could make excellent watch dogs out of such ownerless dogs.

Since then every army in the world has used dogs for various purposes: as watch dogs to sound the alarm at silent enemy infiltration, as patrol dogs to cover small detachments of scouts and to precede them on their march, as mine detectors to smell out mines placed by the enemy in front of their lines or to cut off their pursuit, as guard dogs to keep watch over arms or munitions depots, aircraft hangers, technical laboratories, etc., and as ambulance dogs which are used in conjunction with the most modern means of getting help to the wounded.

What are the differences between police dogs and dogs used in war? Actually, there are very few; the same breeds are used, the same discipline, the same psychology, and very nearly the same training procedures. If we except parachute dogs (which naturally receive special training, but as soon as they land on the ground become like other dogs), only the greater risk of wounding or death in performance of this duty enables us to differentiate between military dogs and dogs used against criminals.

Much more so than police dogs or customs dogs, military dogs can be severely traumatized by fright. They are so trained and hardened to war that after several months of exercises and teaching they can run beneath bullets and shells, gas and flames, or between two soldiers whom they love. With a message in its collar, a dog can assure the precious liaison on which so many lives depend. But some, and they are not numerous, have sensory hyperesthesia, which makes them perceive exterior stimuli with more intensity than others. I have known well-balanced dogs which in one day have been so "shocked" by the effect of a percussion-fuse shell going off next to them, or a mine exploding in the air, that it became virtually impossible to use them afterwards.

Parachute jumping also poses a problem. On its first jump incapable of knowing the real danger that threatens it, the dog jumps without difficulty when its master invites it to or, better still, precedes it. During subsequent jumps they are more conscious of the danger and the anxiety that they show is more eloquent than any words.

The dog used in war is so unlike a machine that persons in the know talk of "education" where we would talk of "training," and few cavalrymen keep a more affectionate place in their memories for their horses than almost any master of a "commando-dog" has for his canine companion. I have met many young men returning from Indo-China and Algeria, and one did not have to wait long for their confidences: "The dogs," said one lad with his right arm amputated, "I thought I knew them

An exercise in crawling for an army dog.

The training of an attack dog.

ZALEWSKI

ZALEWSKI

*German dogs
before
a gas attack.*

ROGER-VIOLLET

before this" (motioning towards his empty sleeve with his chin). "When I was young, my father had a dog, like every farm has, a dog which is chained up during the day and let loose at night. Since then, I have known my 'Flicot.' He was for me more than a chum and more than a brother. For ten months he never left my side day and night, and it is thanks to him that I am still here. . . . But *they* ended by getting him. They shot him down like a rabbit!"

In another distant war *they* also had killed a dog like a rabbit, a very beautiful Alsatian which a young rifleman who had been slightly wounded brought back one night in

his arms, and whose body he threw on our table, his eyes streaming with tears. He swore to avenge his dog, and the next day, it was he who fell in his turn. . . .

And I did not think it at all ridiculous that a few days later both the boy and dog were mentioned in despatches. Between 1940 and 1945 eighteen dogs were decorated by the British. Among them was the famous Alsatian, called "Antis," about which three novels have been written. Antis was brought up by a Czech airman, went with him everywhere for four years in the R.A.F., gave him help through the most dangerous missions, and finally died of old age in arms.

DOGS FOR THE BLIND

Was France the first country in Europe to train guide-dogs for the blind? In the course of World War I Commander Malric and Lieutenant Megnin had the idea. Towards the end of hostilities they had succeeded in getting the British government and then the Swiss government to send missions to the French kennels at Plessis-Trevise, and both Dr. Balsinger and Colonel Richardson were immediately inspired by the French experiment.

Have you ever seen a dog leading a blind man in the street? I am talking about dogs

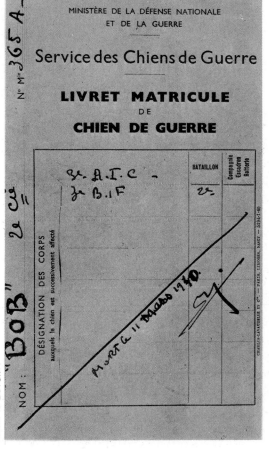

MINISTÈRE DE LA DÉFENSE NATIONALE
ET DE LA GUERRE

Service des Chiens de Guerre

LIVRET MATRICULE
DE
CHIEN DE GUERRE

*"With a kind of anxiety
more eloquent than words."*

Commando dogs.

which have been purposely trained in this work, dogs which are capable of anticipating a shock or fall, of estimating by instinct the speed of a car which is coming towards its master and itself, and which are capable (as has been proved in an incident which actually happened in America and which film, by pure chance, has been able to fix forever) of throwing themselves in front of the blind man they are protecting and being killed by the car which has not stopped in time. I know of nothing more overwhelming than such a sacrifice, doubtless irrational, but in which the instinct of protection, the most total devotion, the most perfect training

enables a dog thus to save the life of a man. This exceptional being, more perfect than a machine and less sensitive than a human, with qualities of complete self-abnegation and loyalty—is not the guide-dog the stuff of legends?

A SORT OF "SYMBIOSIS"

And here we come to the mystery. We once knew in Menton a young twenty-year-old blind girl who one day adopted a young dog for amusement's sake. It was a puppy of less than five weeks, and she raised it like

a child. It never left her. A year later, although having never been taught, it began to guide her from instinct through the streets of the town. Just like a dog which had been strictly trained, it would stop at every obstacle, would not risk crossing a street until it was sure of enlisting the help of some passerby, resisting any imprudent act. Whenever such dogs are themselves blind, it is true, they manage for themselves better than any human being, who is almost totally dependent upon his eyes. But how can we explain the sense (it is difficult to express it in words) which can dictate to a simple animal what to do? Attached to its young

The trained guide dog for the blind is equipped with a rigid leash on a harness.

A blind man in Times Square, Manhattan.

FOR YOU I AM PRAYING
GOD BLESS YOU
Thank You

mistress this dog had achieved a sort of "symbiosis" which is readily admitted by every blind man supported by his guide-dog: "My dog makes me forget my blindness."

And as if it were not enough to record such an acknowledgment, we must recall here that in only one year, because of the grafting of dogs' corneas, fifty disfigured soldiers won through and recovered their sight.

WATCH DOGS AND SHEEP DOGS

And what about the small, unknown dogs without rank? Watch dogs and sheep dogs could rightly claim to be that—these dogs which live unremarkable existences far from towns.

Farm dogs are legion. Many are kept chained up from dawn to dusk for seven to eight years with less than two square yards around an old barrel serving as their inhabitation, to eat their meagre pittance and finally to die.

Their job, say far too many country people, is very simple: they have nothing to do but to bark. And their fate? The majority of them are destroyed when they are found to be too old for service.

And yet, all dogs, whatever and wherever they are, are watch dogs, and especially so if they are sheep dogs. Wherever flocks graze, wherever man has set his steps in the steps of shepherds of old, with the same ancestral concern for defending what was the first "capital" (from capita—number of heads), there are sheepdogs.

In Australia, the crossing of wild dogs with the noble Scottish Collie has given the best results. In Yugoslavia the autochtonous dogs are very similar to the Malinois or the Tervuren (varities of the Belgian Sheepdog). In Turkey, the great wild mastiffs with yellow hair and black faces match themselves with wolves. In Russia, the large sheep dogs with corded hair are heavier than the massive Leonbergs or Newfoundlands. In Lapland the most prevalent type resembles the Husky and guards the reindeer herds. And finally, in England, from the Bobtail (Old English sheepdog) to the Collie, every sheep dog is king.

France has her white Pyrenean dogs, her long-haired Briards, her black Beauçerons with tan feet, her little, panting Labris and a lesser known army of sheep dogs from Languedoc or Provence, which are seen only in summer when the masses of teeming flocks fill the village streets, swarming along the sides of the houses and in a cloud of dust make their slow way to and from the Alpine pastures.

Whether their coats are long or short, they already know their craft when they come into the world. And what a craft! To shepherd a moving sea of sheep along a road, to make it string out when a car approaches, to run along the banks of this bleating river, to follow it in order to contain it, to precede it in order to draw it along, and once they arrive at the pasture, to change their attitude and watch over their charges sternly, to keep them within the limits of their territories, to sally out to bring back a stray, to help the foolish sheep that has slipped in a stream or has stupidly got caught on a barbed wire fence . . . such is the work of these dogs.

How many sheep is one dog responsible for? Two hundred head for a Briard, 150 for a Labri or Beauçeron *"bas-rouge."* For eight months of every year a good sheep dog will cover over 20 miles a day around its flock.

The secret? A common tropism towards all predators, which incites them to pursue every animal which escapes, to overtake it and to dominate it by intimidating it, circling it, or biting it . . . but also a disciplinary in the dog which it has known for nearly 80 centuries. Here again we can only note and admire it.

The story of "Carraya," a bitch which was a cross between a Briard and the little Pyrenean Sheepdog or Labri, has been au-

L. HERSCHRITT

thenticated as the kind of adventure that could never have been invented by a novelist.

She was a mongrel that belonged to a Spanish shepherd from the Estrella region. She had no other virtue, as far as her master was concerned, than that of being keen and conscientious in guarding her flock. Now, one morning, Juan Lopez, a young man from Madrid interested in caves, was in the process of discovering an unknown one 300 feet below ground, when out of the virgin depths arose a long cry, at once soft and plaintive. He stood petrified, for he thought himself alone. The cry immediately ceased, only to resume in a more lugubrious tone. With every sense alerted, Lopez listened, then quickly directed the ray from his flashlight

toward the spot the mysterious sound came from. In the sudden light, the silhouette of a quadruped appeared among the stalactites. Lopez pulled out his knife and approached it. Was it a wolf? No, it was only a dog, an old mongrel was quietly watching him. He made a few feverish pulls on the rope which joined him to his two friends who had remained above, and the speleologist hoisted himself to the surface. He explained his improbable discovery, and of one accord the three young men decided to save the unfortunate dog at all costs. After six hours of patient, gentle effort, they succeeded. Meanwhile, some peasants and neighboring shepherds, having been alerted by the noise, ran to the place. When the dog at last

The most hardened hunter worries over his dog when it is hurt.

In the valleys of the Pyrenees a keen dog is highly valued for guarding the flocks.

J. RIBIÈRE

J. RIBIERE

appeared, several of the witnesses cried out in unison: "It's Carraya! It's old Jan's dog!" And to think that three years earlier he had thrown her down into this abyss, because she sometimes bit the difficult sheep she guarded too hard! It was indeed Carraya, but how had she managed to stay alive? after such a fall, could anything but a skeleton with broken legs remain of the dog? A fall of nearly 200 feet! Such a drop would surely have killed her, but she had plunged into a small subterranean lake. She swam to a bank where piles of sheep bones and two pigs' corpses, which the cold had preserved, supplied her with food. She had remained there ever since. She fed on the animals thrown into the hole, as she herself had been, and on any others that accidentally fell in. It was incredible that in the subterranean gloom she had not moulted, and in fact the thickness of her fur coat protected her. However, the true epilogue of this amazing story was that after being dazzled for a moment by the light of day, she immediately ran to her master's hut and made a great fuss over him! The same evening she returned to her work, the same job that had been interrupted for three years.

HUNTING DOGS

We will not talk of the great slaughter brought about by animals bred purely for hunting in the private sector, for compared to this, ordinary hunting is like the family stew placed beside a fashionable, expensive, exotic luncheon. Genuine hunting is the rediscovered enjoyment of ancient times, when man and dog united their instincts and intelligence to increase their effects.

The only modern form of hunting and huntsmen which we find excusable is that which is prompted by these feelings. Without readily agreeing with this, without even sometimes suspecting it, true huntsmen go hunting more for their dogs' sake than for the arguable satisfaction of slipping a still

*The Retriever
is the perfect type of dog
for bringing back game.*

warm partridge or a young hare sticky with blood into their game-bag.

The dog used by man in hunting has changed much with the times. Mostly gone are the Greyhounds with erect ears and curled tails of earlier civilizations (but the Ibizan Hound of Spain is one survivor) . . . transformed are the powerful mastiffs of the Middle Ages, reduced to the minimum are the packs of beautiful pure-bred dogs which formed the dog nobility from the 16th to the 18th centuries.

The hunting dog of today has been levelled in the extreme. He is of average height and varied aptitudes: the Breton Spaniel, a newcomer; the obstinate Water Spaniel; the Braque du Bourbonnais and the Braque d'Auvergne; also the foreign dogs, the bushy Korthals (Wire-haired Pointing) Griffon; the resourceful Beagle; the ferretting Cocker Spaniel; and the valuable Retriever. These are only some of the more widely distributed breeds.

The dream of the ordinary huntsman would be to mix them, cross them, multiply them in hundreds of ways to obtain a most marvelous dog that would find the pheasant running in the undergrowth, pin down a brace of partridge, catch the hare which the shot has merely grazed, hurl itself into an icy lake in search of a duck.

In short, a unique dog, which would still be capable, after sunset, of making a tour of inspection to retrieve any game that had been lost and to drop it cleverly at its master's feet.

If this type of dog were to exist, the number of huntsmen would double, but doubtless so would the number of abandoned dogs. In fact, we cannot guess how many dogs—both in town and country—interest their masters for only a few months when the hunting season is open. What happens to them before and after? They muddle through as best they can to earn their allowance of food, waiting for their feast days to come around, when something a bit stronger than training, habit, and dependence leads them,

RAPHO — CHATILLON

*The truffle dog
has been shown to have the edge on the pig in
its acute sense of smell.*

FRED BRUEMMER

trembling with impatience, to that ancestral cooperation which is at the heart of all dogs.

These are the truest of dogs. They remain faithful to the pact with such moving ardor that sooner or later man is touched by it. We know many a "hard-hearted" man who mocks the affection which people bear towards lap dogs, and is secretly caught in the trap of this fleeting friendship. He is the sort of man who shows anxiety over a thorn embedded between the toes of his clot of a dog; the sort of man who will spend a small fortune to avoid wasting his favorite spaniel in any useless or dangerous task.

Hunting is just that. It is this "symbiosis" between man and beast, and it is difficult to compare it with the organized pursuit of the "laying of the pack," when the dogs depart together, start and finish together, and remain, in the true hunting spirit, in what is a sort of common mass, having no real communion with man aside from the common goal.

We have come a long way since the ancient days when the noble lord knew his best bloodhounds intimately and bore a jealous interest in them to the point that he opened both his heart and door to them. Such a sentiment no longer exists, and cannot exist today between dogs and modern huntsmen.

And it is because hunting has become more and more the function of private societies, from which all ideals of the true huntsman have been excluded. In the face of this, friends of animals cannot remain indifferent for long to the abuse of hunting. The great age of venery died with Monsieur de Lambrefault, the last of the dog's friends of yesteryear.

TRUFFLE DOGS

The wheel turns. Many dogs which had specific jobs yesterday today have no employment. Our roasts brown by themselves, depending on the heat and length of time that we leave them in the oven. The turnspit dog is unemployed.

Nevertheless, there still remains the truffle dog. It has been shown that it is much more gifted than the pig, because of its acute sense of smell, in searching out "this concentrated aggregate of silicate aluminum, iron, manganese, sulphur, amyloid matter, essential oil, and water" which, Brillat Savarin in his *Physiologie du gout* (The Physiology of Taste) calls the "diamond of cooking." This tubercle was valued highly in ancient Greece and Rome, and Juvenal and Plutarch have sung its praises. The dog with its fine sense of smell can seek it out after very simple training, and much more reliably than the sow or wild boar.

This occupation for the dog is not new. Frantz Funck Brentano states that Louis XV derived much amusement from searching for truffles in the morning beneath the trees of the Parc de la Muette, with a small pick in his hand and with the assistance of specially trained dogs which the king of Sardinia, his grandfather, had sent him. Kipling, the fine gourmet that he was, used to say of the pig that it only had "an appetite at the end of a rope," while the truffle dog "is an artiste to all appearances which is studious in dedicating itself to its art."

The truffle dog has the edge over pigs in that it never touches any other vegetable matter, just as the well-trained Braque will never touch the hare that it brings back to its master. It is, however, necessary to teach it its job, while pigs dig out and unearth truffles from instinct.

How does one educate the truffle dog? The same way we educate dogs to detect mines: by using the principle of association of ideas. A truffle found is immediately followed by reward. It is important never to lose one's patience, and never to scold the dog over false trails or lack of success. The truffle dog digs for the pleasure of pleasing you, so say all the farmers of the Drôme and Basses-Alpes regions, and they also add that one must "caress, congratulate, encourage and then carry on." We can understand the concern that some hunting dogs must feel at being trained as truffle dogs, for some professional truffle-seekers manage to unearth weekly in the winter, with one dog, 150 to 200 kilos (1650 to 2200 pounds) of truffles, for which they can get more than 5,000 Old Francs per kilo.

5
THE DOG
IN THE FACE OF
SUFFERING AND DEATH

16 THE DOG AND MEDICINE

*"It is not a question
of knowing whether animals reason,
but whether they are able to feel pain . . .
that is the whole
question."*
(Jeremy Bentham)

Among the dog's many uses in the service of man, there is one that is common throughout the world today and about which hardly anything is written—the use of the dog in experiments.

In the laboratory the dog is gradually taking the place of the guinea-pig, the rabbit, and the rat, because, with the exception of monkeys, which are too costly or too rare, it is anatomically and physiologically closer to man than any other animal. Because of this, it pays an increasingly heavy price for the preservation of man's health, and has done so since the early ages of medicine.

In spite of his name (from *galenus*, calm) Galen (131 to 201 A.D.) was the first physician to free himself from the Hippocratic ideas of anatomy. The Master of Cos, i.e., Hippocrates (5th century B.C.), considered animal vivisection repugnant, dangerous, and undignified. Galen had no such scruples. He is considered the creator of experimental medicine and surgery, which were evolving, from century to century, over a mountain of dead bodies. Galen, as early as 2,000 years ago, was cutting up, opening, and dissecting dogs. He individualized the tendons and muscles; he divided the bones of the skeleton; he described them one after the other, and gave them names, some of which are still used today. To study the function of the nerves he cut the medulla into different sections, and he demonstrated, among other important things, that the voice is completely dependent on a nerve called the recurrent laryngeal nerve.

After him came Arab, Hindu, and Chinese physicians, and by the Middle Ages the curative arts had become something quite different from what they had been. The Salernitan school taught a philosophic approach; the Montpellier school outlined a surgery which no one dared confirm, for *"Ecclesia abhorret a sanguine"* (the Church has a horror of blood); from this came the very modest "barbers," to whom one surrendered oneself for bleeding. These early surgeons operated from castle to castle under the anxious eye of servants, while the dogs prowled about their legs, not knowing what awaited them.

The Renaissance tried to recapture the time lost over the centuries. Paracelsus and Rabelais did not hesitate to proclaim that they were here on earth to make truth prevail in medicine, and with the help of their Epicurism, they threw themselves into the most audacious follies. The first, despising plants, extolled iron, gold, and mercury; that was chemo-therapy (or alchemy?). The second, just as curious a person, touched on hormone-therapy in an astounding adventure which he recounts in his second book, and for which a bitch paid the price.

"Panurge" wanted to confess his love to a rather arrogant but foolish lady, and was rudely repulsed. Vexed by the outrageous refusal that he had met with, our friend made this threat: "By my soul," he said, "I will avenge myself, fair lady, and I will deliver you to the dogs!" And this was not bravado, but the most ingeniously fiendish of vengeances. To accomplish this Panurge chose a feast day which sent the town's noble lords and ladies out in all their finery. The day before he had secretly procured a bitch in heat. Having stuffed it all night with food and then killed it in the morning, he had removed the ovaries, chopped them up and dried them, and then reduced them to a fine powder. Then slipping the charmed drug into a piece of paper, he ran to the church, and looking contrite, he approached the lady and timidly held out the roll of paper. He begged her to pardon his late breach of manners by accepting this rondeau written in her honor. The lady unrolled the paper to read the gallant speech, and in doing so scattered over her fingers and the folds in her dress the powder which Panurge, hypocritically apologizing, had spread there intentionally. When the service was ended, the lady had hardly stepped into the square in front of the church when ten dogs surrounded her, attracted by the smell. In vain she tried to

From the "Livre de Chasse" ▶
by Gaston Phébus (15th century).
(ARCH. R. LAFFONT.)

*Eye-examination
with an ophthalmoscope.*

Testing a contact lens.

Setting it in place.

"How Panurge played a trick
on a Parisian lady."
(Bibliothèque nationale, Paris)

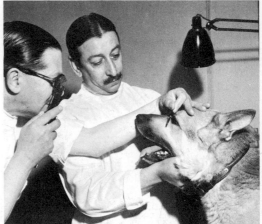

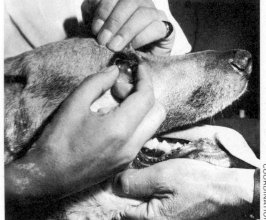

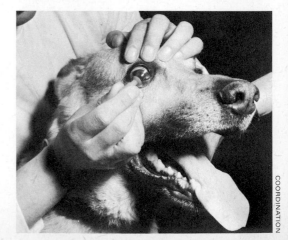

calm them. More started running from all sides and threw themselves upon her, to the great amusement of the passersby who only laughed at her confusion.

Did Rabelais know the secret of such harmone powders that were to be discovered some centuries later? In any case, throughout his books he had shown himself to be an amusing author of science-fiction.

In the 16th century, plagues and epidemics ravaged the world, and in the 17th century scalpels and lancets were readily put to work. There were the great discoveries of the circulation of the blood, and—thanks to dogs—the discovery of the circulation of the chyle by Gaspare Aselli (1581-1626). Some time later Jean Pecquet (1622-1674) completed Aselli's work with the discovery of the thoracic duct in the dog, and showed that what he had been able to study in dogs is exactly the same as what occurs in men.

In the 18th century, Lazzaro Spallanzani (1729-1799) contributed to the knowledge of the action of the gastric juices in digestion; some time later he succeeded in the first experiment in artificial fertilization of a bitch. François Magendie (1783-1855) continued the work of Galen and demonstrated, by using young pups, that there exist sensory nerves for pain and motor nerves for movement (the anterior roots of the medulla direct movement and the posterior roots sensibility).

In the 19th century Claude Bernard's (1813-1878) passion—a passion which often caused him much misery—was for actual vivisection, and henceforward the most important discoveries were linked with it. These ranged from the action of the sympathetic nerves through the glycogenic function of the liver to glandular secretions. "When one enters a laboratory, one should leave one's imagination in the cloakroom as one leaves one's overcoat . . ."—so said this relentless physiologist. He might also have added: "As one also leaves one's sensitivity!"

Fortunately, the 19th century also saw the discovery of anesthetics. As R. Bouissou put it, the surgeons of that time "had almost with reluctance rounded the cape of pain."

The famous surgeon Velpeau officially maintained that he considered such progress "negligible." As far as dogs were concerned, doubtless he was right, for dogs had made this easing of suffering possible, and yet had never benefitted from it until the beginning of this century. However, they owed another great victory over a terrible illness to Louis Pasteur (1870-1914). This was a disease which had decimated their numbers and had for so long been a subject of fear: rabies. For rabies spared no one, and rabies was always fatal.

Pasteur did not give in until he had erected a solid shield against it. For many years he pursued his experiments on hundreds of dogs, at the risk of their bites and even his death, until the day when he prepared a culture obtained from the marrow of rabbits infected with rabies and let it grow. He then realized that this rabic culture had lost its virulence. When it was inoculated in dogs, not only was it not communicable but it immunized them against the disease.

The incredible thing is that dogs paradoxically were the victims of this amazing discovery. In fact a law was passed, stating that any dog which had been in contact with a rabies-infected dog, even if it had been

A monstrosity:
a dog with six legs and three tails.
(Bibliothèque Nationale, Paris)

Dogs were present everywhere
and at all times
(16th century engraving).
(Bibliothèque Nationale, Paris)

neither wounded nor bitten, should be struck down on the spot. And more was to come. The anti-rabies vaccination, which was practically wiping out rabies, was only officially recognized in France for animals which were *not* dogs, while at the same time it was authorized and recommended in all the French colonies and made obligatory in nearly every other country.

On the other hand, it is only fair to recognize that dogs have benefitted from scientific progress in other ways from experiments *in vivo*. From 1920 on, the first diabetic dogs, hitherto condemned to die, were saved by insulin at the University of Toronto. We should especially mention the numerous applications of artificial hibernation, following the work conducted jointly by the École d'Alfort and the Centre at Val de Grâce; the magnificent results of bone surgery (*enclouage* and *restorative synthesis*), which we owe to the methods of Professor Cauchois; the studies of the blood supply of the mesentery made by Professor Leger's team; and the possibilities of delicate operations on such disorders as diaphragmatic hernia or foreign bodies in the thoracic esophagus.

These interventions, which were impossible before the perfecting of anesthetics, now enable us to save nearly all dogs which are victims of laceration of the diaphragm or of obstruction of the back of the esophagus, and also all lesions known to current clinical medicine. Operations on the no less common cataract were equally impossible (or rather were of no interest other than the purely esthetic up to this time), because the problem in this case was that it was impossible to make a dog wear corrective glasses. This treatment, which until then had been neglected, thenceforth was gradually to seem more practical, once English vets were successful in making dogs tolerate contact lenses.

And thus we come to modern medical feats. The operation for blue disease, or cyanosis, which yearly costs hundreds of dogs their lives, enables us today to cure a dog congenitally stricken with this disease. Opera-

217

*A Bleu d'Auvergne
which has complete confidence
in its nurse.*

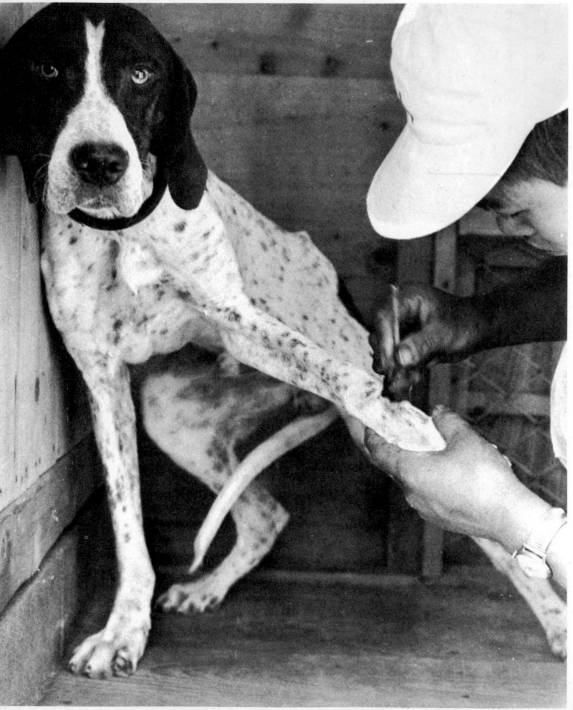

ted on at Broussais hospital with the same care and attention that is given to saving a child, such a dog, which could not run without immediately losing consciousness, leaped around the surgeons five weeks later.

We can also talk about organ transplants, on which we rightly place so much hope. But who has dared to try one out on man, before perfecting the technique and ensuring there can be no danger of failure.

At the Saint-Eloi hospital at Montpellier a Red Setter plays like all happy dogs, and is spoiled by everyone on the staff. Operated on by Professors Romieu and Solassol, it has lived for more than six months with a transplanted pancreas. How many people dying of disease of the pancreas or of cancer of the head of the pancreas would be grateful to survive one extra day. As to the heart transplants, could the most recent successes have been achieved without so many experiments on dogs? In America, a dog lived normally for three years with a transplanted heart.

At the Broussais hospital in Paris, six such dogs operated on by professors Cachera and Lacombe have been in excellent health for four months. They are under the particular care of Professor Alpern, whose task it is to keep them alive after surgical treatment. They have been saved; but this famous immunologist surrounds them with care and affection, because their survival is a token of the incredible success of the anti-lymphocytic serum from sheep which he has perfected. This serum of Professor Alpern is our most promising weapon today against the rejection of transplants, a rejection to which the dog is more sensitive even than man.

But here is a no less surprising experiment. A Rumanian surgeon, Professor Émile Truta, has succeeded in auto-transplantation of the uterine cornua in pregnant bitches. The cornua, with its fertilized egg, was removed and then regrafted. The bitch's time came, and she brought perfectly normal pups into the world without any trouble. What is the use of that, asks the layman? It has a quite un-

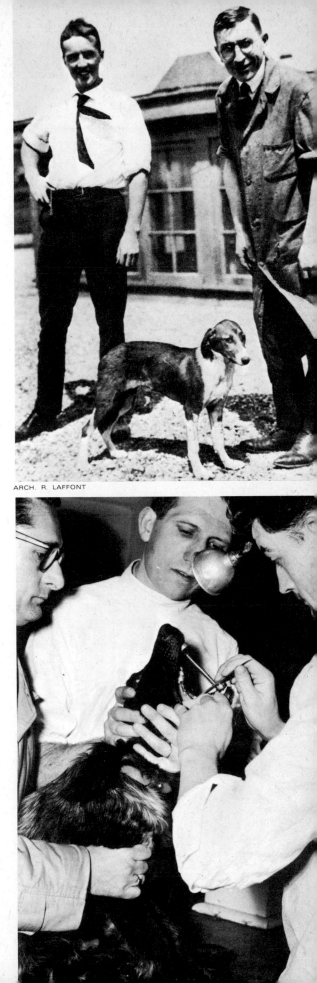

*F.G. Banting
and Charles H. Best on the roof
of the Medicine building of the University
of Toronto with the first diabetic dog
to be saved by insulin (summer of 1920).*

*A fish-bone stuck
in a dog's throat necessitates the immediate
intervention of a vet.*

ARCH. R. LAFFONT

expected use: Once the immunological processes are reduced we can effectively make such a transplant from one bitch to another. The bitch which receives the uterine cornua of another pregnant bitch can give birth to pups which are not her own. "This," says Professor Truta, "is the first step towards the same intervention in women. . . ."

A NECESSARY EVIL

Looking at such a balance-sheet, what is the sincere opinion of someone who loves dogs, someone who has seen them suffer and die and whom certain abuses had formerly so revolted that he has fought for twenty years to soften the fate of these innocent victims?

Experimental research is, unfortunately, a necessary evil. Each day it takes on a wider aspect with the exigencies of progress. We must not impede it, but strict regulations must henceforth be demanded for the authorization of experimental research *in vivo*. These regulations, as yet still imprecise, demand or will demand a strict supervisory control over the selling, buying, transport, and comfort of animals destined to serve science.

Is that everything? No, for we would like to state this truth, which experience has shown us: It is good, it is necessary, it has become indispensable that research conducted on living animals is made the subject of a strict law. But sensitive souls may wish to reflect on this. The most intelligent dog is only sensitive to the unaccustomed. It *has* fear, especially when people it knows entrust it to people it does not yet know, and when people dressed in white (unaccustomed in their eyes) come and bend over it.

But at this point the drama ceases. A simple innocuous injection, and this anguish vanishes. It is then no more than a sleeping dog, a dog which knows nothing, which can know nothing of all that man—in the same situation—can imagine. It is not frightened of anethesia, because it knows nothing about it, nor the uncertainty of awakening; and

likewise it cannot worry about the result of the operation because it does not even feel it.

It reawakes knowing nothing, having neither understood nor tried to understand. Between the dog that is operated on without its knowledge and the man who takes an interest or anxiety in such an operation on himself, which patient—man or animal—suffers more?

Let us not deceive ourselves. I say this, because I know. I say this because I have seen it. There is no delicate operation on a dog today that has any chance of success unless the dog is given the best anesthetic and receives post-operative care as complete and as scrupulous as that lavished on man.

But there are other things more serious than surgery, more dramatic as well, against which we can never protest enough, in order to defend our friend the dog, in the name of the minimum of comprehension, pity, if not human dignity.

Whether it is a question of toxic gases, agonizing deflagrations or fatal radiation, their place is not in this book.

Forgive me for leaving it there. . . .

ANIMAL MEDICINE

Parallel with human medicine, by helping it and inspiring it, animal medicine, which yesterday was no more than the "veterinary art," with all that the word "art" implies of individual initiative, adaptation, and ingenuity, has progressed with such success that it, in its turn, has become a science. However, the term "veterinary" (from the Latin *veterina*, "beasts of burden") today is ill-suited to designate the different branches of the science of animal care.

Of all the animal medicine, medicine concerning the dog has made the greatest progress in the last thirty years. Today all the great European nations, including the U.S.S.R., reserve a privileged place for the medicine of the dog. France has not been left behind. Her modern hospitals at Alfort serve

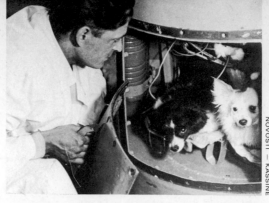

NOVOSTI — KASSINE

The Soviet space dogs "Danka" and "Koziavka."

"The ultimate destiny of dogs is the same as that of man." (Illustration from the edition of 1797.)

At the R.S.P.C.A. hospital for animals in London.

The original Sputnik commemorating the presence of the first dog in space. (Industrial exhibition in Moscow.)

SNARK INTERNATIONAL — MARKER

GIRAUDON

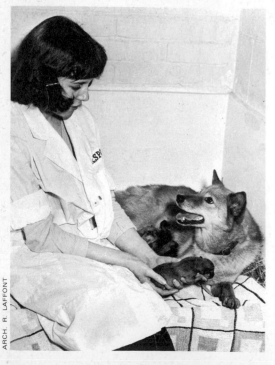

ARCH. R. LAFFONT

as models for all. There even exists a "blood bank" for dogs whenever a massive transfusion is necessary.

However, it is in America, always at the forefront of progress, that the concern for dogs, indicated by the affectionate interest shown in them by man, has provoked the setting up of an important and perfected network to ensure their better care. There are more than 2,500 veterinary surgeons in the United States, who busy themselves with the health of 25 million dogs.

For every urban zone of 20,000 people there is a veterinary surgeon and there are no less than 1,800 canine clinics, distributed throughout the whole country. These clinics, says Dr. de Wailly, are generally provided with equipment excellently adapted to modern techniques. One sees there vast hospitalization wards where ill dogs and dogs recovering from operations are the objects of continuous supervision night and day. The various applications of the laboratory, analysis, radio, x-rays, etc., are widely utilized there.

The Angell Memorial Hospital in Boston is a gigantic foundation dedicated to research into canine medicine alone. Nine veterinary surgeons are attached to it permanently, assisted by six interns chosen for their academic excellence and their original research. The most strict regulations of anesthetics and asepsis are observed there. Instruments, dressings, overalls, and gloves are systematically sterilized; and they estimate an average monthly work load consists of 2,000 medical cases, 500 surgical operations, 500 fracture settings, etc.

In New York, the Ellin Prince Speyer Hospital and the Margaret M. Caspary Veterinary Research Institute at the east end of 62nd Street constitute the vastest, the best organized, the most modern and the most welcoming Animal Medical Center in the world. Founded and maintained by a bequest of six million dollars by Alfred H. Caspary in memory of his wife, who for thirty years was the president of the Women's League for Animal Protection in America, the Animal Medical Center of New York is an enterprise of assistance and research. The building rises to eight floors; it daily employs 110 persons, of which 23 are veterinary surgeons and one a doctor. Among the animals treated, about 70% are dogs, of which more than 20,000 are annually examined, looked after, X-rayed or operated on under the best conditions and according to the most modern techniques. The actual laboratories occupy the four top floors, and one cannot help wondering at how far canine medicine has progressed, when one enters the radioisotope room and sees its impressive apparatus and its disturbing warnings concerning the dangers of radiation.

If one adds that we can estimate at more than 150,000 dollars annually the free care given to dogs whose owners are "financially embarrassed," we can comprehend the indisputable social utility of such an organization, and can smile with sympathy at the wit of Alain Branne when he says: "If one day in the United States I become as sick as a dog, it will not be in the waiting room of a 'sawbones' that I shall go to sit down, but in the Animal Medical Center of New York."

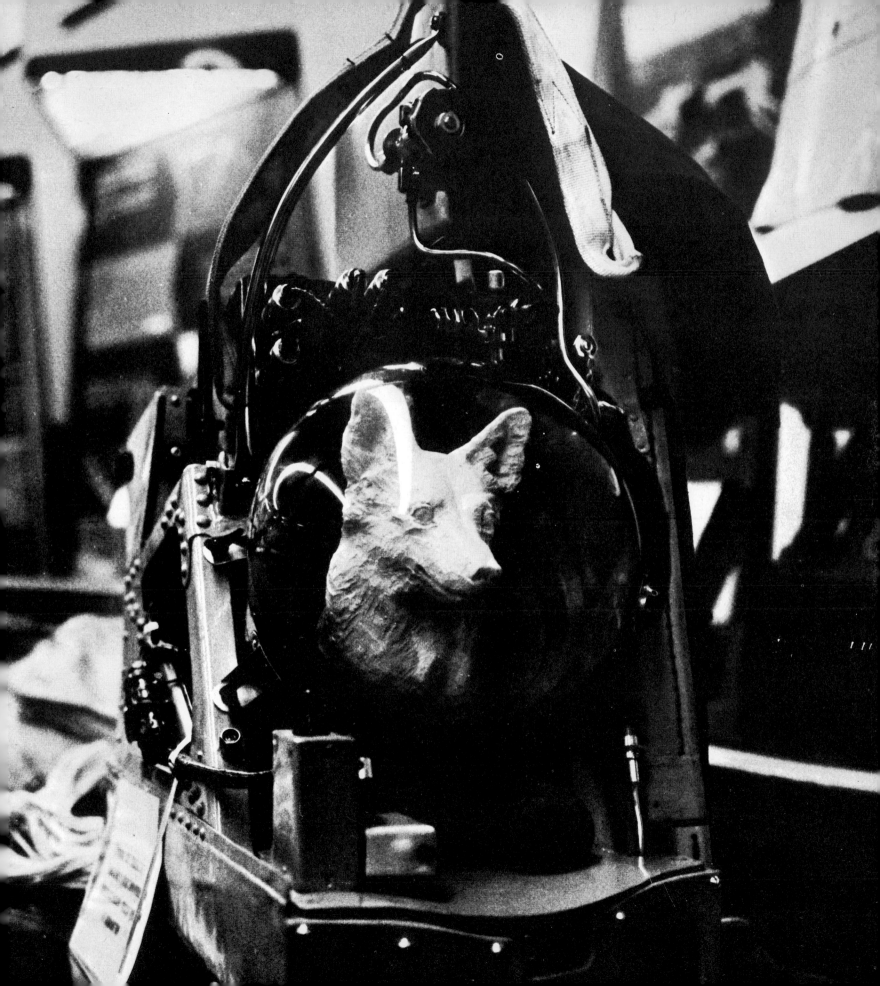

17 THE DOG AND THE LAW

HAS AN ANIMAL ANY RIGHTS?

Renan, Victor Hugo, Clemenceau, Poincare, to cite but a few of the great departed, have sincerely desired and clearly set out what they mean by the idea of "rights," an idea which has never been accepted for animals. Dogs, therefore, have no privileges.

After all that we have tried to learn of the unknown aspects of dogs and the place which they occupy in human society, how can we hide a certain irritation in recording that, in the eyes of the law, this marvelous servant, this immemorial helper, is no different from the anonymous chicken or the dangerous crocodile (if you take a whim to have one as a companion). In principle, the law extends the same protection to a humming bird as to the most savage wild beast, when man takes them under his roof.

The dog, therefore, is no more considered a "subject of law" than any other animal. This state of affairs is disputed and some degree of rights is virtually recognized in the private protection afforded by protection societies. But how far does this extend?

First, these groups are not necessarily admitted before a court of law in any capacity other than that of a private individual. One need only look at recent cases such as that of "live pigeon shooting" (among so many others) to establish that the laws are interpretable according to the animal-loving spirit (or lack of it) of the magistrate.

New laws have set alight great hopes in the breasts of animal-lovers. But they would have been overwhelmed had the law set out precisely in what way ill-treatment differs from an act of cruelty, and had it defined what is understood by the words "cruel acts."

Is the ruling on vivisection for experimental research any better? Perhaps, in the case of the control of supplies of animals to laboratories (though the incidence of this control reflects above all the economic or tax structure). On the other hand, the laws which relate to the transport, the housing, and the necessary care of these animals, and what qualifies as unnecessary suffering, are too vague. Eight or ten of these dogs are crammed together in narrow cages and shunted from one end of the country to the other by clandestine purveyors, with a death rate of two out of five.

These are the cases which must be brought to court daily to bring to an end other tragedies of which the public knows nothing: the short-lived hunting dogs, which are bought just after the opening of the hunting season and then abandoned when the gun is hung up in the rack until the following year; guard dogs which have become too old and which are brutally hanged to save a cartridge; unwanted dogs which are thrown into water with a stone around their necks and those whose masters try to lose them, often with unexpected consequences. . . . Such was the case with Camby, a tough farmer from Oregon who four times tried to rid himself of his dog. He would take the dog into the depths of the forest and quickly return home; without fail the dog would return to the farm. The fifth time John Camby tried to end things for good and all; he walked so far that he could not find his way back to his farm and he had to resort to following his dog!

The laws in force today are both too impressive and too indulgent in everything related to the protection of animals, yet at the same time they are very clear and strict on the prohibitions which affect them.

In the country, thousands of dogs are tied up day and night on a short chain, and are given a meager food allowance. Who cares about them? In the towns, the prohibitions which have been raised against dogs in the last few years have been of all kinds. These have accumulated by successive small decisions; dogs must be on a leash; dogs are forbidden in elevators; dogs are not allowed in food shops, butcher shops, bakeries, and restaurants. Dogs are not allowed in this park or this garden; it is an offence for dogs to foul the pavement; dogs are not allowed on the bus or on the subway.

*Everyone
has the right
to love dogs.*

The problems posed by the presence of dogs in cities are numerous, but the problems are the same everywhere, because dogs are the same everywhere. The law and the rules, however, differ according to how much concern there is to resolve the problems and whether there is taken into account the interests of the society in general or the liberties of the individual.

THE RIGHT TO OWN A DOG

The right to keep a dog in an apartment building was hardly ever contested, until apartments became scarce and certain agents and landlords began to insert in the lease the well-known clause "it is forbidden to keep animals." So, tenants were faced with a cruel dilemma: to get rid of their dogs or to leave their apartment. Overwhelmed by the measures or threats, many tenants gave in.

With more and more people living in close proximity to each other, many agents for medium-priced housing were not slow to introduce a simple prohibition on the presence of any animal in the apartments. The injustice is all the more disgusting when the prohibition affects a poor family who have little hope of finding other accommodation, and even more so when it is a timid and defenseless old person, whose little dog is his only companion and distraction and often his only true source of affection.

There is no precise jurisprudence on this point and if the tenants bring their case to court, they are either discharged or ordered to give way.

THE RIGHT TO HAVE A MASTER

This title might seem rather paradoxical, so long as society—which makes the law—limits itself to dealing with humans. The word "right" as defined by a great animal-loving lawyer, Lespine, "does not only signify the rights and prerogatives of an in-

dividual with regard to others in the exercise of his activity. It signifies also all the rules governing this activity in society."

A very striking case of the rights of a dog which corresponds to the duty of man towards him, as well as towards society, is the serious offense of abandonment.

This is strictly curbed in England, Switzerland, Germany and Sweden, for example, but in France this very cowardly way of getting rid of a dog reaches unsuspected proportions (especially at holiday times). It has been estimated that 150,000 animals each year find themselves overnight without a master.

Legally such abandonment constitutes "ill-treatment" if not "cruelty." It ought and must be punished. Unfortunately, it is not always easy to bring the culprits to justice. In fact, the dog, without a collar, identification disc, and usually of indefinable breed, is most often quite anonymous. It is essential, therefore, that the public authorities take immediate steps to avoid this sort of thing. Firstly, out of consideration for the collective good, for every lost dog constitutes a danger. It can bite, cause accidents, and become a cause of social disturbance, and the law must protect society from such risks. The law must also intervene out of humanity (or, if one prefers, out of pity), for no animal is more unhappy than a lost dog. It does not know that it is abandoned. It does not even know that it is unhappy, say the materialists; but our hearts do not deceive us. We are faced with one of the most elementary duties of justice towards the feeble and the irresponsible, and here we really touch on the human notion of help.

Unfortunately, it is not always easy to find the owner of an abandoned dog. A simple solution would be to make it compulsory for all dogs to carry some sort of identification. It would be enough for them to have an official registration number, which could be entered along with the name and address of the owner, and tattooed on the inside of the animal's ear or haunch (according to its size and breed). This would allow the owner of a

UN HONNÊTE HOMME N'ABANDONNE PAS SON CHIEN

stray dog to be easily traced. The record could be completed by the inclusion of a "nose print," which is, for a dog, as distinctive as a fingerprint is for a man.

Such regulations would surely result in fewer people taking so lightly the responsibility of having a dog. Others (as has been shown by a serious study) would accept a sacrifice to ensure that their animal was looked after in their absence, so long as the kennels could guarantee to look after the pets well at reasonable prices. Unfortunately, there are some very callous people in this field and the law has shown itself regrettably

BIPS

Dogs' bar.

They are not going without me!

indulgent. Why not regulate and control all boarding kennels? Individuals would be able to bring to court those which failed to reach the necessary standards. In England and in many other countries this activity is not unrestricted. It is subject to special authorization and inspection, inspired by the regulations for hotels and boarding houses, and each dog that is admitted must have an insurance policy against illness made out in its favor.

A means of identification of dogs and the application of such regulations would result not only in dogs being abandoned less frequently, but would also make it easier to enforce public health controls and fight more effectively against fraud and theft. At the same time, these controls would serve as a real protective measure for the animal itself.

THE RIGHT TO LIVE

Should not the right to live, which we remove with a light heart from so many animals, be accorded out of gratitude at least to some dogs? I refer to dogs involved in war, police dogs, dogs used in scientific expeditions, seeing-eye dogs, and all dogs engaged in farm work.

The public believes that these dogs are simply put into retirement. Let us make this clear: If it is a question of dogs used in polar expeditions, their repatriation, and thus their survival, is always merely a question of finance. This was well illustrated at the end of the last expedition to the Adélie Coast, when 27 dogs, after serving the men for two years in a climate as severe as one can imagine, were saved from being abandoned by a radio campaign, during which we did our best to make known their plight. The polar mission had ended, the money had run out. There was not enough to repatriate these brave animals. The public was so overwhelmed that in the ten days that followed the launching of the appeal, more than 4,000 offers were received to adopt these obscure auxiliaries.

J. RIBIERE

The fate of police dogs is even harder because, for them, there are no exceptional cases but an inflexible rule. Because of a legal technicality, all dogs used for defense, investigation, and close collaboration with man, are discharged on reaching nine years of age. Do not be deceived. This means that whatever the animal's state of health, whatever services it has rendered, it will be auctioned. This means, no less clearly, that it has become a useless mouth to feed and, unless a buyer is found, it will be destroyed. It is difficult enough to understand how a dog, which has probably faced up to months

*Better to be a mongrel
than a star mannequin.*

of shelling and machine-gun fire, can simply be killed because it cannot be made the object of a financial transaction. One understands even less how dogs which have taken part in Arctic or Antarctic expeditions can be abandoned to fend for themselves in the polar desert like unwanted skis or broken sleds.

One can be surprised by such happenings when one believes that the protection societies are all-powerful. The protection of animals is not a public service. It is made up of a number of separate groups based on private initiative, in which each member does his best to relieve suffering among animals and persuade the government not to lose interest in a cause, of which the importance tends to be minimized because people do not really know the facts. There are many town governments which, without supporting these societies, throw on them the burden of maintaining the municipal pound, which is really part of the responsibility of the public health and safety department. Even more numerous are the people who do not belong to any group—even though it costs next to nothing —and yet who are very vociferous in their criticisms of the various animal protection societies.

To what can this attitude be attributed? To the fact that the notion of protecting the dog as a duty of social order is not yet firmly implanted in the minds of men. The legislators seem reticent about voting in the necessary laws, just as the courts too often hesitate to apply them.

However, the campaign which was mounted in France eighteen years ago (1952) for the revision of animal laws has shown that one in four French people do love animals and are concerned about the lot of dogs. It appeared that the public authorities were concerned at such findings, and it seemed for a while that the laws were designed to give proper weight to the problem, but what the authorities seemed to hold out with one hand, they quickly took back with the other.

ENOUGH IS ENOUGH

Could the exaggerated displays of affection shown to dogs have contributed to creating this attitude of mind? It is possible. One can see so much foolishness and extravagance. What do well loved dogs want with starched collars, sunglasses, or Wellington boots? And fashions in dogs' clothes are ridiculous. To claim that dogs are amused by an artificial chop or a plaything in the form of a rubber bone (no matter if it is impregnated with the smell of meat) is to make them seem very stupid. On the other hand, it is perfectly reasonable to get rid of disagreeable smells by spraying the coat of a Skye Terrier or an Afghan Hound with a few drops of an alcohol-free perfume which, the manufacturer strangely claims, is "free from any allergy."

A much more doubtful gadget is the "umbrella for fragile dogs." Another American firm advertises an inflatable swimming pool for Bassets, and another, "canopied beds with a heated cover," and a young and pretty psychology writer has just written a thick book on the habits of lady dog-owners who are slaves to their animals and who try to bring a little gastronomic variety into Tao's or Bobby's dog food. . . . And a former actress, Miss del Rio, has recently opened in midtown New York an unusual boutique which sells inexpensive paper dresses for ladies of fashion with matching coats for their hound or Chihuahua. If one adds that this collection is modeled every day by beribboned Pomeranians or glossy Bassets, parading on front of the customers, their tails down and their eyes weary, one would agree that it is better to be a very disreputable mongrel belonging to a butcher in Montmartre than a star mannequin at "Carlins."

Enough is enough but, in fact, this social phenomenon, which was the subject of an article several months ago in the serious scientific (though in its attitude to dogs, very British) journal *New Scientist*, has gone further. The canine revolution of which the

New Scientist speaks can be summarized in these words: "It is no longer up to the dog to understand man but for man to understand the dog."

In fact, it will be necessary for us to come to this if we do not wish to prove correct Clifford Simak, the famous science-fiction writer who, in his book *Tomorrow the Dogs,* imagines that the legendary, ultra-civilized and fabulous dog has stolen man's own right to rule on earth.

A whim perhaps, but to what unfortunate ends are all these follies leading? There is a lawyer in Massachusetts who asked the court to adjourn a case for a week so that he could witness in person his dog's graduation from a training school;[1] and a Cleveland industrialist who had no hesitation in hiring, at an astronomical cost, a New York tailor to go to his home to fit his Poodle with a mink coat; and, finally, the Hollywood star who in all seriousness ordered wig-coats in real hair for her dogs which were moulting.

Enough is also enough when one brings to mind the secret slaughterings of butchers' dogs in pleasant Switzerland to satisfy unacknowledged appetites, or in response to a stupid belief that dog fat (from which Scottish medicine[2] made its panacea) is the only remedy against pulmonary silicosis found among Polish miners.

DOGS AND DEATH

And what can one think of the cruel love as the result of which a dog becomes a victim after its owner's death? Some are mentioned in wills, which, in the majority of cases, are contested and become the subject of a legal wrangle.

Others are mentioned in last wishes which are as cruel as they are selfish; for example, the will of Mrs. Gladys Prockter, which required that all the animals on her Pelham estate should be sacrificed on the day after

[1]*Veterinary Medicine.* Vol. 62, No. 7. Page 712.
[2]Walter Scott, in *The Bride of Lammermoor.*

High fashion for dogs.

*From sunglasses
to snow shoes.*

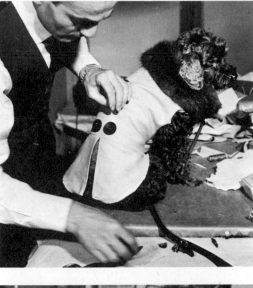

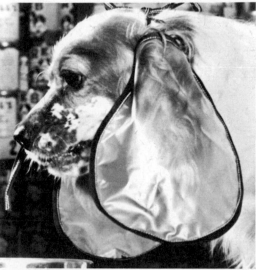

the presence of dogs in prehistoric tombs, but Lactance tells us that the Egyptians often threw living dogs on the funeral pyres of their masters. One can also read in Homer that Patrocles was burnt with his dogs, and Pliny, writing about the funeral of a young man, says, "He possessed several horses and many dogs of all sizes." Regulus cut their throats over the funeral pyre one after the other. Tacitus spoke at length of the custom, which had become a tradition for the rich Germanic peoples, to be buried with their animals. Nearer our own times, in 1781, as part of the rights of the Order, the horse of a Teutonic knight was sacrificed on the coffin of its master.

THE PRESENCE OF DOGS
IN HUMAN BURIAL GROUNDS

Recently in France there was the legal problem in the burial of a dog belonging to M. Blois, an industrialist from the Gironde, who had the idea of putting in the family vault a plain box containing the body of the dog which his children had greatly mourned. When this news got out, considerable feelings were stirred up in the region. The magazine *Point de Vue* began an enquiry. "Unthinkable in consecrated ground," said lawyer Maurice Garçon. "Last wishes should be respected," said another lawyer, Suzanne Blum, arguing that animals were considered as objects by the law and "should be equated with jewelry, decorations or weapons." Two other lawyers, Louis Lespine and Jean-Pierre Sloan, agreed with this. As for Professor René Capitant, he maintained that rights on the usage of a plot in a cemetery were laid down in "article 10 of the decree of the 13 day of the 9th month of the year XII," which permitted the holder of the land to "make it his burial place and that of his children and heirs," always taking into account that "nothing should interfere with respecting the last wishes of the deceased, if it is proved that a dog (as an object) occu-

her death. Too many passionate dog-lovers take their pets to the grave with them because "no one else will be able to give them as much love." This leads us to the delicate question of what happens to dogs when they die and how should they be buried.

The presence of dogs in tombs along with human remains goes back to the dawn of time. We do not know the significance of

pied such a great place in his heart."

All religions are concerned with this problem. Professor Hamza Boubaker, director of the Moslem Institute, thought it "a crime against humanity." Chief Rabbi Schili admitted that "after all, why not?" The Reverend Father Danielou, professor at the Catholic Institute, is of the opinion that "it is a mistake." Archbishop Kovalesky, head of the

Chained up in front of an empty house.

Orthodox Church in France, was less frank: "It is possible, because animals too will be raised from the dead one day . . . but it is wise not to do things which cause a scandal."

Political circles too entered the heated argument. "Above all, liberty, sweet liberty," replied Frederic Dupont, a former government Minister. Jacques Soustelle, a former president of the Council, avowed "I am not at all shocked by this idea." His colleague, President André Marie, smilingly replied, "Taking everything into consideration, like Alceste, I would prefer the company of my dog to that of a human being that I despised." As for M. Pierre Cot, a former Minister and barrister: it is not the emotional, spiritual, denominational or legal problems which worry him but, he says, "he has not the right to impose such a presence in the tomb on those who have gone before him or who will succeed him."

One must cite the opinions of famous biologists such as Jean Rostand, Professor Clement Bressou, or Professor Delauny; writers like Paul Vialar, Pierre Descaves, Christine Arnothy, M.E. Naegelen, André Billy; artists such as J.-L. Barrault, Jacqueline Gauthier, Line Renaud, René Lefevre, etc. to underline the passion that can be aroused on the simple question of the burial of a little dog in a grave where men rest. On such a question all the machinery of Justice, Virtue and Morality was aroused. Rights and duties were set against each other, denominational interests were awakened, philosophers made to think and poets to rejoice.

CEMETERIES FOR DOGS

Thousands of letters from ordinary people, both for and against, flooded into the newspaper offices from all corners of France in the following few months. One can draw from the whole an opinion which can be summed up in the phrase: "To each his own."

This is the judgment of wisdom. Animal lovers throughout the ages have always managed to provide burial places, either private or communal, for their dogs. The ancient Egyptians, Athenians, and Romans built and carved tombs for them. Some can be found which are engraved with emblems of fidelity and inscriptions of gratitude. Modern times have followed the trend. In England the Dukes of York have made a dog cemetery at Oatlands. Frederick II had his Great Dane "Gengisk" buried at Sans-Souci with the eight dogs which succeeded it, in gratitude for having saved him from being taken prisoner by the Poles. Catherine the Great of Russia inaugurated a cemetery at Tsarkoieselo in memory of her bitch "Zemire." Later, the Duchess of Roquelaure had one made on the death of "Badine," and the epitaph written by Sainte-Foix on this mourned dog (which was as ugly as it was bad-tempered, but very intelligent) is well known:

"Here lies the famous Badine
Who had neither beauty nor goodness
But whose mind was as
Systematic as a machine."

These cemeteries for dogs were private installations, like those which have always existed on many family estates and in country gardens. Even monks have not seen it as a betrayal of their mission to mark with a friendly epitaph the corner where they have buried the little companion of the community. Did not the monks of Cordeliers of Etampes at the end of the last century write in Latin the amusing story of a spaniel which had become very dear to them? The dog had understood that if he sat down quite still in a nearby stream, which was full of crayfish, after an hour he could return to the monks with his coat loaded with the little crustaceans, on which they could feast. He became famous and when he died a simple monument in the garden of the monastery immortalized both his services and the affection that he was borne.

Communal canine cemeteries or public gardens of rest are not rare, and one has not to go far to find one. There is one at Monte Carlo. France has three: one not far from

J. RIBIÈRE

the one already mentioned, at Cap d'Antibes another—the most famous—on the Ile des Ravageurs at Asniéres; and the most recent at Villepinte. There are several in America and in England, one in Brazil—at Rio de Janeiro—and one in Japan.

The one at Rio de Janeiro is symbolic. Mausoleums in black marble stand incongruously beside little notices stuck into the earth like labels in botanical gardens. One of the tombs is surrounded by no less than a floral decoration, which is beautifully maintained. It is the memorial to a worthless dog, but one day he pulled from the water, a few yards above a thundering waterfall, his master's grandchild who had fallen into the torrent.

The one at Paris is quite different. There are several slabs of sculpted marble, but the majority of the tombs are simply bordered with leafy plants and some flowers, with

here and there touching inscriptions: "Old friend Bill, rest in peace," and "Brave Drapeau, who was our friend in the war," and —because Paris is always Paris—this unexpected epitaph, more eloquent than any avowal:

"Would that women took as a model
My dog Elsa, who lies here, who was tender
and faithful."

TOWARDS REAL JURISDICTIONAL PROTECTION

One must set out these anonymous tributes in a dossier on the rights of the dog; they are cries from the heart and, in their simplicity, or their bitter humor, they express human truth and elementary justice. Would that we could convince those in positions of respon-

In Rio de Janeiro,
marble mausoleums side by side
in the same cemetery with....

M. COGNAC

sentenced to four months in prison two drunkards who murdered a dog: a big watch dog, a Caucasian sheep dog, which they stole and killed to sell its skin. Bravo, say all the animal-lovers; but, at the same time, the Soviet writer, Noris Riabinine, denounced slaughter which was directed systematically against stray dogs in Tcheliabibsk as well as Oulianovsk and in Uzbekistan. These two examples show well how difficult it is to reconcile legal respect for personal property, the health and economic interests of the society, and the love which we have for animals.

We have spoken of Soviet Russia because the housing problem there, which is not yet completely solved, poses the problems of communal living and the presence in the house of a dog, which is one tenant's personal property. Legally, the problem is just the same in the most animal-loving, capitalist states and it will remain so as long as the domestic animal (and *a fortiori,* the wild animal) is not under the law.

Can one hope that this will one day be changed? Yes, if one is more concerned with justice than with re-election. Yes, if one is prepared to admit that the law which today equates animals with objects (which one can acquire and sell) is only making use of a legal fiction, which is identical to that which under ancient law equated slaves with inanimate objects.

THE ACT OF PIRACY

While writing these lines, we have in front of us the illuminating report of Professor Aurel David, of the Institute of Political Studies at the University of Grenoble, which was read to the twentieth Recontres Internationales de Genève, where physicists, cyberneticians, biologists, psychologists, doctors, philosophers, and lawyers from all parts of the world were gathered together. The subject under discussion was "The robot, the animal, and man."

sibility who would like to protect animals (as one can and as one ought) but who are held back by a scruple: On the one hand they are convinced of the necessity to lay down new laws to protect animals, but on the other, they believe in the classical, legal concept that man alone is subject to the law and that the dignity and the interests of man alone can motivate legislation.

Because they dare not cut themselves off from this concept, they become bogged down in contradictions. In Moscow, a court recently

While reading the report, the words of Alain, the lucid and sensitive philosopher, came to mind: "There is a very important reason why man should protect animals; it is because they are dumb animals. . . ."

It would be wrong to interpret this in a pejorative sense. Alain was the son of a veterinary surgeon and he wrote that he had acquired the basis of his philosophy while accompanying his father on his rounds. He knew that animals were socially and legally "incapable" in the same way as children or the mentally sick are. It is in this sense that we must be their guardians in the face of our morals and our laws.

More precisely, Aurel David had raised in his report a point of law which should please the philosopher. "In the absence of a regular legal organization, any act of cruelty against an animal constitutes an act of piracy in the legal sense of the term."

In fact, any crime that is committed in a place where sanctions cannot be organized or exercised is also a crime of piracy. This is the case where there are total revolutions, mutinies at sea, or in the jungle or on a desert island. The responsibility of the criminal is, therefore, even greater when morality and law rest upon him alone, because good and evil depend solely upon him. This is perhaps why the rules of maritime assistance preceded by 2,000 years the same rules of assistance for people in danger on terra firma. Piracy makes even more disgusting a crime which is committed against a child or any being which is incapable of calling the police or the courts to his aid. So one can say that every time an unjustified act of cruelty is committed towards an animal, an act of piracy takes place, for all the world—so far as the animal is concerned—is a country without police and without judges.

In concluding, Professor David remembered that he was in Geneva and emphasized the fact that Switzerland is at the same time the country which for centuries has resisted war and which has the most comprehensive and best enforced laws for the protection of animals. This seems quite logical.

Today there are no more slaves, and as we are now perfectly familiar with nervous physiology, with the psyche, and, in consequence, the sufferings of some of the higher animals, there must be no more animal martyrs. Can modern justice continue for long to hide behind indifference in considering that "all definitions which are too precise are dangerous in civil law." It is true that justice wrote this last sentence in Latin.

No matter what . . . our generation must

*Dog in the cat-house—
on business or in error?*

*"Troubled by
the great mystery of the dog,
trying in vain
to learn more."*

decide that in truth all the higher animals which live in the society of man are "incapable" in the etymological sense of the term, and they are permanently so. This incapability means that they have an imperative right to justice. This is true of all animals, but does the dog not deserve to be, to some extent, set apart from the others?

Why not? Even if one refuses to recognize in the dog a certain evolution on the intellectual plane, even if one considers that the modern dog, capable of the utmost tenderness, has exactly the same brain as a fierce wolf-like creature of the Upper Paleolithic Age, one must admit that men have

changed. They have—for thousands of reasons—a tendency more than ever to tighten the bonds of friendship with the only animal which leaves them with the illusion that they have not completely lost contact with the other living creatures on the earth. Knowing this creature, whose value is not always measured in profit, how can our mechanized, computerized world not yearn nostalgically for a lost paradise?

How, in the end, can one not agree with the wise and sensitive Maurice Genevoix when he writes: "This dog, which I cherish and which I love, it is on me, his master, that he depends; because I give him shelter and

food, the links are strengthened and show forth in love. I love that which has need of me, which is so dependent on me. Through this creature, I exist and I count. I am sovereign and god. In his loving and faithful eyes I see what I want to see, what I hope to see and what I hardly dare say to myself, looking into my own eyes. . . ."

Having the same sentiments, will we be forgiven for trying to justify ourselves in being troubled by this "great mystery of the dog," for trying in vain to learn more?

"There is always, in what one does," wrote André Malraux, "a certain irrational value from which it is difficult to extricate oneself."